Dear

To Trish,

I Hope You Enjoy It.

Bernie

Dear Daughter

Bernie Donnelly

Disclaimer

This is a work of creative nonfiction. The events are portrayed to the best of my memory. While all the stories in this book are true, some names and identifying details have been changed to protect the privacy of the people involved. I do not assume and hereby disclaim any liability to any party for any loss, damage, or disruption caused by errors or omissions, whether such errors or omissions result from negligence, accident, or any other cause.

Published by Izumi Publishing

ISBN-13: 9781523883257
ISBN-10: 1523883251
Library of Congress Control Number: 2016902624
CreateSpace Independent Publishing Platform
North Charleston, South Carolina

Acknowledgements

My thanks go to the following people for their invaluable advice and encouragement - Joey Korn, Kenny Shusterman, Kristin Reeves, Phil Fleener, Charlie Rentz & John Sampson. Special unadulterated thanks go to my beautiful editor in chief "Keiko."

Foreward

BASED ON A TRUE STORY, *Dear Daughter* will surprise the young and intrigue the adult with its tale of loss and redemption. Its story revolves around the author's attempts to explain to his estranged daughter why he had abandoned her as she had requested him to tell her the truth, but he needed to find it first.

It's a life that no father would ever dare tell his daughter, unless she was an absolute stranger.

The author takes the reader on a journey through his life molded by his family and the many non-archetypal Dublin characters who ensured that the promise he'd made to himself as an eighteen-year-old would come true. *Dear Daughter* is an entertaining and exciting story of how one person coped with a number of unique challenges - from hoping to earn his daughter's forgiveness and wrestling with the pitfalls of a career in business to dealing with a looming corporate takeover. His three encounters with death, combined with his candid and comedic thoughts of murder and suicide, guarantee that no reader will be bored.

Prologue

IT WAS ANOTHER BEAUTIFUL MORNING on the Gulf Coast of Florida, just like every other morning. I always liked routine. I always felt that a person who had a routine was, generally, a happy person, and that morning I was a very happy person.

I put the kettle on for my early morning cup of Irish tea, a habit that I didn't want to break. Well, I tried to, but I couldn't get used to the American cup of coffee thingie. After popping my usual two pills of aspirin and my medication, I sat down to do my usual news reading and e-mail checking on my computer. It was during that process when I saw a message from someone I hadn't heard from in forever, someone I had only seen for barely two hours over the previous twenty-five years. It read:

Hi there,

Sorry if this comes out of the blue, but I was wondering if I can ask a question? I suppose I might have asked it before, but seeing as how I better express myself in writing. . .

I'm just wondering why you left me?

I don't want you to think I am angry with you or that I blame you, I'm not even upset about it, but I want to stop asking myself this "why" question. I won't be annoyed or upset with whatever answer you give me; it will be the right answer because only you can really answer this question.

So there it is: why did you leave me?

Again, my apologies if this takes you by surprise, but I have to send this question out there: maybe you could answer it,
all the best,
Lora

Lora was the youngest of four children from my first marriage. She had two other sisters and an older brother, the oldest child being seven when I left in 1990.

How do I respond to Lora's question? I thought about it every waking moment. My wife was excited for me because she, more than anyone, knew how much I had missed my children. My wife tried her best to get me started on my reply, but she knew that only I could try to explain to Lora why I had walked out on her and her siblings all those years ago and had never been in contact with them since.

So I made my decision: I was going to tell her the truth. I had no idea how she was going to react, and I had no idea where the truth was going to take me. I replied thus:

No apologies necessary whatsoever, Lora. I'm delighted you asked. It's a profound question that demands a concise answer.

I want to make sure I explain myself properly to you, but you will need to understand that it requires a long and detailed response. Is that okay with you? It will take the form of a book, and I hope you will be able to follow me on my journey.
Love Dad

She responded almost immediately:

Sure, thanks for agreeing to this.
all the best, Lora

Oh yuck! This didn't sound good; it didn't sound good at all. She wasn't helping me. It seemed like a very cold response. Why no "Love, Lora" or no "Okay, Dad?"

It didn't get my pulse racing, but the more I thought about it, the more it made sense. I wasn't her dad, so how could I expect her to respond as if I were?

So I sent the following email:

Lora, I don't know anything about you and, as a result, I don't know how strong you are or whether you are capable of handling what I need to say to you. This is very much to my chagrin because, as much as you've been troubled about me "leaving you," I'm asking you if you "care" how much I've been troubled about never having seen you, been around you, or known anything about you? Does it matter to you that I've never known my youngest daughter, continually seeing normal parents every day of my life as they watch their children growing up in front of them, wondering what it would have been like to be a part of their every living moment - good and bad? Does it matter to you that I have suffered just as much as you because, while you were just a child growing up, I was your dad watching from a distance, not being able to be a part of your life? You see, as much as I want to explain "the leaving" to you, it troubles me that maybe you don't care how I was feeling when I left you, what events occurred leading up to my departure, how troubled I was living with your mum, and all the crazy things that happened to me that just don't happen to normal people living normal lives!

I don't want to upset you anymore than you have been already, and the truth could upset you. I have to explain your father to you, and I don't know if you care or are interested in me enough to want to understand.

Is this what you want to hear?

Love, Dad

She replied the same day:

Hi there,

I know writing this will be hard for you. I am asking you to be honest with me. Let's face it: I am a stranger. However, I know what our perspectives and situations are. We are different. I was a child, and I didn't know you so I didn't know what I was missing. Naturally, I understand that it must have been more difficult for you. I have no children, but the mere thought that I would not see my nephew again would crush me.

I have heard only briefly about what you went through around that time. Naturally, I would prefer to hear it from you because only you can explain your feelings. My mom will obviously be a (substantial) part of your answer. I know this. I understand this. However, you two had a completely different type of relationship to the one that I have had, and continue to have, with her. On top of that, it was almost thirty years ago; I doubt either of you are the same person today. I understand your reluctance. You don't know me, and I am not unaware of the upset that I have caused by merely asking this question. So it's your choice. As for my interest in you, if I didn't want to know you as you were and as you are now, I wouldn't have e-mailed.

All the best, Lora

So that was it then, a perfect response from a very intelligent lady who I didn't know. Yes, as she so succinctly pointed out, we were strangers, so it should be easy for me to tell her the truth - a perfect truth - at least as I remembered it.

So I responded:

Lora,

I am going to tell you everything. I've told nobody everything. This'll be a no-holes-barred exposé of my life leading up to my exit from yours. It's the only way I can explain myself to you and, thereby, explain my actions. You have to know all about me if you want to understand how I affected your life, and then you can come to your own conclusions. You will be shocked, but I believe you can take it - maybe more so than anybody. It will be a first for me, also. To do this, it helps knowing that we're strangers because I can talk to you in that context, not as your father, which would be awkward.

As a result of this decision it will take me a lot longer to reply, but so what? We have plenty of time, and I need to do this correctly. I want to take my time to ensure that I have the timeline correct and that I don't miss anything pertaining to the events in my life that affected me, leading up to my frame of mind when I left.

My only hope is that, as a result of doing this, we will no longer be strangers.

Dad

And so it was time to remember.

CHAPTER 1

You see, Lora, two years prior to receiving your email, I decided to clean up my office. As I was going through my old files, a postcard fell from a folder. It was from my eldest son Jack, your brother. He had sent me that postcard around ten years before asking me how I was and giving me his contact details. I examined that card for hours, and when my wife awoke, I told her that I'd sent an e-mail to Jack at the address on the card and asked him to contact me. I also let him know that I would love to hear from him. She was surprised but excited for me, and so we waited to see if I would get a response.

I waited for days, checking my e-mails every hour, thinking that it was almost impossible that he would have received my e-mail because the address he had used was a very old one from a provider that had probably long gone out of business. I had no other way of finding out where he was because there was nobody I knew who would give me information about him because I was persona non grata in Ireland.

Then, about a week later, lo and behold and hallelujah! A response arrived.

Hi Dad,

Still using this address. Better way to get me though is through this new email address.

So I hear from my sources that you are living in Florida now. How long have you been there, and how did you end up this side of the pond?

I am currently living in Ashland, a small town in Southern Oregon. I have been married for almost a year and a half to Angelina; she is from here.

Anyway, I hope you are healthy and happy....Jack

Holy crap-a-rooskie! It was an e-mail from Jack; I hadn't seen him in over twenty-four years, apart from a brief encounter when Jack's teacher had contacted me about Jack when he was about twelve. When I met with the teacher, he explained that he had asked his students to write about what they wanted in their lives, and Jack had simply written "my dad." I choked up when he told me that, and then he told me that Jack was waiting for me in the adjoining room. When I saw him, I couldn't stop crying. I bawled out loud in front of the little fella as he sat and stared at me. I repeatedly told him I was sorry, and that I loved him so much. As the uncontrollable flood of tears streamed down my face, I asked him how he was doing at school, and he barely said two words. I think he was in so much shock at seeing his dad break down.

As I left him I promised to see him often but, of course, I never did. The reasons will be explained later. Now that we were back in contact I was determined that Jack and I would never lose each other again.

He made it very easy for me to get to know him. He called me "Dad." Wow, none of my children had ever called me Dad before - not since I had left. We started to exchange lots of e-mails, and I tried to remember what a father should do, trying not to be overanxious, but I couldn't help myself. I was more than thrilled to have another opportunity.

I had missed all of the great events in his life up to this point, but at least I could be around for of his future events - if he'd let me. I was not going to let him slip away, ever.

Eventually, I needed to hear his voice, so I gave him a call. I was like a child when I first heard his manly voice. I had no idea what he would sound like. I had rehearsed everything I wanted to say, all of the questions I wanted to ask, but I forgot everything as soon as I heard his voice.

He was calm, relaxed, and mature, and he made it easy for me to engage. It wasn't long before a year had gone by, and as we approached our second year, I decided I had to see him in the flesh. I told him I wanted to visit him and his wife in Oregon for my sixtieth birthday, that it would be the best present I could ever have. He was taken aback but was delighted at my suggestion, so we organized everything for the trip.

My wife and I flew into Portland, Oregon, about two days before we were due to meet Jack. When the day came, we drove down to meet him. I was nervous, and I didn't know what we should do when we met, so in true inspirational Irish style I decided we should go to the pub to calm everybody's nerves, especially my own.

We waited outside the hotel, and only having a photograph he had sent me, I looked up and down the street wondering what he would look like in person. Then I saw him on the other side of the street, and he saw me. My god, he was huge, about six feet four, and I couldn't take my eyes of him as we awkwardly embraced. He asked me what we wanted to do, and I said we should go to a pub, even though it was only ten in the morning. I never thought that would be a problem; the Irish never had a problem finding an open bar. Jack said he thought he knew of one place, so we walked around making small talk as he looked up the bar owner that he knew. He invited us in, and we sat down and had a few beers while the girls had coffees. Finally, we were relaxed.

This wasn't going to be a time for a deep conversation; it was too soon for that. This was about seeing one another in person. The other stuff could wait. We spent the day together having lunch at a local vineyard, eating pizza, and drinking wine while a tree protected us from the glorious sunshine. We chatted, laughed, and made small talk, mainly because neither of us was sure how it would go or how we should react. But it was a start - a great start - especially for me and, I hope, for him, too. Not wanting to screw things up by overstaying our welcome, I suggested that my wife and I should return to the hotel because I was tired, and we planned on meeting the next day for breakfast before heading back home to Florida. The next day was even more relaxed. The girls were great. They both knew this was a unique occasion, and they got on great together, which made everything so much easier for Jack and me.

Before we met for breakfast I decided to look around town. I was in a store when I decided to buy Jack a hat, one of those cool fedoras that I thought would suit him. It was a great success. He said it was his favorite type of hat, and that he had recently lost his old one, so I was thrilled. He then produced a card and a present that he had bought for my birthday. I choked up. It was the first present I had ever received from any of my children.

After that, things were so much easier between us, and even though we had spent only two days together, it felt great that we had broken the ice. We're still getting to know one another, and it doesn't matter if it takes the rest of my life, at least we've started.

Jack reintroduced me to his eldest sister May who has since given me two grandchildren I plan on meeting next year. I haven't seen May in about twelve years. We had arranged to meet in a local hotel near her university in Dublin, but in my excitement I forgot to bring any money, so I thanked the Lord that she didn't want anything to eat or drink. We ended that meeting with her not wanting to be beside me and both of us finding things a bit awkward. We never saw each other again, not because we had a fight, but because we were simply strangers. But things have greatly improved with May and me over the past two years, and we speak often.

So, Lora, that brings you up to date regarding my relationships with Jack and May. I am barely into a renewed relationship with my two eldest children, and now you have laid this on me. How the hell do I reply and not lose you again? It's not as if May or Jack hasn't asked me similar questions, but they never pursued it as graphically as you are now.

Lora, because you know nothing about me and, subsequently, nothing about my family or the people around me, I thought it would be a good idea to give you a little background to how I grew up, the people I met along the way, and the things that happened to me because those are the things that molded me into what I am today. Once you hear these stories, I hope to explain myself to you satisfactorily, and then I will explain why I left you. Whether my explanation is satisfactory, only you can judge.

CHAPTER 2

My ninth birthday was the first time I nearly died. We had a small party at the house, and I was drinking an orange soda. I somehow bit off a chunk of the glass. It got caught in my throat and protruded through both sides. I remember exactly where I was standing in the kitchen as I saw my father turn blue in the face as he reached toward me, forced my mouth open, and retrieved the glass from my throat. Everyone panicked except my father. He stopped the bleeding by slapping a lump of Vaseline across my throat. He then poured me another orange soda as if nothing had happened, and everybody went about their business. But I'll tell you this: I'd never seen anybody look as scared as my father did that day.

I hated school—every living, breathing, fart-filled moment. The Irish school buildings were always cold, damp, and filthy, as were most of the teachers. The Christian brothers were as "Christian" as ISIS. Most of them were alcoholics. Some should have been imprisoned, and none was the least bit friendly. They were incapable of imparting knowledge that would make you think, that would bring out your skills, or that would even encourage you to be something. They ruled with the terror of the strap or the ruler in the spirit of the Roman legions. You were their slaves, and they were your masters. The Irish governments of the day were happy to have a cheap educational solution, thanks to the Christian Brotherhood, and the brothers used the power ceded to them to great effect.

There was never a day I looked forward to, never a moment of happiness beyond staring at the hands of the clock, waiting for them to reach four so I could escape. The lay teachers were just as bad as the brothers, with one or two exceptions. There was the English teacher who continually punched students with his ringed middle finger for no reason whatsoever as he patrolled the classroom, and, boy, it hurt. There was the geography teacher who had a major lice problem and would flick the crawling beasts off his arms on to the nearest unsuspecting student. The math teacher continually picked his nose in front of us, and we all ducked when he flicked the snot at us. The science teacher scared the shit out of us. He appeared to be seven feet tall to us twelve year olds, and he only had one bloody piece of magnesium to demonstrate a chemical reaction, which ensured that none of us would be joining NASA anytime soon. They tried to teach us physics and civics, but they soon gave up.

There was an Irish language teacher who took such a major dislike to me that he would immediately say "Donnelly, out!" It became so routine that whenever he entered the classroom I immediately made my exit, saving him the bother of ordering me out. Many years later I was in a restaurant when he strolled in and, I swear, I automatically stood up to leave; that's how much of a hold those teachers had on us.

We had no sporting facilities, no fields, nothing. There was only a concrete yard where running competitions were held, which I always won (preparing myself for the great escape). I was so good that the school entered me in a national athletics competition in Croke Park—a major Dublin venue—but I was so petrified that as I approached the finish line in first place, I suddenly stopped because nobody had told me there would be a cord to indicate the finish line. So as I stopped dead, another runner crossed the line, breaking the cord and finished first. The teacher-in-charge crucified me on the journey home. That teacher was my Irish language teacher, the guy who always told me to get out of his class, hence the ridicule and displeasure I had to endure from him for the rest of my school life.

An honorable mention must go to the history teacher who arrived during our final year. He was a breath of fresh air because, as we opened our boring textbook, he asked us what we thought of World War II. He actually sought our opinion. We gazed at him with shock and awe. We wondered when the men in white coats would be arriving to take him away. It was like that scene from *Dead Poets Society* when Robin Williams tells the class to rip up their books, except this was seventeen years prior to that movie, and our hero was serious about getting us to discuss World War II.

Then again, I couldn't blame the teachers entirely when I considered the rabble they had to deal with. We were sorted into "A", "B," and "C" classes based on intelligence and how bad you smelled. Thankfully, I was always in the "A" classes because I was constantly clean and well-dressed. The lay teachers were usually from outside the city, "culchies" as they were known, and they didn't have a clue about how to treat city boys. They expected us to follow Gaelic games or talk about hurling or Irish football, even if we had no interest in any of it. They considered us totally subservient, so they never treated us with the slightest hint of respect.

I recently discovered that a principal from the junior school had been molesting young boys for years. One poor chap, a man in his fifties, recently committed suicide. He had been abused and had to live with that dark secret all his life. The animal that did that to him has since died; may he never rest in peace.

We knew we could never tell any of this stuff to our parents because they simply wouldn't believe us; instead, they would tell us that it must be our fault, and that we should always do what the teachers told us. So it was no wonder the teachers got away with the awful things they did; they were protected by the society around them.

Those Irish schools were nothing like the ones you attended or what kids attend now. Those schools shed no light on our talents. It was only after I finished school that I realized I had a talent for math, and that I loved history and English.

I kept to myself, changing friends often and steering away from trouble. I didn't have an outgoing personality; it only developed after I left school and started working. I always passed my exams, but I didn't shine in any subject. I stayed below the radar and waited for it to be over. What a waste of fifteen years . . . When I finally finished high school I walked up the street and, without turning around, I said aloud, "Thank God that's over," and I never thought about the place again. We tried to have a school reunion once, but it didn't work. We never tried again as I guess nobody wanted to relive those days.

Sean was my best friend. We often played together, and on one summer day, he arrived at my house and wanted me to come out and play. My father took me to the movies instead. I don't know why, but Sean started climbing the big tree up the road, and he fell, breaking his leg. I found out when I got home, and we went down to St. Michael's Hospital the next day to see Sean. He had developed an infection and died a few days later. Everyone was shocked. My father blamed the hospital, saying it was a dirty place and, as a result of Sean's death, he would never consider taking us there, no matter the emergency. I didn't understand. I just wanted to see my friend, but the next thing I knew I was going to my first funeral. I couldn't make sense of the fact that even my grannies were still alive, yet my best friend was dead at thirteen. I think of Sean often.

A couple of years went by, and I had made new friends. One day we went down to the beach for a swim. There was a spring tide, high and rough. Neither my friend nor I could swim, and we hadn't seen the sea so rough before. I decided to test how deep the water was, so I jumped in, only to be taken out about fifty feet by a riptide. In a matter of seconds, I was way out of my depth, and I sank like a rock. This would be my second unintentional attempt to leave this world. It's true that you come up and down twice when you're drowning, and then you stay down the third time. I came up the first time to see my friend laughing his bollocks off, thinking I was messing about. I went down the second time, and my lungs started to fill with water. When that is happening, you don't have time to be scared. Somehow, I surfaced again and managed to blurt out "Help!" a couple of times before sinking again, and there would be no coming up.

Three blokes dived in when they heard me scream. They were great swimmers and managed to drag me out by my hair, my small nuts, and my leg, and proceeded to pump the water out of me. Strangely, after I got my breath back, my first thoughts were that my parents would find out and kill me, which was stupid, really, but I didn't want them to hear about it. To this day, even though I taught myself to swim, I totally panic if I go outside my depth.

That very same day I returned to the beach because somebody told me I must conquer my fear, that I must go back into the water. But that time I never made it to the water because I slit my foot on some broken glass and had to be carried to the first aid hut. I was spilling blood everywhere.

I was never good at sports except running and boxing. Whenever they picked street football teams, I was the last to be picked, alongside anybody else with an infirmity, which didn't do anything to develop my nonexistent ego. I liked running because I could be by myself, and I was fast. I took up boxing when I was about sixteen because I knew I needed to defend myself as it was a rough town in those days. I had a good trainer who taught me how to fight but, above all, he taught me restraint, and that has served me well ever since.

I always said hello to everybody. It didn't matter who you were; Bernie would always bid you the time of day. I did that from the time I could talk and walk. My mother told me that I would often go missing when I was around five or six years of age. She would go looking for me, and she would always find me in one of the neighbors' houses eating cookies and having a soda. I used to do the same on the streets. On the way to school we used to pass an old man on his donkey with his cart full of pig shit. The stink was awful, and he'd have his young kid on the back of the cart helping him. The kid obviously never went to school, and the two of them always waved at me and gave me a big smile. The other lads would jeer and ask why I was talking to those knackers, but I ignored them because, as far as I was concerned, they were nice people.

Fast forward ten years, and I was walking home from my summer job as a bartender downtown, and I got caught on the wrong side of the road as ten or so thugs were approaching me. One thing you never do is cross the road in the face of such a threat—that would be suicidal because they would know you were scared. You just had to ride it out and hope to Jesus you got through the gauntlet unscathed. Well, they saw me, and I basically said my prayers because I was doomed. I was going to get a good hiding at one o'clock in the morning. I was in the middle of them being shoved around when, all of a sudden from a dark doorway a voice said, "Leave him alone; he's with me." They all looked at a guy with a lit cigarette as he stepped forward into the moonlight.

"Oh, didn't know that, sorry," one thug said, and off they went.

The bloke with the cigarette looked at me and said, "You're a bit outside your neighborhood, aren't you?"

I said yes and thanked him.

"You'll be all right now," he said, and he went on about his business.

Of course, it was that kid who used to ride the donkey cart with his father all those years earlier. I met him again some thirty years later at a charity golf outing. He had become a multimillionaire who owned of a number of pubs and newspapers.

At that golf outing he asked, "Do you remember me?"

"Of course I do. You saved me from a hammering one night."

"Do you know you were the only person who ever said hello to me or my dad?"

"No, I didn't know that, but I'm glad I did."

"And you never knew my name, did you?"

"No."

"Maybe we should leave it that way."

"Maybe we should."

And I never saw him again.

CHAPTER 3

THEY WERE SIMPLE DAYS WITHOUT too many complications for a young kid. There were no computers to destroy our imaginations, so we were sent out to play with everybody else. We played cowboys and Indians, and if there was nobody around, we used our imagination and played with whatever was lying about. Ma's knitting needles could be a sword, arrows or missiles, and the vacuum cleaner could double as a bazooka.

We had three channels on the television. Da drove me up the wall when he made me switch channels by pressing the buttons on the television so, I seldom watched TV because it was a pain in the arse to serve as the remote control. Television is still a pain in the arse, even more so because there are a million channels all playing the same stuff with commercials interspersed throughout the programs. While this technology is great, it appears that people have lost the ability to communicate, which is an oxymoron.

Every house was open to us then with keys in everybody's front door. You could go from house to house and let yourself in. We were safe in those days, although we would find out later about the barbarous acts the clergy had been committing behind closed doors. We, however, never felt threatened. But now kids seem to have parental escorts everywhere they go.

We never got up to much because there wasn't really much to get up to. We didn't have any money, so we didn't take drugs. We didn't drive until we were about nineteen or twenty, and we looked forward to our birthdays. We were especially excited about Christmas; it was magical. We received things we only dreamed about. We were always excited with anything new, and I appreciated everything my parents could provide.

Going to your granny's was great, too—depending on your granny. If it was Da's mother, that was no fun. Her house barely had running water, no fridge, and all you got was lumpy soup with fat and barley. But Ma's mother always gave us money, and that was always welcome. The best visit of all was to my dad's sister, Auntie Bridie, who always gave us jelly, ice cream, biscuits, and cake, so we absolutely loved that. The highlight of a weekend was when my parents would meet my uncles in a pub, and we were told to wait in the car—sometimes for hours. They'd send out bottles of orange soda and packets of potato chips to keep us quiet, and we loved it. We wondered about everything—how the planets worked, what made the world go around, what boobs were for—and we came up with all the wrong answers.

You must remember that, when I was born, Ireland was a tiny country of only three million people, just eight years after the end of World War II and five years after Ireland had been declared a republic. There was high unemployment, and the economy was wrecked. It was also a political mess that ran on old war factions led by old men. But there were some young intelligent politicians who used their ingenuity to try to get the country back on its feet. They were responsible for introducing free education for everybody up to intermediate level, which was revolutionary for its time. Without it, none of us would be where we are today.

When I was twelve, the church sent folks to our school looking for altar boys (they wouldn't do it now), so a group of us decided we'd do it. It was down in the local hospital run by the nuns, and we used to get up early every morning and take turns either ringing the bell or pouring the wine and water for communion.

There was an old priest, Father Fitzgerald, who used to say mass. One day he didn't appear. Instead, a strange man walked in looking for all the world like a six-foot-tall Tom Cruise. We'd never seen anybody younger than about eighty, including the nuns, so we were surprised that not only was he a good-looking bloke, but he was also a really nice guy who didn't scare the shit out of you.

Every morning in the church, a beautiful facility that was looked after diligently by the nuns, there would be the same number of faces, mainly old deaf nuns and a few nurses who attended mass every day. Then one Saturday morning as we stood at the door and waited to go out to the altar, Tom Cruise says, "On you go, boys." When I opened the door and we all walked out, there was an audible gasp from the nurses and the nuns who could see. We never took any notice of it. We did our thing and were told to be back again the next morning for seven o'clock mass. The next morning, Sunday, it was time for the usual procedures, and as we were standing at the door, Tom says, "Everything good, boys?"

"Yes, father," we said in unison, and off we went.

Well, Holy Jesus, the place was packed to the rafters with nurses, novices, cleaners, and doctors, and every one of them was female. I looked at my mate, and he shrugged and said, "Women, huh?" I told him we were not gonna have enough wafers, so when it came time to serve communion, I was elected to hold the paten under their chins in case they dropped any of the hosts and, I swear to God, there was a run on communion. The priest had to break each wafer in half, then quarters. Some of the women had their eyes open staring at the Cruiser, and I noticed that some of them were coming back for seconds.

"Hey! You were here before," I said to one of them, but the Cruiser moved me on. I wasn't happy, and apparently neither were the nuns because that was the last we saw of the Cruiser. He's probably working in some jungle in Africa with his good looks eaten away by some tsetse flies.

I loved getting summer work, and I'd jump at anything that would earn me money. My friend Declan had been working as a porter in the local hotel, so he managed to get me a job in the dungeons below the kitchen where I was enslaved to a huge Neanderthal whose jobs included anything that normal humans wouldn't touch. I wasn't mad about it, and after about two weeks, the call came down from the kitchen that we were required to remove something horrible from behind the ovens because all of the waitresses were screaming. The hulk and I went upstairs to the kitchens and, I kid you not, the hulk lifted the massive oven away from the wall all by himself. As we peered behind it we saw this white football that, on closer examination, seemed alive. It was a steamy ball of crawling white worms that I'm reliably informed is common in all old hotel kitchens—enjoy your soup!

The hulk grabbed the ball of worms with his bare hands and proceeded to parade the aforesaid nightmare through the kitchens and down to the basement, but not before yours truly was last seen riding his bike home to his mammy at a furious speed, arriving home long before the hulk made it to the basement. I never went back there, and I certainly never ate there again. I was so appalled by that vision that I didn't even bother to collect my wages. Declan told me that he gave up his job there when, during one Sunday lunch service, as the waitress was bringing a flaming baked Alaska into the dining room, the flame from the baked Alaska ignited on the lacquer in her beehive hairstyle, which was all the fashion for women in those days, and the poor lady went up in flames. The hotel never recovered, and baked Alaska was never on any hotel menus from that day forth. Declan then had an idea that he would make a good bricklayer like one of his brothers who had a construction business. Having just finished school and not having a clue what we were going to do with our lives, both of us thought it wasn't a bad idea at all.

One weekend he said he had landed a job just up the road in Glenageary, one of the more affluent parts of town. It seemed that his old man—who worked as a porter in one of the Dublin hotels—got talking to a guest who needed some building work done and, of course, his old man knew Declan was looking for a start, so he told the guy that his son would do the job. He assured the guest that his son was more than capable and would do a fine job, and as he'd been porter for over thirty years in this salubrious hotel, the guest could rest assured that he had a full comeback in the event anything went wrong. So Declan got the job and asked me to help. I agreed because I needed the few shekels.

Off we walked up to this bloke's house on a fine Saturday morning. We met the guy who said all he wanted was for us to put a window into his old garage. "No problem," says Declan. After the guy disappeared, having agreed on the price, I said to Declan,

"What do we do now?" He pointed to the place in the wall where he wanted me to start hammering with the sledgehammer. After about a half hour of taking turns swinging at that wall and not making the slightest dent, I asked Declan if he was sure he knew what he was doing. Was he not supposed to mark stuff, make drawings, put up support beams, or do something that would make us look like we knew what we were doing? "Not at all," says Declan. "Just keep belting away." After another while, I was knackered, so Declan took the sledgehammer and charged at the wall. The next thing we knew, the entire garage came crashing down, roof, walls, everything. We were lucky we weren't hurt—not so much as a scratch.

After the dust cleared, I said to Declan, "Holy crap, Declan! What do we do now?"

"Run like the clappers," he said. So off we ran down the hill with me bursting my hole laughing all the way to my house and Declan shouting, "This isn't bleeding funny! Say nothing to nobody," as if the owner wasn't going to notice that his entire garage had collapsed! The owner of the house went raving ballistic and drove into Declan's old man's hotel fuming and raising hell and, as a result, Declan's brother had to make amends by building the owner a brand new garage—with a window of course—which was the beginning and the end of our construction business.

Around that time I worked as a part-time bartender during summer breaks from school, and I loved the work and the money, especially the tips and meeting people. I hung around with a bloke named Stewart, another bartender, and we had great fun. Stew used to bring me into his flat in a rough area of town, and we'd have a few drinks before I went home. My job was to keep watch while Stew went downstairs to a neighbor's flat for a ride from one of the daughters, and I was to make sure nobody saw him. I would have liked a ride myself, but she only had one sister, and she was so fat I was scared of her.

One evening Stew asked me to go to the racetrack with him. He was a terrible gambler who was always looking for an easy way out. We went to the dog track after we had been paid our wages. By the time we'd gotten off the bus and walked in, Stew had already placed his entire week's wages on a dog in the first race; that dog was last and is possibly still running. I couldn't believe that someone would want to lose all their money so quickly. As a result, I made sure it would never happen to me. Gambling was for suckers.

My mother never liked Stew, and I told him that under no circumstances was he ever to come knocking on my door, or my ma would run him. I was due to meet Stew downtown, and as I was at home getting myself ready to go out, I heard Stew at the door. My ma was shouting at him: "Never darken this doorstep again! You're no good, and you never will be, and stay away from my son!" I was mortified, and I never saw Stew again.

Fast forward some twenty years and I'm entertaining some clients in a Dublin pub for lunch. I go up to the bar to get some refreshments and, lo and behold, there's Stew serving some customers at the far end of a mile-long bar. He turned around and immediately recognized me, even after all those years. He then shouted out at the top of his lungs, "Your mother was right. I'm no good and never was." He had never forgotten it, and we laughed. That was the end of Stew. But it's funny how your mother is always right.

I worked as a bartender at large private parties for one of the big pubs who were commissioned to supply all the booze, cigars, and staff. Ireland had no strict laws about underage people working as bartenders, or drinking beer for that matter. I was only sixteen and was delighted to get the money working the parties because I was good at my job. I had worked quite a few parties without any trouble, except for one time a part-timer called down to my house to collect me in his old Volkswagen to bring me to the gig. He seemed pleasant enough. We were working hard at the party when, near the end of the evening, he approached me to offer a lift home. He said he was going to grab a few bottles of beer, and I was to meet him outside. I didn't think much about it; it was pretty normal for the guys to have a beer or two after a gig, but when the foreman came up and asked me where all the cigars had gone, I was shocked to see that the whole cigar case was empty. Those weren't your cheap cigars; those were your "Hello Castro's." I told the foreman that I hadn't a clue, and off he went in search of the cigars. I had a feeling in my groin that Herr Volkswagen had done the dirty deed and, sure enough, I found him outside with the trunk full, not only with the aforementioned Castro's but also with a variety of quality spirits. I nearly died with embarrassment. I wanted to kill the guy, but he would have beaten the crap out of me. I got out of the car and told him I didn't want any part of it. I was fired the next day. I was brought into the manager's office. The manager told me that things were quiet, and they didn't need part-timers. In other words, they were telling me to piss off and not bother coming back.

About two years after that I landed a job with Ulster Bank. One lunchtime I went over to the local pub for soup and a sandwich, only to find that "the foreman" was behind the bar. He recognized me immediately and asked me what I was doing these days. When I told him I was working at the bank across the road, he shouted, "Hey, lads! You'd better get your money out of the Ulster Bank before your man here gets his hands on it!" I laughed and told him I never had anything to do with the stuff that went missing at the party, but he didn't believe me. He's long dead now, the little bollocks.

CHAPTER 4

I HAD NO DEFINITE CAREER plan. For my parents it was a case of feed him, clothe him, push him from the nest, and let him fly as soon as possible. I have always been a loner in one way or another despite my apparently extroverted personality. I can engage anybody in conversation, talking about any subject you care to bring up and fooling you into thinking that I am knowledgeable about what we are discussing. I enjoy a person's company and, above all, I can make people laugh. But behind that façade is a person who enjoys his own company. After all, if you cannot enjoy your own company, how can you expect anybody else to enjoy it? I will always abandon people if they disappoint me, ignore me, use me, or are unappreciative. I am not greedy—except where cake is concerned—and I am always the first to offer my assistance. I don't get involved in fights or aggressive behavior, and I have never hit anybody, although there were a number of times that I wanted to. I always walk away.

My parents, your grandparents, Tommy and Rose, were typical working-class people with little formal education, primarily because they came from poor families and were expected to be earners as soon as they could. They were from the inner city of Dublin, from corporation and council housing, barely existing from week to week. Even though my father was registered in a school, he never attended classes, unbeknownst to his parents. Apparently he used to leave the house in the morning, dump his schoolbag, and head into the city. Nobody knows where he went. I had assumed he had attended school like everybody else. The funny thing is that he was maniacal about any of us not attending school and, as a result, we never missed a day.

My mother attended a nun's school that she hated, so her mother took her out of school when she was about twelve. Rose had to look after her mother from then on. They did everything together and appeared to be especially close all of their lives. My mother was a good-looking woman, and she met my father in a cinema where she worked as an usher. My father worked as a projectionist at the same cinema. They hit it off pretty quickly and got married when she was nineteen and he was twenty-three.

My father hated city life and everything about where he grew up. Being the adventurous type, he decided to move away from the city to Dun-Laoghaire, a town which was being developed about twenty miles from the city center. This was like living in the sticks as far as my mother was concerned. She being a city girl, availed herself of every opportunity to jump on a bus to visit her mother and get back home before Tommy realized what she had been up to. Her clandestine operation went on for years. The house they bought was in one of the new housing estates that were being built in Ireland at that time, which allowed families to grow up together in closely knit communities.

I loved my parents; they were good people whose main priority was to survive, improve their own lives, and raise their children as best they could. My father always told my mother that she was there for him and that he was there for her, that he was to be her priority as she was his. As long as that happened, everything would be fine. The kids came second.

He was apparently a jealous man and a bit of a control freak, which I only found out during the final years of my mother's life. It happened one day when I was visiting Ma, as I did a couple times a week. I would take her to the local cinema and then to a pub for a drink and something to eat. We both enjoyed it. That was about fifteen years after Tommy had died. I asked her one day why she never mentioned Tommy anymore, and if she still missed him. Expecting a standard response, I was shocked to hear her say that she didn't miss him at all. She explained that her life with Tommy was good, but that he never gave her a moment to herself. He would leave the house to travel barely two miles to work and would immediately phone her to find out what she was doing, and she would tell him that nothing had changed since he had left the house. He also hated to arrive home to find a neighbor talking to her.

He expected her to be waiting for him with his dinner on the table. He was extremely jealous if another man looked at her in any meaningful way. I had never realized any of that was going on.

She said that her life post-Tommy was full. She was independent. She had fun with other people. She could play bridge, which she loved, and travel around the country and abroad, which was something she could never do when Tommy was alive. She was free to do anything she wanted. I respected her for saying it but, as I said, I was shocked by her revelations.

I am proud to say I have many of my father's characteristics—his humor and his outlook on life. Am I the jealous type? Probably no more than most men. Am I a control freak? Absolutely not. I love nothing more than for people to assert themselves, and I have always given everybody absolute freedom to do as they pleased.

My mother raised, clothed, schooled, and entertained us. She did everything and, because of the nature of my father's work as a cinema projectionist with anti-social hours, he was working while we played, came home while we slept, and worked weekends. But we always knew he would come home, that he was always there for us. I couldn't imagine the alternative, the alternative that I imposed on my own children.

I could never go to my father and have a heart-to-heart with him; that wasn't done in those days. You had to sort it out yourself and muddle through, invariably getting it wrong. He never played with us, but most fathers didn't play with their children, so we didn't see anything wrong with that. How things have changed—some for the better and some for the worse. My father would never attend school functions or watch me play football, and that was wrong, but you knew he was always there if you needed him. He left you to figure things out for yourself because he trusted you. Your father was always your "Da," your mother was always your "Ma," and everything worked somehow.

I have a sister Barbara whom I've grown fonder of over these past years, and we have a special bond, the sort of bond you have with your sister Cathy. Barbara is five years younger than I am, so we weren't close growing up. She was just a kid when I was in my late teens, so I don't remember doing many things with her. She had her girl pals, and I was a typical teenage boy. She has always been reliable and good, the sort of sister you can easily trust and love. You'll read about how I credit her with saving my life.

My brother Joe is a different story. He is four years older than I am, and I would safely say that we spoke no more than twenty words to each other in the entire sixteen years we lived under the same roof. If I asked him a question, he ignored me, so I never sought his advice. He constantly looked down on me and never stood up for me. He was always hitting me, and one day when I was about fifteen he was chasing me around the house and beating me up again when I fell on the stairs and pretended to be dead. He got a fright, and then I jumped up and grabbed him by the throat and told him, with steel in my eyes, that if he ever touched me again I would kill him. And I meant it. He never touched me after that, and he never knew I was pissing in my pants at the time. He hated my father more than he hated me. On the day of my father's funeral, as Tommy lay in the open casket, Joe asked my sister if we should take a photograph so we could all remember his corpse. She said that Joe was smirking. Had I known about it, I would have taken him down on the spot.

My mother taught us the difference between right and wrong and protected us like a mother hen. She could use the rod (back of the hand or the dishcloth) and give us the evil eye, but only when we truly deserved it. She also had a great sense of humor. The only thing she couldn't do was show affection. It wasn't in her nature. She never had it while she was growing up, so she simply didn't know how to impart it. She would never say she loved you, and rarely would she kiss you. She found such displays of affection awkward. She hated it when she saw other women kiss their children. We never expected affection and, as a result, it's only in the past few years that Barbara and I are able to say we love each other in a demonstrative way. It's still a bit awkward, more so for her than me, but at least it happens.

I think it's important that kids be told they are loved as often as possible, but without going over the top. My father was even worse when it came to showing affection. He never said he loved me once. Again, it was the way he was reared. I would say that of the three of us, I would be the one who wanted to be told he was loved, the one who was looking for attention. I wanted to know they were proud of me. They'd say heartfelt stuff if they had a few drinks in them: "Aw, Bernard is a great lad, never a moment's bother, one of the best." But the next morning and thereafter, nothing was said. I remember distinctly bringing my father down to my new offices—I was so proud of the way my company was growing—and I expected they were all proud of me, too. I looked at my father and said, "What do you think, Da?" He just looked at me and said, "It's a bit big, isn't it, son?"

One of the most important people in my life was Tommy, or "the Da," as most fathers were affectionately known. It wasn't that we were close. We never played football or went to sports events or anywhere together. He was just the "Da."

I never knew him to raise a hand to any of us, although he could throw you the evil eye now and then. And when he did, you knew when to shut up or steer clear. He had a wonderful sense of humor and enjoyed a good laugh. I'll always remember some of his sayings: "Don't be always worrying" and "Do you know how Colman's mustard made their money? It's due to the amount of mustard people leave on their plates." He also offered some philosophical sayings like, "Only take advice from those who have nothing to gain" and "Never think that you have a weakness; lie about it."

He didn't have many friends. I can't say I remember anybody coming into the house that wasn't someone who worked with him. His whole life revolved around Rose. He was infatuated with her to the point of being a control freak, as I've already told you. He did everything for her, and as long as they did everything together, he was a happy man. So that was the environment in which I grew up. These are some of the stories that made Tommy a legend in his own lifetime, and stories that were to change me forever.

CHAPTER 5

THESE ARE JUST SOME OF the stories that I remember about my Da. They are not in any particular order but give you an idea of the sort of man he was, the man that I loved very much.

Joe and I were finishing off breakfast before school when in walked Da and closed the kitchen door behind him. Now, I was about thirteen at the time, and I never remember anybody closing that door. It was a non-door as far as I was concerned. So Da walked over to the net curtains on the window, opened them, and pointed to the roundabout outside our house.

"Boys, do you see that?" he said. We both looked down the road and saw nothing.

"What, Da?" I said.

"That there," he said, pointing again to the roundabout.

All I could see were two dogs screwing one another, so I looked over at Joe, who shrugged and said, "Yeah, right!"

Da said, "Well, let that be a lesson to you," and off he went, back into the kitchen where he announced to my mother, "That's done then, Rose. Now what's for breakfast?"

I looked at Joe and asked him what all that had been about, and he said, "I guess we've just had the facts-of-life talk."

Armed and dangerous I was, for now I was fully educated in the facts of life, and I never looked at a dog in the same light after that.

My first introduction to entrepreneurship occurred when I was about fourteen years old. The Da decided that I had the wherewithal to start my own business. He thought that I should start by selling vegetables, as one of our neighbors had been selling them all of his life, and had done extremely well. The neighbor only worked a few hours every other day, delivering fresh eggs, potatoes and vegetables to a number of households in the vicinity. We only found out some years later, after he died, that the main reason he did so well, was he never paid any taxes. We scoured the commodity pages in the local evening newspapers, and I have to say I got rather exited about the whole project. It sure beat having to study for school. Soon I was entertaining thoughts of houses in Dallas, a very popular television program at the time, and possibly one or two Caribbean hideaways. We made our way to the markets at the crack of dawn. We stocked his old Morris Minor with a couple of crates of eggs, and boxes of fresh cabbage and potatoes. The Da had planned our route to include most of the working class dwellings in the bad neighborhood, mostly because nobody knew us there. Our first day on the course, I started knocking on doors with major aplomb and excitement.

"Would you like to buy our vegetables, potatoes or eggs?"

"Fuck off sonny" as the first non-customer slammed the door in my face. Welcome to the real world of door to door selling.

The Da stayed in the car motivating me onwards and upwards. Finally, after about the second tier of long houses, just as I was becoming despondent about my future career, and knocking off one of the Caribbean properties, an old woman said

"How much are they sonny?"

"Two shillings a dozen eggs and ten pence a head of cabbage"

"Give me a dozen eggs, a stone of potatoes and a head of cabbage." The Da hopped out of the car, cigarette hanging from his lips, as he put the potatoes in a brown bag, together with the head of cabbage, and handed her the lot with a tray of eggs saying

"That'll be three and six missus." I'd never heard him call anybody "missus" before and took a mental note to add that to my selling vocabulary.

The next thing another woman came running out

"What's that you have Mary?"

"This bloke is selling the stuff cheaper than the supermarkets."

Pretty soon a small line had developed, and within the hour, our precious cargo had been sold out. We headed home, ebullient and totally satisfied. Over the next two days, we couldn't wait to go back to the market and replenish our stock. This time we bought a week's supply and the da said it would be a good idea to pre-package the potatoes for easier distribution. I spent hours weighing and packing the goods. The next two days it rained non-stop which meant we had to wait until the weather got better. I had stocked them in the shed out back. Unfortunately it was not refrigerated. Blindly we re-traced our selling route and our reputation had obviously spread, as there was a small crowd waiting for us, who quickly emptied all of our stock as we handed out pre-filled bags of potatoes, eggs and cabbages.

That night I went out to the shed to see what we had left, only to find that all of the potatoes had sprung tails. Not knowing that they were rotting away quickly, I loaded up the car for a quick dash to sell the remainder. As we approached our route, we were confronted by an angry mob, who had obviously heard we were in the neighborhood.

"Your eggs were rotten and your potatoes had things growing out of them"

"We want our money back." shouted the angry mob. I had immediate thoughts of *"Crucify him, release Barabbas (hoping that I was the latter),"* when the Da, quick as a light, jumped out of the car

"Sorry missus, must have been a bad lot from our supplier. How much do I owe you?"

With that, I saw our profits, together with our capital, deplete rapidly, as we made our very quick exit. Lessons had been learned;

- Don't think that starting your own business is going to be easy.
- Pick a product and a market that you know something about.
- Don't sell in rough neighborhoods.

The Da was at his best when you least expected anything. We were at home on a wet winter's Tuesday night, watching the television, when Da came home very early, around 5:30. We all got a shock when he walked into the living room and told Joe and myself to grab our coats, that we had to catch a bus. Rose sat up and asked Da what was going on, only to be told, "Leave it to me, Rose. I'm taking the boys to the greyhound track, and we'll be back around eleven, so don't wait up."

He marched us down the road to the local pub and when we walked in asked, "Right boys, what'll you have to drink?"

I looked at Joe, and he said, "I'll have a pint," whereupon he looked over at me.

I said, "A Club Orange, Da."

"Now son," he said, "I know you've had a beer or two, so you'll have a bottle of lager." Holy crap, I was only fifteen and already I'm out drinking with me Da, which made me really proud. I couldn't wait to tell the lads about this one.

"Okay," I said, and we had our beers.

"Now what do you smoke?" Da said.

I nearly fell off my chair, but I boldly announced, "I'd like ten Rothmans, Da," and Joe asked for the same, except the little bollocks said twenty Rothmans.

Then we hopped on the bus into the dog track, and he handed us both a fiver, which was a lot of money at the time and represented a large chunk of his wages.

"Now off you go," he said. "Pick your dogs, and when the monies are gone, then we go home."

I'd hardly finished my third bottle of lager before I was reduced to only a few shekels remaining, and Joe having lost everything, we scooted off on the bus, arriving home to a frantic Rose, so we trekked upstairs to bed, in a very happy but confused state.

Da turned to Rose and said, "Leave it to me, Rose." He followed us upstairs, put on the bedroom lights, and said, "Now boys, never let it be said that your father ever denied you or stopped you from drinking, smoking, or gambling, because tonight you did all three with your father. Now you won't be doing it again, so goodnight boys," and he closed the door.

I lay there in the dark and asked Joe, "Does that mean that Da has to go with me when I get my first ride?"

Then there was el Classico, never to be repeated. It was another wet winter's night—Mother of God it was always raining—when the Da came home, except this time the Ma was fully informed of his intentions, and she had us wrapped up for the weather. The Da had hired a truck. This was during the days when nobody hired a truck. I must annex something here about Da's driving ability: it didn't exist. Da was quite simply the worst driver on the planet, but you couldn't tell him that or he'd go through you. He drove only in fourth gear. He started the car in fourth gear and never deviated, and when I asked him why he didn't use the other three gears, he said they were only spares. So he drove the streets of Dublin chugging along in fourth gear, even from a stationary position, driving all and sundry to distraction as they honked at him from all angles, but that never bothered the Da as he blocked the fast lanes all over the city and never drove over twenty miles an hour.

For the Da to drive a truck was a beacon to the drivers of this world to get off the road, immediately. We climbed aboard all excited, without a clue as to where we were going, and soon we arrived in the city center, or the inner city as it's known, at Aunt Sissy's house, who had just died about six hours previously.

It appeared that Aunt Sissy hadn't had a bank account and had made known to all and sundry at her dying bed that she had her money hidden in her house but had died before disclosing its exact whereabouts. So the people in that room, which included the Da, did a runner as soon as the doctor announced her death and the priest said the obligatory three Hail Mary's. They ran in all directions, the Da heading straight down to some bloke who would rent him a truck.

Da may not have had any formal education, but he was very street wise. I learned a lot from him, as you can imagine. His education was primarily sourced from Hollywood movies because as a movie projectionist, he saw thousands of movies over his lifetime and took note, especially of crime dramas. He had zoomed in on Aunt Sissy's standup piano from the get-go, as that's where Hitchcock would have hidden the money. He told the other two relatives, who were tearing the place apart at the time, that he only wanted the piano, so not having a problem with that, they even helped him load the piano onto the back of the truck, and we headed home. We still had no idea what we were doing, and we didn't know anything about this until we got home. We pushed and puffed our way, helped by the Ma, who always had reserves of energy whenever money was involved, and plonked the piano in the back room, whereupon Da told me to get down into the back of it, as I was skinny and nimble, and look for anything unusual.

The Ma was losing her knickers, saying, "What are we going to do with this thing, there's no money inside of it?"

"Hold on there, Rose," said Da, and holy hallelujah if he wasn't correct. There was a big plastic bag stuffed down between the strings, and I managed to bring it up. It was as if Lazarus himself had walked into the room. There was a stunned silence while we stared at a fortune, all big Irish currency notes the likes of which we'd never seen before. There were fifty- and hundred-pound notes, massive things, and the Da took control immediately, saying, "Right, get the beer, Rose. Boys, start counting the money."

There were two thousand pounds in that bag. That's equivalent to sixty thousand pounds or eighty thousand dollars in today's money. An absolute bloody fortune it was, considering that Da's take-home pay was around seven hundred a year. Holy caramba, we danced around that room, but the Da warned us never to tell anybody because the relatives would come after us looking for their share. He gave each of us forty pounds, took fifty for himself, and gave the rest to the Ma, telling her, "That's all yours, Rose."

The next day was a Monday. Because we never ate meat on a Monday, the Ma bought five big sirloin steaks, and we couldn't believe it. Then as luck would have it the nosy neighbor came in, and we had to do a runner with the meat until she left, and by that time it had gone cold and hard, but we still dived in anyway. That money paid off all of their debts and couldn't have come at a better time for them, as Tommy had been on strike for over a year. What a victory, what a night!

Nobody gave a fiddler's curse about cinemas being on strike, as it didn't mean anything in the real scheme of things in mid-fifties Ireland. The Da had to bring in the money any way he could, so he decided that for the duration of the strike he would be Ireland's number-one electrician. The fact that he had absolutely no qualifications didn't seem to matter. Now I can honestly say, and he would kill me for saying this, but the Da was nearly as bad an electrician as he was a driver, if that was possible. He used to get me to help him, or in other words get me out of the house and from under the Ma's feet. He landed this big job from a hotel owner who really liked Da—it was impossible not to like him—and the man wanted the Da to re-cable the entire hotel. I think the owner took pity on Da, as he knew he had a young family. Tommy was thrilled to get the work, and no matter what you might say about the quality of his work, his dedication and application were never in question. We were up in one of the many attics of the hotel, an old hotel badly in need of refurbishment, when I noticed he was using matchsticks to keep the wires in the sockets. Being only twelve, and always asking questions, I queried the safety aspects of carrying out such a procedure, only to be told, "Your father is a genius and knows everything," so I shut up. That night around two in the morning the phone rang—yes, we had a phone—and the person on the end of the line enquired if this was the home of Mr. Donnelly. Then Tommy was informed that the hotel was on fire, and would he mind making an appearance, as the fire officer would like to speak to him. We were told to get back into bed as Da went off to face the music. We found out later on, much later on in life, that the owner didn't press any charges, and the verdict was an electrical fault. Da never admitted anything, but needless to remark, his electrical days were numbered.

When I finished school, I came home one day to find the Da standing in the breakfast room, all chuffed with himself and smiling. So I said, "What's up?"

"Have you seen what's in the front room?"

"No, what is it?"

"Go in and see for yourself."

I went into the front room and found a dog, a puppy dog, mongrel style.

"What's that for?" I said.

"That's for you."

"For me? I don't want a dog."

"You've always been asking me for a dog, all of your life."

"Yes, Da, that was when I was ten, but now I'm eighteen, and I need a woman, not a dog!" I explained, exasperated.

He was disgusted, and the Ma said, "I told you he wouldn't be interested. I told you. Now what do we do with the dog?"

I felt bad about it, but, hell, I wasn't going to look after any dog, I had things to do, girls to mount. I called the dog Scoopy, as I used to like this television program called Scooby Doo, but I thought he was called Scoopy. The name stuck, and the Ma put the Da in charge of Scoopy. I swear that dog never got an ounce of exercise, never put one leg in front of another. He was even lazier than Tommy, who never exercised in his entire life and never had any intention of doing so.

The dog was terrified of other dogs. One day I saw him lined up, last in the line behind all the other dogs, as they mounted the only bitch in the neighborhood, only for Scoopy to get nothing at all by the time she had been mounted from all directions. I felt sorry for him because I knew how he felt.

Under a lot of duress, Da took Scoopy for a walk downtown and along the pier, a total journey of approximately one and a half miles. He left the house around ten in the morning and by nightfall there was no sign of the Da or Scoopy. We were worried as we had no way of contacting him, when around eight o'clock that night up came a taxi, and out poured Scoopy and the Da. We broke our shit laughing at the pair of them, and the Da announced, as he walked by, "Never again, Rose, never again."

Da had bought his first new car, a Vauxhall Viva, a red one, a total piece of shit, but it was his pride and joy. One day not long after buying it, he and Rose went to do the weekly shopping at the local supermarket. When they came out, they approached the car only to find there was a huge scratch running right up the side of it. Tommy was fit to be tied down without an anesthetic.

"Leave this to me, Rose," he said as he eyed some bloke sitting in the adjacent car reading his newspaper and obviously the guilty party.

"Tommy, don't do anything," said Rose.

"Leave this to me, Rose," Tommy said as he knocked on the bloke's window, pointing to the scratch on his car.

His face was growing redder as Rose was tugging at his coat, saying, "Tommy, Tommy—"

"Rose," Tommy barked, "I'm dealing with it!"

Seemingly, the bloke in the other car hadn't a clue what Da was going on about, when the Ma shouts, "Tommy, it's not our car!"

"Oh crap!" says the Da and looks at the other bloke, saying, "Nice day, isn't it?" They walked very quickly into the car park, cringing and not looking back. He was always getting himself into embarrassing situations, but it ran off him like water off a duck's back.

Another time I had given him a new calculator. He thought this was the dog's bollocks as the Da was not the most technically gifted person, a calculator was as much as he could cope with. He couldn't wait to test it out, so off they go that week to the supermarket, and the conversation goes like this:

"Pound of butter, 22p," says the Ma.

"22p," says the Da as he enters the number into the calculator.

"Cornflakes, 35p."

"35p," says the Da.

On it went until they completed the shopping and arrived at the cash register, where some bird with the intelligence of a dead rat yawned at the Da as he told her about his new Japanese calculator and how he knew how much all the groceries were going to cost.

The bird dinged her way through the groceries and said, "That'll be seven and six pence."

"No, it won't," said the Da, with the line forming behind them and Rose looking straight ahead, as she always knew her place in such matters.

"Wha?" says the bird.

"Look, this Japanese calculator says I only owe you four and ten pence," he said and showed the LCD display to her.

"Look-it, I don't know anything about your bleedin' calculator, but my machine says you owe me seven and six, so there!" she said, wanting to throttle him.

Da was having none of it and said he wanted her to do it again, much to the anger of everybody standing behind them. Three times the bird counted the groceries, and three times she got the same answer, and now the line behind was huge.

"It's seven and six. That's it, right!" says the bird, ready to clock him one.

"These bloody Japanese, they can do nothing right," says the Da. "Pay her, Rose, I'll be outside," as he cringed his way out of the shop.

The only time there was a major confrontation was with Joe, the brother. He was always trouble. I remember the Da and him having another argument one day, and the Da went into the kitchen and asked the Ma, "Are you sure he's ours, Rose? Did the hospital make a mistake or something?"

Joe never did anything good in his entire miserable life, and he grew up never wanting to be a part of our family. Things had reached a boiling point when Joe was about eighteen and I was fourteen. Joe had won a load of money playing poker the night before. He was blowing his own trumpet about how brilliant he was and bragging that the Da couldn't play poker to save his life, which was true. Joe wouldn't shut up about it, and he droned on and on when the Da, having had enough of it, said, "So you think you can beat me at poker?"

"No problem," says Joe. "You're a crap poker player."

So Da got a deck of cards and said, "I'll play you for what you won last night."

There was a stunned silence in the room, the Ma dropping the kettle because she knew Da was a lousy poker player too. I just wanted Joe to lose, but I knew that wasn't going to happen.

"Let me see your money," said Joe.

"I have the money," said Da.

"Yeah, well what are the limits?" said Joe.

"No limits," said Da as he announced that they'd play just one game, and one game only, until somebody won the pot.

"You're on," said Joe, and in silence they dealt the cards.

Now I knew how to play poker, but I'd never seen that much money in the pot.

Joe kept three cards, and Da bought three. It didn't look good for the Da.

So Joe said, "I'll raise a hundred pounds." A hundred pounds back in the mid-sixties was huge. Da looked at him without moving a muscle. The Ma stood at the kitchen door looking very worried. I was entranced.

"I'll see your hundred and raise you three hundred more," said Da.

At this stage I think the Ma farted because there was a lousy smell like only the Ma could let one go. Though come to think of it, it might have been me, or then again, Joe might have farted due to the fright he got.

"Let me see your money," said Joe.

So the Da went over to his drawer, took out his bank book, and said, "There's over a thousand pounds in there, and you'll get your money if you win. Now where's your money?"

Joe says, "I have me post office savings book, and there's four hundred in it."

"You can't use that," screamed the Ma.

"Leave it, Rose," said Da.

"Go get it," the Da said to Joe.

So off Joe runs upstairs, produces the post office book, and throws it on the table.

"So what have you got?" said the Da.

Joe threw down three sevens with a big grin on his miserable face.

The Ma and I looked at Da. He seemed motionless, not a flicker on his face. I remember that stare as he looked at Joe.

"A run to the King," said Da. Holy crap, he had filled it from nothing! Unbelievable! I whooped around the room, and Joe got up and left the house, banging the front door. We didn't see him for three days after that.

The Da turned to me and said, "Never ever gamble, son. Let that be a lesson to you."

The Ma was crying, saying, "What will we do? he's not coming back."

"He'll be back, and hopefully he will have learned a lesson," said the Da.

I had a feeling that the Da had rigged the cards before he had dealt them, but I never found out for sure. Joe never learned any lesson. In fact, it made him even more resentful of all of us, and he refused to take back his post office book, even when the Da offered it to him. He eventually took it about four years later. The money was still there, untouched.

I was about fourteen or so when I was involved in my only fight. I was playing outside on the roundabout with a group of about a dozen lads, messing around as young boys do, when someone got it into his head to start fighting me and the next thing I knew the whole group of them on top of me and I ended up with a bloody nose and crying, so I went home. When the Da saw me, he asked me what had happened, and I told him. He grabbed my arm and brought me out into the street, whereupon everybody did a runner.

"He'll take you on one at a time," the Da shouted down the road. "One at a time, you cowards, come on out and fight him now!"

"Eh, Da, could we talk about this?" I enquired as I wasn't at all as confident as him that I would be successful in carrying out his challenge. Surprisingly or unsurprisingly, nobody accepted his challenge, much to my relief, and nobody ever bullied me again. It was as if a statement had been made and my territory had been won. I was very proud of my Da that day.

One final note about the Da. I was about twenty-one and still living at home. I was having my dinner looking at the television, happy as a little piggy, when the door opened and the Da popped his head in, saying, "How are you, son?"

"I'm great, Da," I said.

"Do you not think it's time for you to be moving on and start living your own life?" he asked in a very matter-of-fact sort of way.

"Eh, would it be all right if I finished my dinner first?"

"Aw yeah, finish your dinner son, but let's say six months, okay?" And with that the Da walked away, and I looked at the wall and thought to myself, "I suppose that means it's time to be getting my skates on, as it looks like I won't be getting any more free dinners!"

CHAPTER 6

I WAS EIGHTEEN WHEN I finished school and I had no idea what I wanted to do. I knew I had to look for a job. There was no possibility of me ever going to university. The idea never arose as there was no money to pay for it, so end of story. I applied for forty-seven jobs (I remember the number) without any success, every one of them replied with a "Dear sir, we regret. . . ." I thought about becoming a pilot, so I applied for a job with Aer Lingus. I passed the initial interview, and when I arrived for my second and final interview, the guy asked me to look at some book and tell him the numbers that I saw on each page. When I looked at the pages, all I saw were colored paintings or drawings of trees and stuff, and so I told him I couldn't see any numbers. He told me that I was colored blind, badly colored blind, and they couldn't accept my application. I told him I knew I was colored blind, as was my father and my brother, but not my sister. My blindness is quite severe because reds, browns and greens all look the same to me, and I cannot distinguish the difference between blues, purples and pinks. Colors such as tan, magenta or violet, don't exist for me. He explained that they couldn't take the chance of having me flying one of their jumbo jets, telling me to push the green button and have me crash the plane into the Irish sea with the loss of their aircraft and a couple of hundred lives. I noticed he mentioned the loss of the aircraft before mentioning the loss of lives! I sort of understood his point of view, so there ended my flying career as well as any thoughts I may have had about becoming a vet, doctor, astronaut, architect, fashion consultant, paint manufacturer or anything else to do with colors, which severely limited my options.

People have asked me how I have managed with traffic lights all of these years, and I tell them it's been pure luck.

I also got a second interview with one of the largest supermarket chains, and I attended a final interview out in Sutton, on the other side of the city, which was a pain in the arse when you had to rely on buses. I was ushered into a smoke-filled office, and the interviewer asked me some questions.

"What would you do as a manager in one of our branches if you found out that you had no Kellogg's cornflakes, it was late in the day and your store was due to close in three hours?" he asked?

"I'd ring one of the other stores and get them to send some over," I said. This seemed to please him no end because he grabbed the phone, pushed a button, and told whomever was on the other end of the phone to come and see me. I felt excited, and he told me the owner would be in shortly.

"If you bought something for twenty pounds and fifteen pence and sold it for twenty-four pounds and fifty-eight pence," he then asked, "what would your gross margin percentage be?"

Crap, I thought. "Eh, could I have a calculator?"

"No calculators," he said.

I panicked. I tried to do the maths, and my brain shut down. I was screwed. I sat there in a cold sweat. As the door opened behind me, I glanced over at the owner, who looked at the interviewer, who shook his head. The door closed, and I was told they'd be in touch. And that was the end of my supermarket career. I was playing golf thirty years later in Portugal, and who should be in front of me, holding up play, but the owner that closed the door in my face. I shouted up the par three, "Get a move on, you dopey bollocks!" It felt really good.

I even applied for a job with one of the banks. Every Tom, Dick, and Harry was applying to the banks, and even though I knew I'd hate it, I was desperate. The entrance exam was up in Belfast at the height of the Troubles, and I was quite excited about it because I'd never seen any armored cars before. I think Ireland possessed about three Datsun's that doubled up as the army's armored personnel carriers, so to see the British army and all their paraphernalia out on the public streets was a real novelty for someone like me. I was so excited that I took my Brownie camera and tried to take a photograph of a passing armored car when all of a sudden the car screeched to a halt, and out jumped about six heavily armed soldiers pointing their guns in my direction. I froze. They saw that I was obviously not a threat and scooted off. I nearly pissed in my pants. I stayed in my room that night. I got the job, but I only lasted one day as I thought that when the banks shut their doors that was my cue to go home not realizing that they were only shut to the public, the work still went on on the inside. It was not for me, besides I didn't like counting other peoples money, I wanted to count my own and I didn't see any future in that.

With no sign of a decent job on the horizon, my father arranged for me to follow my brother into an accountancy firm in Dun-Laoghaire, a small firm run by an old codger who had no time for me, loved my brother, and used any opportunity to make my life miserable.

I don't know what he had to complain about because he didn't pay me anything, and I worked hard. Having hated every subject in school, but somehow managing to pass all the exams, it was around this time that I found out that I had an affinity with mathematics. I actually liked the damned thing, and I even started to read maths books. I found that I was good at it. I enjoyed the accountancy, at least for the first couple of years. I liked having somewhere to go every day. The people I met were an understanding lot, and I became friendly with a couple of them.

The firm had some notable clients, particularly in the entertainment field, but clients only came to us when they had tax problems, or better still, if they didn't want to pay any taxes. Our firm had a bad reputation with the tax people because we were always coming up with excuses for clients as to why they hadn't made their tax returns. The boss used to send us kids into the tax appeals courts, and we'd give angelic reasons for why our clients were late with their returns, such as, "Our client fell into a bucket of tar your honor, and as a result he's been laid up in bed" or things like the-dogs-ate-the-returns type of stuff. Things you used to say to your teacher if you hadn't done your homework. Infantile stuff really.

I managed to pass three of the four exams I needed to qualify as an accountant. I was more interested in women than studying, and I began to get disillusioned with working in that firm. One day I was in the boss's office, opening the mail, and he said to me, "How old are you now, Bernie?"

"Eh, twenty-one, boss," I answered.

"Well, do you not think it time for you to be moving on?" I just looked at him without replying, knowing full well that he wanted me to hand in my notice and soon. I went back to my office, and I told one of the guys that I thought I'd just been fired. I left there about two months later.

I know it must have galled him to have witnessed my subsequent career successes because he had considered me as being of average intelligence and a bit of an idiot. I also ended up selling him all of my junk computer equipment, dressed up as new, and I felt no shame in doing so because I had been his slave, working there all those years for peanuts.

It was also around this time that my personality came out of hibernation, and I began to blossom. I started to notice that I could be quite funny. People would laugh at the things I'd say and I was very quick with retorts, without being a smart ass. I became more vocal and opinionated. I liked my developing personality, and so did people around me. The more attention I got, the more I thrived. This period of my life was like my rebirth, as I gained in confidence and started looking after my fitness and health. I retried dating with some successes and more failures.

I was a very determined individual, and I used to run the legs of myself every evening down at the seafront, the West Pier specifically, as it had fewer people and allowed me to think. When I reached the end of that pier, I'd made a definite plan to achieve three things that year. Firstly, I wanted to pass another accountancy exam. Second was to find a gorgeous girl and have sex, the sooner the better. My third target was always the same. I had reached one definite conclusion very early in life: I wanted to be a multimillionaire. Not just a millionaire, I was going to be a multimillionaire. I even knew when it was going to happen. It was going to be when I reached forty years of age, not a moment sooner, and certainly no later. Forty was the number that gave me sufficient time to achieve my ambition, and achieve it I would. How was I going to achieve it? I had absolutely no fucking idea.

CHAPTER 7

I WAS HOPELESS AT MEETING girls. I ogled many, but I had no success whatsoever in dating the ones that I dreamt about. I envied my school friends who seemed to have no difficulty in having a bevy of beautiful girls whenever they chose. I was like Scoopy the dog, always at the end of the line and hoping for the odd stray. As a result, masturbation played a big part in my life as my metamorphosis took me from teenager to young man. I was still a virgin at nineteen, and I would safely say that had there been an Olympic event for masturbation, I would have been gold medal material.

After I'd left the accountancy office, I got a part time job as a lowly paid book-keeper in a local business while I tried to find something that I liked and gave me some career prospects. My friend Joe begged me to go with him to Majorca on holiday. He neglected to tell me that he was bringing his girlfriend and that he intended to propose to her over there. I was greatly pissed off. First, he had never mentioned it before. Second, he spent the whole time ignoring me totally as he devoted the entire two weeks to her. I was left sucking my thumb while they became the engaged couple. We went night clubbing, and who should walk in but Maria, who was going to be your mum. I fancied her. She looked cute with her long blond hair and her min-skirt showing ample legs and best of all she was Irish. We danced and got along famously. The rest of the holiday I saw her on and off, and we were on the same flight home. When we arrived at Dublin Airport, her dad was there to pick her up, so we exchanged numbers, and shortly after that we started dating. I was in awe of the fact that she was the first female chemical engineer in Ireland. She was also earning a lot more money than me as I was still scraping along with my miserable wage as a book-keeper, but she didn't mind that. Maria was the first girl I had dated who wasn't from the city. She was a country girl through and through. She also happened to work in the same factory as my mother, which was more than a surprise, a surprise I could have done without, remembering that my girlfriend was chief engineer and my mother a distinctly non-chief assembly line worker. This was a part-time job for my ma to get her out of the house. It was not good from the outset. My ma didn't like Maria.

Maria was a very determined woman. When she wanted her own way she would run over you, no matter who you were. I didn't mind this part of her nature. I was very easy-going anyway. Maria was painfully shy. People having met her for the first time would think that she was a bitch, the way she ignored them. I would correct them by explaining that she was shy or that she probably hadn't noticed them. Unfortunately, she did it to the wrong person, namely my mother. Oh God of all the people. I had told my mother I'd met Maria and that unbelievably she worked in the same factory. One day Maria was walking through the factory. My mother tried to introduce herself, and Maria walked right by her, ignoring her completely in front of my mother's friends. When I heard it, I told my ma that Maria obviously hadn't seen her, that she wasn't like that. But my mother is not the person you should cross; she didn't believe me. As a result, Maria was going to be the recipient of my mother's famous evil eye for evermore.

Of course I only briefly enquired of Maria about the incident, and she knew nothing about it. I believed her, knowing her as I did, but the damage had been done, and if my mother was annoyed, then so was Tommy. Maria did this all the time with everybody. Her shyness was her worst enemy. She hated crowds, went puce if she had to stand up in front of people, and smoked to calm her nerves. I found that she hid behind me a lot. Again, I didn't mind, as I was used to her. She left the factory soon afterwards and got a job as a patent examiner. She enjoyed working in the patents office. It suited her, being locked away from the general public with people of her own intelligence, in a calm and unexciting atmosphere. It also meant that she didn't have to work with my mother.

We continued dating for about a year. One day I was over at her apartment, and she dropped the bombshell on me. She said she was pregnant. I was shocked and didn't know what to say or do. Maria said she was not going to have the baby or tell anybody she was pregnant, as she said it would kill her parents. She had already decided what to do; she was going to have an abortion. This was typical Maria at work, as I found out later in life. There was no discussion. That was that. I know it's the woman who shoulders everything in times like this, and to be honest I was just a kid who hadn't a clue. There was no time to think of the ethics of having an abortion. This was sheer panic and had to be resolved quickly. Maria had arranged where to go for the abortion. I had no idea how she had found the clinic in Harley Street, in London. She wouldn't say. These were the holy Ireland days where you were damned for even mentioning abortion, let alone acting upon it. It had to be done in such a clandestine manner that nobody could ever find out. We set off on the mail boat from Dun-Laoghaire, then took the train to London. It was my first visit to London, and we never spoke the whole way there. We arrived at the clinic, paid over the money, and I asked her if she wanted me by her side. She said no, that I was to come back in a few hours. I walked around killing time, and when I went to meet her she said she was fine. We went home, just like that, like an ordinary day at work. She didn't want to talk about it, and we never did.

After that things cooled between us, and about two months later I broke it off with her. I can't remember the exact reason I decided to end it. I didn't think anything of it, and I never missed her. They say that when you split with somebody that you should never go back to them. They say that you split for a very good reason and you are asking for trouble by getting back together again.

I applied for a job working for a British computer company as their financial controller. The idea was that I should work in their London offices with a view to setting up their Irish operation. I was delighted to get the opportunity to go overseas, so off I went to London for about a year or so. I loved London, meeting new friends and going out. It was during this spell away from Ireland that I really started to get to know myself. I enjoyed the simple things, like riding the underground, seeing all the tourist sites like Buckingham Palace and the Tower of London. I also loved how huge London was compared to Dublin, the many ethnic cultures and foods that we didn't have in Ireland. It was also my first time living anywhere other than with my parents, and boy was that an eye opener. I could no longer dump my dirty clothes in the linen basket or go the fridge and grab some food, never thinking how it got there in the first place. I used never had to think about paying bills or wondering where the electricity came from.

My employer had put me up in a two story house, sharing with six other Irish graduates who were employed as programmers. When I first arrived at the house I couldn't believe the mess and the sloppiness of these people, so after a couple of days I set about reorganizing this rabble. I was sharing a bedroom with possibly one of the hairiest gorillas I'd ever seen who left his animal traces everywhere. He never washed the sink after he shaved, and he left his smelly clothes everywhere. The other rabble never seemed to care whether there was a clean dish in the house. It all just blew my mind. I had been well reared, and I had principles that included cleanliness. That was a priority of mine, and I called a meeting of these deadbeats. They may have been academically brilliant, but that's where their graces ended. I told them there were going to be changes around here. I showed them a roster of who was responsible each day for cleaning, cooking, shopping, etc., and when they looked at me as if I had two heads, I told them that unless it happened, none of them would ever get paid. I would ensure that they had nothing but trouble financially, as long as they were employed by the company whose finances were controlled by me. That got their attention, and things improved for about three days before it all fell apart again, so I succumbed and tried to stay away from the pigsty as best I could by working late at the office. I just about barely slept there, never touching anything, especially any foodstuffs.

I was watching television with the piggies when the doorbell rang. The next thing I knew, I was confronted with four very good-looking Irish girls who proceeded to tell me that they would be living there and asked me to point out their bedrooms. I was still gaping at them as they passed me on the stairway. I figured somebody somewhere had made a huge mistake. I followed them upstairs. They took one look at the rabble in front of them scratching their balls, then turned on their sneakers as their leader announced, "Right girls, let's get out of here. We are going downtown." They quickly turned around and marched past me in regulation file. As they went downstairs I shouted after them, "Wait, hold on a second! I'm coming with you." I was a person that was always in a state of readiness, it must have been my Boy Scout training. I was running down those stairs with my bag packed and out on the street in a matter of seconds, pleading with them to take me with them. I explained who I was, that I was a clean, good person, and that I was an accountant and definitely not a programmer. They said absolutely not, but relented when I told them that I was responsible for paying their wages and could be a total bollocks if they didn't agree. So began my one-year of living with four good-looking Irish girls in the up-market town of Hampstead, where my duties included buying the groceries, cleaning, and serving as chief bouncer for all parties that would ensue. There was only one other rule: any messing about and I was out on my ear.

We got on great. Life was very good. I had arranged with my boss that the girls get an upmarket four-bedroomed apartment, but I neglected to mention that I was also staying there. The girls and I got on great, and after a while we were all very comfortable around each other. It didn't matter if they were half naked or whether they had a boyfriend staying over. Everything ran like clockwork, and my enthusiasm for the female gender soared after that.

I was so relaxed in female company that at lunchtime—our offices were on SOHO Square beside the aforementioned Beatles offices—I got to know most of the prostitutes that had their lunch there or who picked up customers on the square. They got used to seeing me around, and they'd say, "Hey Bernie, how is my little Irish bloke?" Charlie, the blonde prostitute, would tell me all about the tricks she'd covered the previous night, how much she earned, and what her dreams and aspirations were while we were having our sandwiches like working colleagues or brother and sister. I really liked all the girls, and there was never any question of me doing anything untoward. They obviously recognized that about me, and that's probably why they liked me. I'd listen to all of their stories. They were an eclectic mix of girls from every walk of life, the educated to the uneducated, the slum dweller to the well-off kid who abandoned her family. I found they were all good people, each and every one of them, far better than many so-called normal people that I'd met in my life.

After a year or so it then came time to set up the Irish operation, and so I headed back to Dublin. I was excited about the prospect of being in charge of the finances and having a senior position.

Maria had written to me asking me to contact her when I returned from England and I did. She said she had missed me a lot and as I was alone we started to date again, but more seriously this time. We suited one another. We never loved each other, but we liked each other's company. We were both loners, although I was beginning to spread my wings. We had very few friends, and we bounced well of each other. Maria never had a girlfriend, and I don't remember her ever having a girl's night out, primarily because she was an academic who had been surrounded by men when she was at university, not to mention the fact that she was a country girl, meaning she hadn't made any friends in the city. I on the other hand had a blossoming personality after I went to London. It was a personality I developed and liked, and so did everybody I met. Whatever friends we developed over the years, I developed them. It made Maria happy that she could coattail me, and I was happy to let her. I don't believe we would have gone anywhere if it wasn't for me. The fact that I was two years younger than her didn't seem to matter. There were huge cultural and personality differences. She was not street smart; I was. Her natural inclination was to head for her parents' home; I didn't. I wanted a big house, big things, to explore the world; she never did. She was a great cook; I sucked. I had a major sense of humor; she didn't. I liked to keep fit; she didn't. We were as different as chalk is to cheese, yet we made it work, at least for a time.

So there we were. She was twenty-five; I was twenty-three. She was a qualified chemical engineer with a great job, permanent and pensionable, bringing in a great salary while I was starting out on a career, and I had no idea where it would take me. I soon found out that my new company expected us to operate on a shoe string. There was very little money, which surprised me, considering the amount of revenue that the Irish programmers were generating for the company. I think they were robbing Peter to pay Paul. I learned a lot trying to get the company to work, making it efficient and profitable.

Everybody was young and around the same age. We had great parties, and Maria and I made some good friends. I remember being at a party one night when I was asked who my best friend was. I said that I didn't really have a best friend. He said that his wife was his best friend. I remember staring at them, thinking how amazing that a guy could say that his wife was his best friend. I had never thought of Maria as being my best friend. When I mentioned it to Maria, she just scoffed at the notion that your partner could be your best friend. It was also a thought that stayed with me all of my life.

One night I was the last out of the building. I got into the elevator, and it shut down between floors. This was the first time that this had ever happened to me, and I didn't know until that moment that I was slightly claustrophobic. I was stuck in that elevator the entire night, absolutely terrified that I would suffocate. I'm not mad about them. After only about a year I had to leave my job, as I saw the writing on the wall. That company was going down the toilet as tensions unfolded in the Middle East when the ayatollah arrived in Iran from Paris and all hell broke loose. We were screwed. We had been owed vast sums of money that we knew would never be paid. The Irish operation was going to be the first to suffer, so it was time to get something concrete on my resume.

I applied and got the job as a financial controller with a very large printing and paper company, one of Ireland's largest companies. I was glad of the job and the position, as it would finally cement a career for me. The money was a lot better, the work was engrossing, and I had the bit between my teeth. It was around this time I decided to marry Maria. I hadn't given it enough thought at the time other than, like other guys I knew, we were prompted by everybody we knew that we should be getting married. Parents would be talking about looking forward to having grand children and all former friends were already married, so it seemed like the thing to do.

CHAPTER 8

One hundred and forty people worked in that printing company, and some of those people had been there forever.

Bob, our managing director had hired me, and I liked him a lot, as I did all the guys, including the worker bees on the floor. I met many characters in Dublin, particularly in that printing company. We had a large transport department delivering all around the city, and I needed the gas receipts to complete my monthly financial reports. The department was run by a union guy called Dave who had a great ability to talk to you with a cigarette hanging from the side of his mouth. No matter how long he kept bobbing the cigarette up and down, the ash never fell to the ground. It could have been four inches long, but it never fell off. I wonder how the hell he managed it. I was pissed one day, and called him into my office.

"Dave, I need those gas receipts for the past seven months. Have you got them?"

"Yes, Bernard, I have." He always called me Bernard, not Bernie like everyone else. We sat down at my desk, and he took out new blank receipt books from Shell, Esso, Texaco and began to write up the receipts in front of me.

"Dave, what are you doing?"

"I'm writing up the receipts you asked for!"

"Dave, you're meant to give me legitimate receipts that you got from the various garages, not make them up right in front of me."

"Well, do you want me to turn my back on you so that you don't see me?"

"Jesus, Dave, I'm the financial controller. You could at least show me the respect of not treating me like a total idiot."

"No, Bernard, I like you. I wouldn't do that," he said in all innocence.

"Where did you get the books?"

"We print them outside in the factory."

"Get out of my office, Dave! Oh, and get me some of those books on the quiet," I said.

"No problem."

Around this time the company was under extreme pressure from head office to produce results, and we hadn't been doing it. Quite simply, Bob, our beloved boss, had lost control, and I was worried about him. It's always the simple things that give you away. For example, Bob had lost one of the lenses in his glasses, and no matter how many times I told him to get them fixed, he continued with a lop-sided frame that made him have to bend his head sideways to see you correctly.

One particularly sunny day, Tony, the litho printing manager, knocked at my door and asked had I got a minute. Now Tony, or any of the machine guys, never bothered with me as they usually went to Bob or the sales director if they had printing questions, but this particular day I was the only senior person available.

I said, "Sure, what's up?"

"You know the big printing job that we are doing for the GAA, that's the Gaelic Athletic Association, the largest sports body in Ireland, responsible for organizing Irish sporting events?"

"Of course," I said. It was our most profitable contract. They were great customers who always paid us on time and never gave us a moment's bother. "What's up?"

"Have a look at this sheet we've produced for their calendar and tell me if you notice anything wrong."

The sheet was divided into twelve individual months for next year's GAA calendar, which was hugely popular in all Irish households. As I looked at the sheet printed in four beautiful colors, I asked, "What am I looking for?"

"Keep looking and tell me if you notice anything peculiar about any of the months?"

I looked at the month of January: nothing there. February was okay, as was every month through to December. "I can't see anything wrong, Tony. Don't tell me we made a leap year out of February. Is this a leap year?"

"No, nothing as simple as that," he replied.

"Do we have two or more days with the same numbers?"

"No, it's more obvious than that," he said as I got more frustrated. "Have another look at April."

"Oh mother of divine sorrows!" I cried out. "Oh Holy Jesus, what is that?"

"That," says Tony, "is probably the greatest screw up in the history of the printing industry."

There, in four living colors, was a dramatic photograph of an obviously very fit GAA all-star player jumping up with another guy, reaching to the blue skies with their hurling sticks, and there for everybody to see hanging down his thigh was probably one of the finest specimens of Irish cock and accompanying hairy testicles that any man would have been proud to own.

"Did nobody proofread the negatives?" I asked.

"Yep, it passed proofreading in all three departments," said Tony.

"How many have we printed?"

"Four hundred thousand."

"How many have we delivered?"

"Probably four hundred thousand."

"Well, that's it," I said. "I'm off to look for another job because I'll be damned if I have to tell Bob about this nightmare."

"That's not the biggest problem. When four hundred thousand Irish households wake up next April and turn the page in our kitchen calendar, we are going to have to deal with the whole Catholic Church as well!"

With that Bob came into my office. Tony and I exchanged looks, and I said, "You'd better sit down, Bob."

So he adjusted his glasses, and tilting his head he asked, "What's wrong?"

It's funny, whenever a person or a company is going through a bad patch, people always assume the negative about everything.

"Wrong? Eh, worse than wrong Bob," I said as I pushed the printed page over to him.

When we resuscitated him, he ran around like a headless chicken. Now, I've never seen a headless chicken, but I am assuming when a person starts mumbling incoherently and going in various directions it must be something fatal, and Bob certainly qualified himself for that title.

"Who spotted the error?" I asked.

"One of the women in the bindery department," said Tony.

That was typical. It had gone through a full screening test with three departments, all of them checking the negatives and the photographs before putting them into production. They get printed, checked again, then bound and checked again in another department, and it was only one of the old women in the despatch department who noticed some young bloke with a very large dick. None of the men, all one hundred of them, ever noticed a thing, not even someone who had the prowess of a large elephant.

After the deliveries had reached the head offices of the GAA, the phones rang off the hook, unsurprisingly. The president of the GAA would only speak to Bob. When we had calmed Bob down, like they do when the boxer is about to go back into the ring against a lean young Muhammed Ali, he reached for the phone as we all crowded into his office to watch the final round, towels at the ready.

"Tell me it's a hockey stick, Bob," says the GAA president. "For God's sake, please tell me it's a fucking hockey stick!"

Needless to remark, it wasn't long before Bob departed the scene. Funnily enough, we never got paid for that job.

My one weakness in life was trusting people. I could never understand why people could be mean to one another, especially so-called friends. This outlook was obviously going to change as I went through my life, but not before I had let it happen to me a few times. Every time it happened to me, I was hurt deeply. My first encounter with something like this happened while I worked at that printing company. I had become friendly with a colleague who had the same position as me with another firm on campus. I'll call him Judas because that's what he was, and even today I cannot bear to even think of him. I used drop into his office every now and again, and we'd discuss the gossip of the day or sports.

It was coming up on Christmas, and we were expecting our usual bonus. I mentioned to him that I had devised a way of ensuring that we could make more of a bonus if we operated the calculation using my formula, even though it was against company policy. I might also add that the two of us had put our names forward for a promotion within the group as a vacancy had recently arisen. He thought it was a great idea, and I suggested that he should implement it in his own company.

Two days later I received a command to appear in front of his divisional boss. I walked into his office to find the head guy telling me to sit down as Judas stood at his shoulder. The boss guy threw my formula back at me in detail, telling me he would fire me for doing something totally against company policy. He said he would be informing my divisional boss about the matter and that I should expect the worst. All the time I couldn't take my eyes off Judas, and he couldn't bear to look at me. I couldn't believe somebody could be that callous. I wanted to jump across the desk and throw him out of the window. He got promoted a few days later for being a good company boy.

I sat at my desk for the next few days waiting to get the call that I was fired. I hadn't told anybody. Then my door opened, and in walked David, my divisional boss, an imposing man, well over six feet tall, handsome and commanding. I thought to myself that this was it as I rarely had any dealings with division people. He approached my desk, asking me how I was. I said I was fine, and with that he threw an envelope on my desk and asked me if I could deal with it. I opened the envelope to see it was a bill, a very large bill for work done refurbishing his house. I looked up at him and said, "No problem, David."

"Good man," he said and exited stage right. What a bloke. He obviously came to the conclusion that I was also his type of guy, as he ignored the calls for my head and instead trusted me to bury his invoice. Said invoice was never seen again. I was good at that stuff. If you wanted a body buried and never to be found, then Bernie was your guy. However, not to be outdone and in my usual manner, I grabbed the baton and visited David the next day in his office, telling him that I had arranged everything. As he thanked me I asked him if he could help me get a mortgage for a house I had my eye on. He looked at me with a glint of admiration in his eye, as he knew I certainly had balls, remembering I had been only a foot away from the executioner's noose just two days before. He said, "Sure thing, no problem," as he gave me the number of a guy who would look after my needs. That was the final time I spoke to him as David passed away very shortly after that, may he rest in peace.

I was looking forward to my annual salary review as we all did at the end of the year. Money was always scarce, so anything additional was always very welcome, and as I had not received any increase the previous year, I was expecting something very good this time. Bob had completed the reviews for everybody except me, and I was getting anxious. I was relieving myself in the men's toilet one day when Bob walked in beside me. He gave me my salary review as I peed away.

"You're doing a great job, Bernie," he said as he proceeded to relieve himself.

"Thanks, Bob," I said, wondering what he was getting at.

"I've decided to give you a five percent increase. Unfortunately there won't be any bonuses this year due to the disappointing results," he said as he shook himself off, washed his hands, and walked away, review being over.

I stood there for a moment staring at the wall, and I said aloud to the wall, "That's your annual review, Bernie, given to you by your beloved boss as we both peed against the wall. Not 'Have a seat, Bernie, and would you like a cup of coffee.' Bernie, it's time to go!"

After making a number of job applications, I got offered the position of computer manager with a consulting firm, and off I went, little knowing that this was to be the catalyst for fulfilling the pledge I had made to myself all those years ago running down that pier.

CHAPTER 9

My new employer had recently got involved in the "new" personal computer technology that was due to change the world, and they needed somebody with expertise to sell them. My expertise stretched to about three pages ahead of any potential customer. They also offered me the use of a Volkswagen Scirocco, a snazzy little car in its day but consigned to the junkyards a long time ago. The only reason I got the job was because I knew a lot more than the guy who interviewed me, and he knew nothing.

My first day on the job was not good. I had arrived dressed in my accountant's suit and crombie coat, looking very dapper. I was shown to my office, an office I was to share with the three partners, which was very disconcerting and made me very nervous as they would get to see how I operated. I had no idea how I was supposed to operate. I was like a bartender being told to conduct brain surgery. It took me about twenty minutes to move my pen around my desk, all the time thinking about running back to my old job and begging them to forgive me, giving them some excuse that would make them reconsider my nervous breakdown and telling them that I would work twice as hard in the future for half the salary. I was shaken from my thoughts when one of the partners threw the yellow pages at me and told me to start phoning around looking for customers. I had no experience in selling anything, and I looked aghast at my manager who appeared to think that I would have no problems whatsoever. I was terrified as I stared at the phone and even more so as I desperately needed to be alone. Cold calling was what desperate people did, like bible salespersons knocking on doors in the Midwest of America or when guys had to sell you insurance or pension policies. It was my worst nightmare come through.

The days turned into weeks, then into months, and I still hadn't made a sale. In fact, I was further away from making a sale than I was the first day I started. I hawked my demonstration around Dublin, from one place to another. People had heard about computers, but they hoped it was just a fad and would go away and leave them alone. The machines looked great, but the software was abysmal. They simply didn't work properly. When I pushed a button to make an enquiry on screen, the printer would go ballistic, spitting out reams of paper, giving you what the writers termed an audit trail. Why somebody would need a ten-foot paper audit trail to disclose the fact that they had made a simple enquiry beat the pants off me. Then when it wasn't destroying copious trees from the Amazon jungle, the software would stop working just as you were at the most important part of your demonstration. It would display meaningless explanations for the sudden abrupt stops with spurious excuses like "input past end" or "end of string," whatever they were supposed to mean. It was like somebody doing a streak during the final moment of the world's most exciting Super Bowl. It was not necessary. Demonstrations would come to a speedy end, and I would be shown the door and told never to return. The software manuals were as bad as the software itself. When you tried to figure out how something was supposed to work, the writer treated you with contempt for daring to ask something so stupid.

One day, in total exasperation, I said enough. I needed good software, something that worked, and something that I could easily understand. I needed to specialize. I wrote down my strengths and forgot about my weaknesses. I was a qualified accountant, so that had to stand for something. I knew what accountancy firms needed, it was a question of finding of finding the software that could do it. Then it should be a simple matter of persuading them to buy it, or so I thought. I had worked in an accountancy office for four years. I knew that accountants would be more likely to buy computers for their number crunching than anybody else out there, and I also knew how they operated, so they were going to be my first target. If that didn't work, I was immigrating to Tibet and becoming a monk, if they'd have me.

I set about searching the world for my elixir of salvation. There was no Google in those days, no Internet. The only source of information you had was the phone book and the yellow pages. I happened across a little software company in Horsham in Kent, England, that had products specifically designed for accountancy firms. I jumped on a plane, and when I met the owner, we hit it off straight away because when I arrived I was greeted by his wife, who said that her husband was in the pub. It was only ten o'clock in the morning, but this was my kind of guy. She shrugged, gave me directions, and off I went to meet James, as he liked to be called. It turned out this guy was a total genius, an egghead, but a total genius. When he showed me his product I nearly wet myself. This stuff was sexy, and what is more important it worked. It didn't crash. I had to have it. He wasn't a bloke who believed in contracts, being a former gunsmith who had decided to turn his acumen to programming. He was the type who believed in a handshake and would use his guns if things turned nasty. I sort of believed him, and I was happy to bring his products to Ireland. I studied his stuff night and day to the point where I knew it backwards. I believed that I should know everything there was about those products, and I was not going to embarrass myself in front of Ireland's elite accountants.

The time came to confront my first potential customer, and I failed. I never got to first base because the guy didn't like the fact that I knew more than him. Now I had to learn about selling because even though I now had the products they needed, I had to develop my individual style. The other major problem I had: nobody was using it. I had no referrals, nobody who would say that my products were great, that it had made all the difference to their practice, that they couldn't survive without it. In other words, nobody wanted to be first. What could I do?

I remembered what Tommy had told me all those years ago: "Never think that you have a weakness. Lie about it." So I did. I told one prospect after another that of course we had dozens of clients. It was only a matter of time before I found somebody who didn't care whether I had a customer or, better still, who actually believed I had dozens of customers and didn't want any names.

I was off and running. When I had one customer I told them I had a dozen. If I had five customers I had fifty, and so forth. By the time I had fifty customers it didn't matter anymore. End of problem.

I loved selling, and as my confidence grew so did my love for my job. The products were great, and pretty soon people started to talk about us. For the first time they started to ring me. I then needed staff to support my growing customer base, so the company really started to take off. I declared myself a fully qualified salesperson based on my achievements. It's an unbelievable feeling when someone says that they'll buy your products, and I never tired of hearing it. People actually believed in you, and they were willing to part with their hard-earned money based solely on your actions and your promises, so I was duty-bound never to let them down, and I never did.

My bosses, to their credit, had an unwavering belief that I could do it, that I could make a success of it, and I was delighted to oblige them.

Billy and I attended the annual accountancy function. We looked great in our dress suits and dickie bows, standing outside the hotel waiting for a taxi in the freezing cold and snow. The night had been everything you'd expect from a night spent surrounded by 4,000 chartered accountants: a total waste of time. My boss turned to me and said, "Have you ever had a hooker?"

Now, to my mind this was not something that your boss would normally ask you, and I said, "Eh, no. Why?"

"Come on, let's go, I know a place where they hang out." Not wishing to disappoint him, I said I'd go along. We approached the aforementioned ladies of the street dressed in micro-mini skirts, freezing their knickers off as the snow blew around them.

"Are you up for it, girls?" asked Billy.

"Yeh, you wanna date?" says one of the birds. I got out of the car and stood in the freezing cold while one of the birds got into the passenger seat.

"I won't be long," said Billy, "and then you can have a go with the other one."

I turned to "the other one," who looked like she'd seen better days. She had blue varicose veins running up and down her legs under whatever sort of handkerchief she was using as a dress, and they reached her neck, where the veins continued their journey to her forehead. She didn't look great.

About ten minutes later Billy returned, jumped out, and told me to "do it" around the corner. He said to pay her in cash as he handed me a twenty. I hadn't a clue what I was supposed to do. I couldn't have got my great friend Oscar up if I had been in a warm Jacuzzi surrounded by naked International supermodels. I decided that as we were only minutes away from our offices that we should avail ourselves of the warmth and head back there to do the thing properly. We arrived at the office. I explained to her that everything was fine, that I worked there.

"Have you got me money?" she said.

"Yeh, I have the money." So I took her downstairs to the basement and into the kitchen. "Would you like a cup of tea?"

"Wha?" she exclaimed.

"I said would you like a cup of tea?" Something inside my brain told me not to lower my standards, no matter what the circumstances, as my mother would not be impressed.

"Yeh, alright," says the bird as she goes off to the toilet.

So I put on the kettle and stripped off. I'm standing there bollock naked when she came back into the kitchen. I had surprisingly managed to get Oscar to semi-rise to the occasion, and I was pretty pleased about that.

"What the fuck are you doing?" she shouted as Oscar deflated, never to return.

"What do you mean?"

"Jesus, sonny, have you ever been with a hooker before?"

"Eh, no."

At that precise moment, I kid you not, there was a loud knock on the front door upstairs and somebody shouting, "Open the door!"

"Crap, who the fuck is that?" I said.

Remembering it was about two in the morning on a freezing cold night, we ran up the stairs and looked over at the front door only to see what looked like a uniformed cop shouting at us to open the door while the flashing blue lights of his squad car lit up the background.

"Bollocks!" I said, and the next thing that bird was out of there, running down the stairs. I swear to you that it was like watching a gazelle in full flight as she cleared the back gate with one flowing movement, never to be seen again.

Meanwhile I got my clothes and hid in the toilet. Eventually the cops left, and about four in the morning the front door opened as Billy came in.

"Where the hell did you go?" he asked.

"Aw, Billy, you have no idea," and I explained about the cops.

"I know, I was watching them while freezing my nuts off. Come on, let's get out of here."

The following Monday, I was upstairs in my office when the secretary said that there was a cop downstairs and he wanted to see me. *Bollocks*, I thought, *I'm screwed*. In the hallway was the biggest cop you've ever seen. He must have been about six feet eight inches tall, and I looked up at him as he asked me to go get my boss. Billy was about five feet nothing, and when I told him that the cop wanted to talk to us, we both went downstairs and must have looked a sight as Billy looked up at me and we both looked up at the cop.

"Lads," he said like somebody was about to give you bad news, "I know it was the pair of you were with those prostitutes last Friday night because I was the one looking through your letter box, and I saw you." He pointed in my direction. "I'm not on official business. In fact, I'm on my way home to lunch, but I thought I'd give you some advice." He folded his arms and looked in particular at me. "That girl you were with the other night was stabbed not too far away from here. She is currently in hospital, in a very bad way. She's expected to live, but it was a close call." I stood there open-mouthed and in some shock. "You see, had she died, you would have been our chief suspect, as you were the last person to be seen with her. However, we caught the bloke who stabbed her. It was her pimp, and he's now under arrest." I was nearly passing out with the fright. "Take my advice, lads, and don't mess around in the gutters because there are nothing but rats in the gutters."

He then turned around and made his exit without waiting for either of us to respond. I was shocked and turned to Billy, who said, "Bollocks! What a load of bollocks!" as he made his way back to his office, leaving me standing there thinking that was definitely the end of prostitutes for me. It was a salutary lesson.

CHAPTER 10

So it was that Maria and I were married in her home town, and over three hundred people were in attendance. Her parents were delighted. Maria and I were excited. This was a major event for the Dublin people. Da took charge of the organizing, which resulted in a journey covering a distance of one hundred and forty miles, which he estimated would take two days, stopping off in a hotel for the first night and many pubs along the way, to ensure that nobody got lost. I don't believe that one of my relations had ever left the city boundaries before this. They experienced things for the first time, such as green grass and the funny farm smells that seemed to be everywhere. When the two herds met for the first time, it was strained, to say the least, and I just wanted the whole thing to be over and done with. On the day of the marriage, as Maria strolled down the aisle, I turned to my best man and said, "I'm making a big mistake, I shouldn't be here!"

"You can't walk out now!" He exclaimed. "There's over three hundred people here."

I shrugged my shoulders and did the deed.

Thankfully everything went off better than I expected, and we made our getaway for our honeymoon to the former Yugoslavia. God knows what it's called nowadays as there seem to have been more countries created there since the war, and I don't know who the good guys or the bad guys are. Things soon got back to normal after the honeymoon, and we started our new lives together.

Our jobs suited us as we suited each other. I'd drop Maria off at her workplace on my way to mine. I made new friends, as did Maria, so generally over the next six years we got along.

There was a huge culture clash between me and Maria's people. I really tried my best to align myself to their way of life, but as hard as I tried I just couldn't. I put up with it. When we bought our first house it wasn't long before the country clans were visiting us all the time. At first I didn't mind, but by the time we'd bought our second house, the big house, it was like Grand Central Station. There was hardly a week went by when someone from the country would drop in and stay for days or even weeks. I would arrive home and never know who was in my house. I began to hate the intrusions. I should have put my foot down, but I wasn't like that. I hated confrontation as I still do. They could never see how they were interfering with our lives.

Buying our first house together was as exciting as it is for everybody. We had fun building our future. We enjoyed our new friends from the housing estate, our neighbors.

However, it was about three or four years into our marriage when Maria, for whatever reason, changed. She was no longer interested in going out together. She stopped having a drink, going to the movies or restaurants, and above everything else she let herself go. What I mean is she didn't care about the way she dressed or how she looked. This was very important to me, extremely important. She started wearing terrible clothes and didn't look after herself. I was embarrassed, and I know it might sound shallow, but it's not. It's very important to most spouses that they can be proud of the way their spouses look after themselves. I believe many women appreciate it when their spouses appreciate them. When we met, I liked her because of what I saw. I married her for the same reasons, the way she enjoyed herself and had fun, but it all stopped because we stopped communicating. Rather than confronting the issues together we became separated, doing our own thing. I knew it was happening, but Maria refused to believe that anything was wrong. I spoke to her mother many times during the final years of the marriage, asking her to help me to get Maria to shape up, look after herself, put on some makeup, do her hair, anything just to make an effort to please me. She ignored my pleadings, and it was a very touchy subject with her. There was one time I'd arranged for a top-end makeover for Maria with one of those celebrity hair guys in town. She went off very reluctantly, having being forced to do so by her mother and myself. She came home hours later looking great, went straight upstairs without any comment, and washed it all out—hair, makeup, everything—down the sink. I was shocked and I know her mother was shocked also.

Buying the big house was a huge undertaking for us, but we were both earning good salaries, we were young and adventurous, so we went for it. I had always wanted a big house, and an opportunity arose when I spotted a particular house that was going to be auctioned. It was an executor sale, which meant that the property had to be sold. Now this house was worth at least sixty thousand (about half a million in today's money), which was a huge amount of money when you consider that the average house was selling for around twenty thousand. I had used my contact from David, the divisional guy in the printing company, to get a mortgage. They said they'd back me to the tune of thirty-thousand, so armed with that and the ten thousand we had saved ourselves, we went off to the auction. Neither of us had ever been to an auction before, and we didn't know what to do. We noticed there were only two old women in the auction room together with ourselves and the auctioneer. So when the property came up for auction we were the only bidders. He had started the bidding at 60,000, and as there were no bidders he reached the reserve price which was 50,000. I bid 40,000. He then closed the auction and invited the two of us upstairs to his office.

"It's a beautiful day, isn't it?" he said as we looked out of his office window overlooking St. Stephens Green on a beautiful summer's day.

"Yes," I said, "and the ducks look great."

"All right, cut the crap," he said. "You can't be having this property at such a ridiculous price."

"Well, it may seem ridiculous to you, but to us it's a fortune."

We stared one another down.

Now you should know this about me: you don't win a staring competition with me. I was born to stare, which has made me a decent poker player through the years and a damned good salesperson.

"I need 55,000 to close this sale," he said.

"Well, I know it's an executor sale and that you have to sell it. All we have is 40,000. Take it or leave it."

After leaving the office for a few minutes I heard him muttering to one of the old women outside in the hall. She was to be the only beneficiary to the will. I also heard her gasp, telling the auctioneer that he couldn't sell it for that amount of money, that the property was worth at least twice that amount. So we sat there. I told Maria to leave the talking to me, and back came the auctioneer, saying, "Look, I can't hang around all day. Give me 45,000, and I'll close it. You're getting a great deal."

I've always been a believer in being fair and leaving something for the other guy, so I said without flinching, "42,000 and we have a deal."

"Okay," he said, not looking at all happy.

We were ecstatic as we knew we had stolen that property.

It was around this time that I met with serious back problems. I was closing a sale, and as I lifted a printer—they were very heavy in those days—I collapsed and fainted. Everybody thought I was dead, including the customer.

I was taken by ambulance to the hospital, one of the nurses asked me if I could stand up, and I managed to hold on to her and lift myself up, only to find that the pain had disappeared. It was going to be like that, pain then no pain, for the next twenty-five years. It would attack without any warning, usually when I least expected it, traveling up and down my hips, then my legs and back up my spine. It was relentless.

Maria was not good where sick people were concerned. She would close down her support department whenever sick people came near. She was unable to show any sympathy for your plight and subliminally told you to snap out of it. On her plus side, I would never have qualified as an accountant if it wasn't for her. She literally locked me away and made me study. I had always hated studying when I was at school and would only do it as a last resort, usually when the exams were imminent, with only a week or two to go. I always managed to scrape through. I did fail one or two subjects in the accountancy exams and had to repeat them. It annoyed me because I didn't want to let Maria down, as I knew she wanted me to qualify. I liked her. I didn't want to disappoint her. I wanted her to be proud of me. I was getting more frustrated with myself as I just couldn't seem to pass the final exam. I managed to pick up some letterhead belonging to the accountancy body, and I typed out a congratulatory letter to myself saying I had qualified as an accountant. I showed it to Maria, and she was delighted for me. It may have solved one problem, but it meant I had to qualify for real. I took private tuition from a tax expert, and fortunately I qualified legitimately that same year. Nobody knew anything about it.

When I put my idea to her about starting my own business she was fully supportive, never blinked an eyelid, and it gave me the courage to act upon it. Many wives would have been afraid to let their spouses follow their dream, but not Maria. She supported my business startup without hesitation, giving me the total freedom to do what I wanted.

I had become frustrated with the computer firm. I had been responsible for bringing in all the revenues, and I had asked them on two occasions to consider making me a partner, but they were having none of it. I couldn't understand their objections as I was the one scoring all the goals, and it was in their best interests to keep me happy.

One day my secretary told me that she hadn't been paid her monthly salary, and two other girls said the same thing. I told them not to worry that I'd sort it out. It was only when my own bank manager rang me the same morning and told me that my cheque hadn't arrived that I panicked, as my mortgage payment was due the next day. I made a bee line for Billy's office, and when I told him about the problem, he turned to me and said that the staff would have to understand that we were going through a cash flow crisis and that they'd have to grin and bear it until next month.

"Next month!" I exclaimed, not believing my ears, knowing the girls downstairs would be out of there like a hot curry gone bad if they didn't get paid. I tried to reason with him, and it was only when one of the other partners intervened that things got sorted. But the writing was on the wall: it was time to abandon ship.

You only get one chance, at most, to avail of opportunity. There's the opportunity that comes along that people never see, the one that people see but are afraid to grasp, and finally there's the one that you grab and run with, as fast as you can. I was always on the lookout for my opportunity, and this was it. I took the bull by the horns and asked my British software supplier if he would supply me with his products if I went out on my own. Neither of us saw any problem as there had been no written distribution agreement with my current bosses. Without a penny to my name, I planned my escape and set up shop over a local pub, courtesy of a great friend of mine who said that I could pay him the rent whenever I had earned enough money. I brought a young guy with me called Des, whom I thought had great potential: zero qualifications but sharp as a razor, the way I liked them. Besides, he knew more about the technical aspects of computers than I did, and the customers liked him a lot. What I didn't know was that my previous firm had put a private detective on me who followed my every move, trying to gather enough information that they could use against me in court. I met the detective in question at a party many years later, and he told me that he had followed me for six months, that it was a very boring assignment as I led a very boring life.

It was an amazing feeling, starting my own business. I'll never forget my first day as Des and I arranged the two pieces of furniture around the one hundred square foot room. It didn't take long! I had enough potential customers lined up that were willing to let me supply them, even though they knew I was a two-man operation. They trusted me to look after them, and I didn't let them down. I sold everything I could lay my hands upon: computer disks, paper, ribbons, and of course the computers themselves and the software. As I told Des, I would have sold my mother a number of times if I knew I could get money for her. She would have appreciated that. It was so much fun knowing that every penny you earned was all yours. I could control what I spent it on. I was in charge of my own destiny—at last. This was the challenge I had set myself all those years ago as I ran the pier, contemplating my future. My future was here.

I got my demonstrations down to a fine art. I learned everything about the products I was selling. I found I could read people, know their idiosyncrasies, what they liked and disliked. If they liked something, I showed them more of it. In a very short time I was making more money than I'd made in all the years working for somebody else. What was more important: it was all mine.

We only needed a few customers because our costs were so low. I had always understood the concept of good business, and that was keeping your costs as low as possible. Don't put yourself under pressure to sell to pay for any unnecessary costs. You don't need fancy cars or expensive office equipment. By the end of the first month I was well able to pay my rent, and I was more relaxed about my very high mortgage. I needed to accrue as much cash as I could in as little time as possible because the banks would not give me a loan. They weren't interested in a small two-bit software company. They were only interested in properties that they could put a value upon. They didn't understand the computer business, so it was up to me to ensure my own survival. By the end of my first year, I had enough money in the bank to take on a couple of additional staff to support my ever-growing customer base. I will always remember a customer of mine calling into my office and asking me how many staff I had. I said, "Just the one," as there was no point in lying to him.

"Keep it like that, Bernie," he said. "Never change it, and don't be tempted to expand your operation."

He went on to explain how his building business had been going along nicely year after year when his accountant advised him to expand his operations. He was a gifted carpenter, and his accountant said that he could earn a lot more money. His wife and he used to take a couple of vacations a year, had very satisfied customers, and got referrals all the time. They took their accountant's advice and continued to hire a lot more employees. Pretty soon they had no time for vacations. Their revenues exploded, but so did their costs, so much so that after three years they found that even though their revenues had quadrupled, their profits were approximately the same as they had been before they expanded.

I should have taken his advice because eventually I ended up in the same trap. We were running along nicely when one day I received an order for four computers and various printers from a guy I knew, we'll call him shithead. It was a huge order for my little business, and I was delighted to get it, little knowing that the customer had no intention of ever paying me for the machines. I was about to learn another lesson. I tried to get paid, chasing him for weeks and then months without success. I was furious because this could have ruined me. He ignored all of my calls, laughing in my face, knowing I was a young bloke who had just started and who hadn't a clue. But I knew something about myself that he wasn't aware of. I was a much more determined little bollocks than he was.

I decided to kill him. Not just injure the little bollocks but actually kill him stone dead. I knew I wasn't going to be the one to do the deed, and I wondered how a person should go about it when all of a sudden I thought of Smithy. Knowing my home town as I did, I also knew many of the gangsters, and Smithy was one of them. I had never resorted to anything like this before, but this was a special case. As far as I was concerned, nobody was going to con me or steal my money. This was war.

I knew where Smithy hung out, and I have to say we had always got along well. I think he admired me as I was one of the few who didn't look down their noses at him because he had a low intelligence and had been kicked out of school at an early age. I met Smithy in his local pub, and he asked me what the problem was. I gave him a rundown of events, and he said, "No problem, Bernie. Let's go see Andy."

Now Andy was one guy I only half knew, and his intelligence level had yet to be analyzed, except that nobody could be bothered with that assignment. We sat down in one of the local pubs, and Andy informed me, "A kill would be about ten grand." He said it as if reading it off a menu about to order his lunch.

"Ten grand," I said. "That's more than twice the amount he owes me. Have you anything cheaper?"

"We could break a leg for a grand, fifteen hundred for the two."

"What about the two arms?"

"Five hundred for the two. It's not worth our while doing anything less."

"Okay, let's go for the two arms," I said, thinking that at least the bastard won't be able to lift any of my computers again for about a year. That would partially satisfy my appetite for revenge. I bought another round of drinks as we discussed the when and where of the plan.

"Right," said Andy after a while, "Smithy, go out and get us a car. We'll do it tonight. Do you know this bloke's address?"

Now, I wasn't expecting it to be carried out this soon, and I certainly wasn't expecting to be part of the action either, so I got a little scared. Smithy pokes me in the ribs and says, "Come on, Bernie, I'll show you outside in the car park. It's easy."

With that we go out to the back of the pub where Smithy got a car started in about five minutes and told me to get in. It occurred to me that if I chickened out now, I might be the one to get my arms broken for pissing them off and wasting their time. All three of us got into the stolen car and headed off in search of shithead's house.

I knew everything there was to know about this bloke, including his house address, car registration and all personal details about him and his family, so I gave Andy the wrong address. We waited outside the house belonging to a friend of mine who had just bought it, so I knew nobody was at home. After about an hour of hanging around outside I suggested that we go back to the pub as it looked like the bloke wasn't coming home. Andy agreed, especially when I said I'd be buying the beer, so I spent the next few hours buying them drinks, and about a week later I made contact with Smithy, telling him that my brother had met shithead and beaten the crap out of him and as a result I had been paid in full. Smithy was delighted and called off the contract, and that was the closest I got to a life of crime. It was also the closest my beloved brother ever got to helping me out, albeit symbolically.

However, I still had the problem of the outstanding debt, so I bought two white coats, one for myself and one for Des. We waited like two good detectives outside shithead's offices until I saw him leave. Then about a half hour afterwards we went inside and told his secretary that we were from the computer manufacturers and that her boss had told us we needed to take the computers away for an upgrade. She was a bit doubtful at first, but I used the old charm, and in minutes I had retaken the lot: computers, printers, even his newspaper for good measure.

That night I was at an accountancy dinner dressed up to the nines when over the speakers I heard, "Would a Mr. Donnelly pick up the nearest telephone?" I picked up the phone only to hear a lieutenant Dixon on the other end telling me that he had a very irate gentleman in his office accusing me of stealing his computer equipment. I tried telling him the story that in actual fact they were my computers and that I had never been paid for them when he interrupted me by saying that he knew the full story. He appreciated that I was more than likely the injured party in all of this, but regardless of the circumstances I had committed a crime by stealing the equipment. He said that if I returned said property to the police station tomorrow morning he would not arrest me.

"Bollocks," I said telling the detective that I would return the equipment. I also had to endure the ignominy of watching shithead grinning at me as he re-stole the stolen property!

It transpired that there was another guy in the same building as myself called Roger, who was in the debt collection business. I told him my tale of woe, and I offered him fifty percent of any monies he collected if he took the job. Roger accepted the challenge, telling me it would take a long time but that he would get it, he would recover the full debt.

"Go for it," I told Roger.

He and I became good friends. It was my first time associating with an alcoholic, and Roger was one of the finest specimens of alcoholics that you could possibly meet. When Maria and I would go out for dinner with Roger and his wife, Roger would go missing, and I thought he had a dicky bladder and never thought anymore about it until one day I was looking for him around the office and I found him lying up against a wall, totally out of it. He told me that he was an alcoholic and that anytime he had gone missing when we were out together, he had gone to the nearest pub or liquor store because we hadn't been drinking fast enough for his liking. He would down a half bottle to a bottle of vodka in ten minutes, which would keep him going for the evening. He also said that his business was in bad shape. He used to be the collection agency for some very large companies who contracted their debt collections to people or companies like Roger. Roger would grab the mail every morning and take out the checks and deposit them into his account then continue to meet up with his other up-market alcoholics in a five-star hotel in the center of Dublin, where they would continue to knock back many bottles of champagne and vodka from mid-morning to late afternoon, whereupon the hotel would favor them with free lodgings to sleep it off.

I had no idea anybody could consume that much alcohol. Happily I can report that Roger has been sober for over thirty years and is a major benefactor to the AA in Dublin, a stalwart no less.

Back to my story. I can tell you that Roger was brilliant at his job. Every morning on his way into the office he would stop at shithead's house. He would park outside and wave as shithead pulled back the curtains in his bedroom. It was unfortunate for him that he lived on the same work route as Roger. After many weeks of this harassment, shithead came out to Roger one morning and invited him in for breakfast as Roger had told him that he would be outside his house every morning without fail until he had paid the debt in full.

I was in my office one day when an envelope was thrown on my desk containing two grand. It appears that shithead couldn't take the harassment anymore, as his wife was giving him hell. Roger was more pleased than I was: mission accomplished.

We were doing so much business that we ran out of manuals to supply with the software. Despite pleadings to the manufacturer, I was left with no other option but to go over myself and bring enough manuals back to Ireland. I told Des to go up town and buy the biggest suitcase he could find because we were jumping on a plane and going over to the UK and getting the damned manuals ourselves. We arrived at Gatwick airport with an enormous empty suitcase. As we approached the customs, the official ordered us to put the suitcase on the table and asked us what was inside. I looked at young Des who started to smile, and then I looked back at the officer and said, "Nothing. There's nothing in the suitcase."

"What do you mean nothing?"

"Well, exactly that. Nothing."

He turned the massive suitcase around towards him, opened it, and said, "There's nothing in here!"

The funny thing is that even though both of us knew there was nothing in the suitcase, the two of us walked around his desk from either side and looked inside our suitcase. As all three of us were looking into an empty suitcase, the officer asked, "Why is there nothing in this suitcase?"

"Do we have to have something in it?" I enquired, and with that he radioed for assistance and told us that we were to say nothing until the police arrived.

"The police!" I said.

Sure enough, within two minutes two of Britain's finest helmeted bobbies came over and asked, "What's the problem here?"

The customs guy explained that upon searching our suitcase he found there was nothing inside. What do the cops do? They only walk around to have a look for themselves. Now there were five people looking into an empty suitcase. At this stage young Des cracked up and couldn't control his laughter, and I quickly followed.

One of the cops said, "This is no laughing matter," which only made us worse, the tears now rolling down our faces as one of the cops started to laugh as well, suddenly seeing the hilarity of the situation. Then he asked us had we just come from Dublin, and we nodded.

He closed the case, saying, "That explains everything then," and sent us on our way.

We were still laughing as we arrived at the offices of the software house, whereupon we loaded up the famous suitcase, and we then had to book ourselves into the Hilton Airport hotel. I asked the receptionist how much a room was, and he said, "Is that for one or two people?"

"Two people, of course," I responded, thinking what an idiot that guy was, seeing Des was standing right beside me. I didn't know that the bloke behind the desk thought that Des was my toy-boy, as he was dressed in denim from head to foot while I was in my suit. Not wanting to appear too awkward, I told him to give us a twin room. He said he only had a double room, so I took it. When we went up to the room, I couldn't open the door as it was the first time I'd come across those new card keys, and the damned thing wouldn't work. We tried kicking the door down when who should appear but the bloke who checked us in.

He looked down the hallway at us and said, "In a hurry, are we?" as he opened the door for us, bidding us goodnight with a smirk on his face.

Des refused to share the bed and went off to sleep in the bath. The only trouble was he went sleep walking during the night, and I couldn't find him the next morning. I had to ask about him at the front desk. The shame of it! I eventually found him sleeping in a lounge chair. Needless to say I never went back to that hotel again. What a day!

CHAPTER 11

I MET SOME REAL CHARACTERS as I toured around demonstrating, installing, and training my customers on the UK products. On one memorable occasion I had arranged for my agents in Scotland to come over to Dublin for a couple of day's training, The owner of the firm, a tremendous character called Wally, and his two senior people arrived over to our offices one fairly blistery day in October. Wally and I got on great, having had a history of some very late nights together in Glasgow. I really thought that he was keen to learn all he needed to know about our products so that he could emulate our success back home in Glasgow. What a silly boy I am sometimes!

We had barely sat down, and as I started to go through my opening presentation, Wally dragged me aside and asked, "What time are the pubs open?

"Can you hang on until around the five o'clock mark and we'll go off then?" I said.

At this juncture I need to give you a little insight into my good friend Wally. Wally was big into horse racing, his brother being a well-known and highly respected race horse trainers in Scotland. Wally was the owner of most of their stable, and the business had been in the family for eons. When I first met Wally I didn't know that he had a drinking problem and that he could react in a violent manner. This had happened that same year when Wally was arrested and charged over an incident in a local hotel when a political discussion ensued with some client. Wally had enthusiastically argued his side of the argument by ramming a glass vase into the client's face, causing extensive injuries. Wally was lucky to get off on a misdemeanor charge having squared things off with the client in the usual manner, but it didn't do his reputation any good because it was blasted all over the newspapers. But Wally never worried about such trivialities, and I made sure never to imbibe too much in his company and to make my escape when any fog appeared on the horizon.

I asked him one day if he had made much money out of the horse racing business, and he immediately answered no, which surprised me as his family's horse business was very large. He explained that the horse business is extremely time consuming and very costly to maintain, that you needed many winning horses to break even, let alone make a profit. The feeding and veterinary bills were huge, and you obviously couldn't cut back on those expenses. He said that they had made much money out of one particular horse and sent that horse to stud, and when the first foal arrived, they nurtured that foal until he was a two year old, with the view of retiring that horse to stud after he had won all his planned twelve races, including the Gold Cup. Everything had gone according to plan: the horse duly won all of his eleven races, and he was second favorite as the day approached for the running of the Gold Cup. Wally and his brother had placed much money in ante post betting, long before the horse had won his tenth race, so they had received the best odds. They had mortgaged their property, as this win was going to finance both of their pensions and their families' pensions. Everything was riding on this horse in this particular race.

On the day of the race the weather was perfect, a sunny day with going conditions hard, exactly what suited the horse. The vet had given the thumbs up the day before. The trainers had timed him against similar competition, and the horse had easily achieved the best times. The only person they hadn't heard from was the stable boy, who had gone missing the day before. As the horses paraded around the parade ring, Wally's horse was sweating, sweating a lot and looking very anxious, not a good sign. The jockey couldn't understand what was wrong with the horse as he was the stable jockey and the only one who had ever ridden the animal.

So the race started, and Wally and his brother watched from the stands as the race unfolded. The horse placed last by a country mile. There was a post-mortem meeting at the racetrack because punters had lost much money, nobody losing more than Wally and his brother. It transpired that two nights before the race, the stable boy was brushing the horse in an indelicate way, hurting the horse because the lad's girlfriend had just broken off their engagement. As far as the horse was concerned, it was obvious that the stable boy didn't love him anymore, and, according to Wally, the horse had been heartbroken. Seemingly, horses are very sensitive that way, and as the stable boy was the only person the horse had known since he was born, the horse considered the stable boy as a brother.

Wally wanted to hang the lad from the nearest tree, but remembering his prior arrest, he decided it was better to let things go. The lesson from that story was that you couldn't win even though the animal was perfect, the weather was perfect and the conditions were perfect. As they say, "If you ain't got the love, you ain't got nothing."

Back to my story. I knew Wally wanted a drink, and I knew a local place down the road, so off we went. He then told me that he had a horse running in the two thirty at Hereford, a small out-of-the-way racetrack in Britain, and he wanted to place a bet. He said that it was going to win because his stable were on the list, the list being it was their turn to win. It seems that there was a type of arrangement in those days that if a certain stable wasn't doing well that one or two of their horses could "win" in out-of-the-way places.

As luck would have it, that particular race was being broadcast on the television that very same day, and there was a small bookie's shop a few doors down the street. As the time approached for the race, I went into the bookie's shop and asked the guy if he'd take a bet of a thousand pounds on the horse. The bookie wet himself when he saw the cash and took it without a word, a grand at twelve to one. I saw a bloke I recognized and told him that the owner of that horse was in my place and that he should have a flutter himself. I put a hundred on for myself, and a couple of my boys put whatever they had on it too.

The horse walked home. It looked like somebody had shot all the other horses in the race. The bloke that owned the bookie's shop got cleaned, but I was delighted. I'd won twelve hundred smack-a-rooskies while Wally had cleaned him out. That bookie closed shortly afterwards, unsurprisingly, but I was a major hit with all the locals.

I learned very quickly as I went along. There was the time when I was over eager to close the sale of a computer system to the accountants for a band called U2. Now, I had never heard of U2, and when their accountant told me that they only needed enough software to handle a few transactions every year, I only sold them what I thought they'd need. I explained to a chap called Bono—a funny name I thought—and his accountant that I couldn't justify selling them any more than they needed (not knowing anything about their financial situation) as I thought that money was a bit tight for them, so I quoted them for just the one computer and one copy of my software, assuring them that it would be more than adequate for their needs. I lost the sale as one of my competitors ended up selling them the kitchen sink as well. Of course it was nothing to the boys in the band as they were already making their fortunes, leaving me at the altar without the bride. The song "With or Without You" always held a particular meaning for me every time I heard it on the radio, and the radio seemed to play it every five minutes. Bollocks, I thought, that was the end of my being Mr. Nice Guy from that moment on! I learned from that experience that good salespersons should know as much as they can about their potential target before they meet them, like any good general will know everything about his enemy before he sends his troops into battle. He has to learn when to speak and when to shut up. After you've competed your demonstration, taken all the questions, and answered them all satisfactorily, then you must ask the one and only question you want to ask, but most people screw it up. So steady the nerves, look the punter in the face, and ask in any of the following ways:

"Do you want to buy?"
"Will I write up the order?"
"When will I deliver?"

My favorite was always "I can deliver next Monday and start the training the following day," which didn't ask him a question, didn't depend on him answering you. Instead, it got him thinking about having all this beautiful equipment lying around his offices with a happy staff. When you ask for the sale, it's absolutely imperative that you remain stonewalled in your silence. You must not break, don't even breathe, and if the potential customer is any good, he can stare you down for a long time, waiting for you to weaken and pounce for a discount. It's akin to two buffalo locking horns, but the best salespersons never falter, continue with their blank stares, and go in for the kill.

I also managed to get my own back on my first boss, the accountant who paid me nothing, because as my products were the ones every accountant needed, he thought that I would do him a favor and give him the stuff at cost. I did the complete opposite. I got every piece of old equipment I couldn't sell and laid it all on him at full price. That was payback time, and it felt good.

With things going really well in the business, Maria and I started to discuss having a family. I knew she wanted to have kids, and I was easy either way. We knew there would be no trouble physically since she had already been pregnant before, and as she had a government job, she could easily take a leave of absence to look after the baby and not lose any of her benefits, so we decided to give it a go. We tried for months. She couldn't get pregnant. We decided to get ourselves checked out. I was first. I was to bring a sample of my sperm into the hospital within one hour of producing it. On the appointed morning we had action stations, and we went off to the hospital with my little brown bag. When I arrived at the outpatients and quietly whispered to the check-in nurse that I needed my sample tested immediately, she blurted, "Sperm sample! Sperm sample!" with the delicacy of hyenas arguing over a dead corpse. Jesus, the mortification as everybody in the place took a good look at the wanker over at check-in!

Needless to remark, all systems were thunderbirds as far as I was concerned, and it transpired that Maria's fallopian tubes were blocked. When I told the gynecologist that Maria had been pregnant some years previously, he told us that the pregnancy would not have gone full term, that it was an ectopic pregnancy. Crap! All that hassle years before, and all for nothing. The gynecologist blew the tubes, and within nine months May was born and we couldn't have been happier.

Maria's idea of an idyllic life was like the one portrayed in *The Sound of Music*. She wanted to be Julie Andrews, singing songs as we all rode out on our bicycles, dressed in curtains and over the Dublin Mountains. She wanted kids from the start. I never imagined that we were going to have four babies from the get-go. This was not what I had in mind. I was 28 years of age, and I wanted fun and excitement. I was too young to be settling down. I had only started to enjoy having money for the first time in my life. Sure, I wanted my wife and I to have a family, but I also wanted us to have fun together. Maria was having her family whether I liked it or not, and she was damned if she was not going to start singing "The hills are alive. . . ."

Both sets of grandparents were thrilled with May's arrival, especially Maria's, as she was their first grandchild. They doted on her, and Maria's parents practically lived with us and were a great help. I never really noticed that they were around so much as I was all consumed with the business. Just as I was saying that everything was going great with the business, I received a call one day from James, the owner of the UK supplier, who told me that he had sold his business to one of my rivals. I nearly fainted because his products represented over seventy percent of my revenues, and I knew the new owners would drop me like a hot potato and let me wither and die. I was really pissed with him, and I couldn't understand why he was selling out at this time when his products were just starting to take off. He didn't care. He had been offered two million sterling, and he ran with it. I suppose the temptation was too much. And two million was a lot of money in those days. It would still buy many happy meals today.

I was scared because I knew how ruthless these new owners would be, as we had had arguments on many occasions in the past, particularly as I had always beaten their company to every sale. So I knew they didn't like me and would be only too glad to get rid of me. I also had no written contracts with James, the original owner, as we both thought we would never need them. Our word was our bond—bollocks! Sure enough, we were told to get out of town almost immediately, which forced me into a corner, and I was officially in the shits.

Desperate times require desperate measures, and as captain of the ship I considered myself up to the task. Fortunately, we were still IBM main dealers, albeit at the back of the pack, but at least we could continue selling the hardware while we waited for some miracle to occur. It was of major importance to keep paying the wage bill, which wasn't exorbitant as my numbers were relatively small. My overdraft facility of eighty thousand was totally busted. My actual overdraft was more like a quarter of a million, and my bank manager was already very nervous, so I had an endless juggling of cash flow.

Being an IBM dealer may have been prestigious, but it was also a major pain in the arse as you were effectively working for them. They decided how much stock you should hold and when you should pay for it. In addition, I was competing against another twelve high-volume dealers who had been in the very competitive and small hardware marketplace a lot longer than me. One day I received an invitation from IBM to join all the other dealers on an exclusive, all-expenses-paid, ten-day excursion to Barbados to include accommodation in a five-star hotel, all dining and imbibing, together with the ubiquitous games of golf, and all the while basking in the glorious sunshine. It was the chance of a lifetime, so I immediately confirmed my acceptance.

I had no intention of going.

It was a dream come true, all right. All the cats would be away, and this mouse was going to play. I even knew what days they would be missing, and I also knew that their bosses would be joining them on such an extravaganza so that nobody would be in charge in any of their companies. I was going to be the only supplier in the country for ten glorious days, so I got my troops of sales people trained and ready, and then I explained my plan. We were going to discount all IBM hardware across the board, something that was blasphemous to the IBM hierarchy. We were going to launch a nationwide campaign in all the daily newspapers, offering 25% discount for ten days, starting on the first day the dealers were due to leave Dublin for their trip. I didn't want to waste a single day's opportunity, and even though they would possibly see the first edition in one of the newspapers, I reasoned that it would be too late for them to do anything about it. I hoped that they wouldn't see it until they were airborne.

Two days before the event, I telephoned IBM to say I had the flu and that I wouldn't be making the trip. In those days you could easily cancel airline and hotel reservations without suffering any penalties, so it wasn't a problem if someone cancelled out. The day came, and I arranged to be at Dublin Airport myself to make sure that they all got on board. I watched from a pivotal position in one of the upper floor restaurants, and I looked down at them from on high as they were all in ecstatic and jovial mood about their trip. None of them had yet seen the advertisement. It was seven in the morning, and then I noticed one of them had bought the *Irish Times*. Damn it, I thought, they were going to see it, but he never opened it, and as they made their way through security I saw him look at the back page of the newspaper. He nearly threw up. He shouted at the other guys, pointing out the advertisement. It was too late. They couldn't turn back.

I rang my sales force and told them that it was all systems go, that they were to exhaust themselves getting new business. The mayfly were up for the next ten days. The phones never stopped ringing, and with each passing day we got busier and busier as the advertisements screamed "eight days to go" then "seven days to go." By the end of the tenth day we had generated over a half million pounds worth of new business at a handsome profit. The ten days were not without a number of overseas phone calls demanding that I cease my campaign, combined with threats on my future existence as an IBM dealer and as a human being, not to mention a splash of somewhat colorful language.

I was ecstatic. We managed to generate enough profits to bring down the bank overdraft, and we also had a whole flock of new customers. It was a one-off coup. I still had to balance the cash flow on a daily basis. It was relentless, and I tried everything to keep us afloat. One of these opportunities involved not paying the rent, which was considerable. The landlords had not looked for any rent for over a year, and I used the breathing space it provided. I had asked my lawyers if I could be locked out for not paying my rent. They said I should be fine, that the landlord would have to give me notice in writing.

So much for the great lawyers. I arrived in early as usual one morning only to find my office door was secured with the mother of all padlocks. I ran around to the rear entrance to find the same thing. We had been locked out. I nearly crapped myself. It was just after seven in the morning. The staff would start to arrive around eight thirty. There was still time to get the doors opened.

I jumped into the car and headed uptown to a locksmith I knew would be open at that time in the morning. Thankfully they were. I explained my circumstances to the owner of the store, telling him that one of my people had changed the locks while I was overseas, that he was now sick and in bed, and that as a result I was locked out of my own offices and needed him to open the locks for me. I neglected to tell him the locks were actually padlocks so as not to raise any suspicions. I told him I would pay his top rate but that I needed it done immediately before my staff arrived. He took sympathy with my plight and the fact that he would be earning a nice bundle of money, and he ordered his ace locksmith to follow me down to my offices. Thankfully the guy he sent was not blessed with the greatest of intelligence, so I told him a story that one of my staff had locked the door when he left the offices the night before, and as we had a lot of valuable stuff inside we had been afraid we'd get burgled.

"Jesus, he's gonna be in some trouble when he gets in this morning, wha?" he said as he stared at the huge padlock on the door.

"You better believe it," I said.

At about this time my new manager, Ted, arrived, so I grabbed him outside and told him what had happened. I told him to keep an eye on any incoming staff and divert them at all costs because if one of the staff had seen what had happened, they would be looking elsewhere for employment and the rest of the staff would soon follow. Loyalty only stretches so far.

The locksmith was working away when I noticed Ted frantically trying to get my attention from outside the window, pointing at the inside of the door, and when I looked I nearly collapsed. The landlord had bolted the inside of the door, with a chain this time.

The locksmith managed to open the outside bolt, and he couldn't understand why the door wouldn't open.

"Jesus," I said, "don't tell me my bloke has locked the inside of the door as well!" looking aghast at the door and then back at the locksmith in an I-can't-believe-this sort of way.

So we both peered through the window, and sure enough he saw a huge chain on the inside handle, so he looked at me in a suspicious sort of way.

"I'm gonna kill him, the prick!" I shouted, as I knew this was the only sort of language this bloke was going to understand.

"Jesus," says the man, "I don't know how I'm supposed to open that."

With that I produced a fifty-pound note and said, "Will that help?"

We were inside within five minutes. This guy was an absolute genius as far as opening locks was concerned, and I had no doubt he could have entered Fort Knox for fifty pounds if he was asked to do it. Thankfully, it never dawned on him to ask how my guy could have got out of the building if the doors had been locked from both sides! The staff arrived and never noticed a thing even though they could see I looked like an animal who had just been chased by a hungry lion. I arranged a payment schedule with the landlords, but I never trusted them after that. I got myself a big dog and left him in the offices every night. It never happened again.

The problems continued with my lack of cash, and they just wouldn't go away. The banks were giving me grief, wanting more repayments on the loans, so early that year I was called into the bank and asked to explain how I was going to solve the problem. All I could do was rationalize the company, and my manager Fred and I set to work firing some of the staff. We needed to reduce the staff numbers to around twelve. It wasn't pretty. It never is when you are firing people no matter what the circumstances. In one scene a techie guy came into the room. Fred told him not to take off his coat as he wouldn't be staying long. Talk about being subtle.

The business went from worse to terrible. One day I came in and the electricity had been shut off. Another day the phones were cut off because I couldn't pay my bills. Our cash flow was a constant struggle, borrowing from Peter to pay Paul all the time. I factored our debts, which was like putting an alcoholic in charge of a brewery, it was our access to easy cash as long as we were producing the goods. Some months we needed to doctor the books to get the cash to pay our bills in the hope that the next month would be better, but it never happened. The numbers didn't add up. As an accountant myself I knew something was wrong, but whenever I asked my financial controller about it, he always assured me that everything was okay.

I needed to get inside those books, preferably when the accountant was missing. This was the only time in my life that I had ever considered suicide. I was in my office around four in the morning with Des, my trusted lieutenant, examining the books to find out where all the cash was going, as things did not add up. We weren't having any luck finding it. I had been immersed in keeping the sales coming in, and I had left all financial matters under the accountant's control. Even though I had asked him repeatedly to explain things over the previous two or three months, he kept assuring me that all was well and that he was handling it. Neither was true. That morning, as dawn was about to break, I looked down at the ground from my fourth floor window and seriously considered ending it all as I didn't want to face failure.

I opened the window, looked down, and thought, "At least they can get the insurance money and get by without me!" But as you look upon ending your life, you know that deep down you don't want to die. In my case I had already cheated death twice already and I definitely didn't want to die. I looked across at the Irish Sea, and it felt like my good angel slapped me across the face, telling me, "I'll probably only break my legs and be paralyzed for life, knowing my luck," so I pulled myself together and found a cigarette buried in my drawer (I was constantly trying to quit smoking).

At that particular moment my door opened, and Des announced that he had found a stack of money, some one hundred thousand pounds in checks, stuffed inside my accountant's locked drawer and not deposited for over six months. Most of them were now out of date. I couldn't believe my ears or my eyes when I saw the checks. All of that time I had been frantically trying to keep my ship afloat, and my accountant had over a hundred grand in un-deposited checks. Here I had been thinking the unthinkable! I couldn't believe it. We hollered and hooped around the offices as dawn broke because he knew as much as I did how serious things were. He didn't know what I had been thinking only minutes previously.

I tried to make sense out of why the accountant had all that money locked away. Was he hoping to cash it himself? If so, why were they hidden away for so long? Des had to restrain me from paying a visit to the guy's house as I wanted to hang him by his goolies. I bided my time and waited for him to come into the office. I sat him down with Des by my side. He turned a whiter shade of pale when I threw the envelope, stuffed with customers' checks, down on my desk. He broke down and cried, explaining that he was having a nervous breakdown, that it had started about a year previously, that he had lost control.

"Lost control!?" I shouted as my restraint vanished. He told me everything, how he had fabricated the figures to keep me happy, how he couldn't handle the pressure. I also found out that he had also ignored all the demands from the tax authorities looking for all taxes that were due. Going back for over a year, nothing had been paid, and to think that this all came to light when the electricity was cut off. In other words, things became known when the lights went out! What a mess! I fired him on the spot and told him to get out of my sight.

As an aside, he became very successful in business many years later. I did meet him once. We shook hands, and I congratulated him on his success, thinking to myself that he may have been having a nervous breakdown at the time, but I was in a much darker place. We were able to contact our customers and get them to reissue their checks. We were saved again for another while! I took control of the finances, cleaned up the mess, and got us back on course. It had been very close. I kept wondering to myself when I was going to get a clean run. In other words, when was I ever going to be able to relax and enjoy the rewards of running my own business? It seemed to be one disaster following another.

CHAPTER 12

I KNEW I HAD TO do something. I couldn't keep going on like this. I needed my own software products for the accountancy market, and I needed them fast. This would be the first time that we had ever attempted anything of this magnitude, and we had no idea how long it would take. But it was a case of do or die.

Designing a software product that works takes a very long time. Back then at least, you needed thousands of lines of software code to instruct the computer to do the basic things, so attempting to produce products that could handle company legislation as well as produce deadly accurate tax computations was an entirely difficult process that would take years to perfect. I set about designing the type of products I would want myself as a practicing accountant. I wanted my products to be sexy and efficient, sexy because I wanted my demonstrations to have the maximum effect, efficient by way of smart programming done by smart people, ensuring that the user got from point A to point B as fast as possible without any spurious lines of code.

From my experience I found all programmers used a weird logic. Their lives seemed to emulate their coding. For example, if you asked them to design a car, they would complete it, it would look great. Then as you test drove the car you'd find that they had put the foot brake and the hand brake in the trunk, which is pretty scary when you are fifty feet away from going over the cliff!

I designed the main system, which I knew would blow the rest of the competitors out of the market, but the tricky part was knowing if my developers could produce it. My top guys said that they could do it. It was going to be risky because we had to delay other things that were important to our existing customer base while we tried to develop this new technology. I gave them the go ahead and told them that I would keep everything else ticking over so that they could devote all of their energies and ingenuity to producing the products.

Over the next few months I locked them away, and I told them that I would look after bringing in the money. It was not going to be easy from a number of viewpoints. First, my existing customer base would get scared of switching to something new, especially when it had not even been written yet. Second, I needed to keep my customers from jumping ship so that I could continue receiving their annual support revenues, which were considerable and now all the more important because I had nothing to sell to the accountancy market since I had been effectively fired by the new owners. On the plus side, I knew that our customers liked us and liked our support services as much as the products themselves, but I knew they were concerned that I couldn't keep them up to date with the latest versions of their software, which were now out of my control.

We lost a good few customers initially, but we managed to keep the majority, telling them that we would have an even better product for them shortly and that it would be a free upgrade. Of course we had no idea how long it was going to take to produce such a product. I imagine it was like when John F. Kennedy proposed the moon landing and the folks at NASA puked in their cereals when they heard his plans. I was puking too but on a somewhat smaller scale.

We had to take three steps backwards to do this, and it wasn't easy. We had some very large multi-national customers who were very demanding, insisting that we should amend our software to match their specific needs. Meanwhile we had to ensure that our products were always up to date with compliance and taxation laws. Then there was also the little fact that our competitors were not sitting idly by sucking their thumbs. They were out to kill us too. The months went by, and we took much flak from both our customers and competitors. We were losing business because our products had already been falling behind technically and we still had nothing new to offer. I needed to do something drastic to keep my existing customers, so I announced the launch of our new products, much to the dismay of my technical staff and the complete bewilderment of my sales force. I booked the conference room in one of Dublin's biggest hotels for one morning only, and we flooded our customers with marketing material, telling them not to miss the event of the century. Our marketing was, as usual, a major success as nearly everybody confirmed their attendance.

Now for the tricky bit, trying to fool them into thinking that their new products were just around the corner. My plan was to show them the new car with all the bells and whistles but without any engine. I downed tools and had my programmers manufacture as many screen shots as they could based on as many crazy ideas I could invent to whet my customers' appetites and keep them locked into my company. I figured it would have the dual purpose of scaring the shit out of my competitors who would undoubtedly hear about my intentions. I could see my staff were feeling scared about everything, but I assured them that everything would be fine. I was not entirely convinced about my own confidence. I needed to produce our new products faster. I needed more expertise as my existing guys were struggling with the technology. I had identified a techie called Ronnie whom everybody had been talking about. I had met him a couple of times, and we had got on well together. You learn as you go through business life that you should always have the best team in your corner, and good lawyers are a very important part of that team. I thought I had the best, as I had one of the senior law partners from one of the larger firms working on my behalf.

We tried to come to an agreement about how much their company was worth. Unfortunately, my lawyer was academically brilliant if you were buying the likes of Ford or Walmart but not when you were buying a two-bit software company. He hadn't a clue, God bless him, and our personalities collided right away. Meanwhile, the other party had employed a young, eager lawyer who was crippling me at the meeting as I tried to complete the takeover. My guy droned on and on, referring to case law as their side got basically everything they wanted, including some shares in my company. Towards the end of the meeting I was asked if I was happy with the deal or if there anything else that I wanted, and I blurted out, “I want him,” pointing to their lawyer, much to his astonishment and my guy’s embarrassment. That’s how I bought their company and how their lawyer became my lawyer. I had acquired Ronnie, my programming genius. I then proceeded to employ a damned good systems analyst, and I set them off to finish our products.

The day arrived for the product launch, and the crowds packed into the great room. I was seriously considering having some semi-naked girls dishing out the coffees, but I was convinced otherwise by a rather perplexed marketing manager who convinced me that the accountancy bodies would not have approved. I dragged out my technical manager to lead the way showing the audience how to get over some problems they may or may not have encountered on their existing systems, and we managed to fill in two hours with two more to go. That’s when I pushed Ronnie, my new technical guru, on stage. After his initial nerves, he then cajoled them with one screen shot after another, dancing his way around the proposed product to the oohs and ahhs of the audience.

We had managed to get to the final fifteen minutes, which was my cue to turn things over for the deadly question and answer session. I noted all of my staff were now neatly positioned at the back of the room near the emergency exit. With one customer after another congratulating me on a wonderful job, I was then interrupted by somebody asking, “There’s a lot of talk these days about the Internet. Will that mean I will be able to review my clients’ financial affairs without having to be at my office?”

The question earned the approving mutters of everyone in the audience. You have to bear in mind that the mid-nineties were the coming of age of the Internet. It was now more than a passing fad.

“Of course you will!” I said enthusiastically. All the technical staff looked to Ronnie at the back of the room, who was looking decidedly aghast.

“How will you do this?” the customer continued.

“Via the cigarette lighter in your car!” I boldly announced as Ronnie now left the building, Elvis style. “We have developed a unique method of plugging your notebook computer into your cigarette power outlet, which allows you to download any files from our system directly over the Internet." At this stage I thought it wise to put an end to the conference and told them that refreshments were now available in the hallway where my staff would be eager to discuss all of the exciting developments they'd seen today.

I managed to avoid one annoying guy who kept asking when he could expect to receive the new product by pairing him with one of our more attractive staff members, whom I always had available for such emergencies. I pushed the last customer through the door, locked it, and turned to see Ronnie with his arms folded, saying, "A fucking cigarette power outlet!"

"Ronnie," I said, "I had to say something."

It took many pints of lager to gradually yield him around to my way of thinking, but the conference worked. I only lost a couple more customers before we were eventually able to produce something.

We were also badly stretched by having to support our other markets, like the legal and veterinary professions, which badly curtailed our proposed killer new product. I took a long hard look at my business and decided there was too much clutter, too many half-baked products being worked on that were interfering with the products I was trying to develop.

I took a big chance. I was going to shed my remaining products and put all of my money on producing my world beater. We were overexposed by trading in too many markets. We were not dominant in our market segments. We had some inefficient staff. We also had the constant cash scourge that arose every month, distracting us from our main tasks. In short, we had many problems that needed to be addressed. On the plus side, I had a very loyal team of four or five individuals who never doubted me and worked tirelessly for me.

I had to get cash. I couldn't keep getting distracted all the time running away from debts. I asked my accountants to find me an investor, and in fairness it didn't take too long. A Canadian guy invested over a hundred thousand for a ten percent stake, and I was happy to have a company valuation of a million pounds. Any positive valuation was very welcome then. Then I received a call one day from a venture capital bank who were interested in investing in my company. Even though I was very wary of vulture capitalists, I didn't want to let that opportunity go by. I figured that even though I would be a minority shareholder in my own company it would feel very good to have a pillow of cash to rest my head upon. It was a mistake in one way to lose control, but when there's only one oasis and you're dying of thirst, it's good to have a pride of lions watching your back as you quench your thirst.

This major new investment meant that we could develop our new products without any further distractions. It also gave me the opportunity to start thinking outside the box for the first time since I had started my company. The first thing my management and I did was get rid of the products that didn't work for us. It seems to be the fashion for companies to struggle with mediocre products because they don't want to admit they were wrong in producing them first. We were no different. This is a big mistake, and the shrewd owners will cut their losses by admitting their mistakes and throwing out the deadbeats, in other words swallowing their pride.

I abandoned the legal market by selling the entire coding system to another dealer who felt he could make a success of it. I abandoned the dental and veterinary markets in the same way, selling them off for a reasonable amount of money. It was like finally seeing through the fog. It became obvious how much time our programming teams had been spending chasing their tails and how stretched our support department had been supporting too many products. I could downsize further, keeping the best programmers, beefing up the teams on our main products without having to recruit from the outside. The support department now had more resources to devote to a smaller, more profitable user base, giving a much better service. We found that the products we had abandoned had carried most of the day-to-day expense of support services. As a result we implemented a state-of-the-art bespoke support system that we designed for ourselves, which allowed us to respond to our customers' queries instantly, thereby improving customer service and getting their referrals by extension. I was also able to rid myself of the sales people whom I knew would never cut it, and I kept the very best, those who were delighted to be focused on just a handful of products rather than trying to sell too much and never achieving their goals.

I had been toying with the idea of outsourcing our programming to another company. This arose mainly because programmers were demanding too much money, and I always maintained that when you employed somebody, it took you at least six months before you knew if they were any good. That's bloody expensive.

I had known an Indian chap called Skip, who was working with one of our London competitors, and we had become friendly. I approached him with the idea of setting up an Indian operation to do all the back-breaking programming work, leaving the Irish companies to do the design and development work. He jumped at the idea because he and his gorgeous spouse had been wanting to return to India for a long time, as his wife was involved in a cancer charity in Calcutta. I also knew that I could trust him implicitly. He was very smart and reliable, and besides I had known him for years, so I decided to set it up.

Skip was true to his word, hiring the best programmers at very little cost compared to western rates, and he ran that company from his own house. Within a month the operation was up and running with the Indian and Dublin programmers organized so that we had a continuous twenty-four hour operation. In no time things progressed at a pace. This was long before Bangalore was ever invented, and soon we had about thirty employees, good people who were producing the code we wanted while we slept, and we tested the code while they slept. It was brilliant, and as a result we were producing products faster than anybody else, twenty-four hours a day.

Normally I would have had a heart attack if I had had to employ thirty employees as I had in India, but remember that, in my usual manner of leaving the managers to manage independently, my manager had a budget to spend as he saw fit. One of the employees was there solely to make tea for everybody at the enormous cost of one pound a day while another bloke stood under a tree outside the building being paid a similar amount to keep the generator going with gasoline. So generally I wasn't too concerned. Of course it was my first real introduction to international business and understanding different peoples and their cultures. For example, I had been jumping up and down for three days looking for my Indian manager, who had not returned my calls. When eventually I got him on the phone and was balling him out for it, he asked me did I receive CNN over in Dublin. He said it might not be a bad idea to look at it every now and then, as I would have known that half of Calcutta was under water from a tremendous hurricane, that, in fact, at that very moment we were speaking, he could see his chief programmer coming up the main street, paddling a canoe. Another time he rang me, as he had heard I had been ranting and raving looking for him again, and as he was speaking to me he suddenly went all quiet as if the phone went dead. A few minutes later he was back on the phone telling me that he had to run over and save a little girl as she was about to play with a python. It's a different world!

It reminded me of the time I had been speaking to my Northern Ireland agents during the height of the Troubles. As we spoke on the phone there was a huge explosion followed by a deep silence. I shouted down the phone, "Are you all right, Conor? Are you all right?"

"Yes, I'm fine," he said. "There's an RUC officer in my room with a submachine gun, and the office wall has disappeared, but I'm fine. What were we talking about again?"

It makes you think long and hard about the true meaning of life as we all seem to get wrapped up in our own worlds, totally divorced from reality.

All of these changes had dramatic effects. Ronnie solved one problem after another, training my existing staff in all the new technology, which seemed to change every other week. The Indian operation performed all the time, consuming programming in record time and super efficiently. However, I am not the most patient of individuals, and I was getting very anxious as my competitors were rolling out newer versions of their products.

We had reached a stumbling block in the final part of the development of the most important product, and it seemed insurmountable. They had tried everything for weeks to no avail, and I didn't tell them that I had made enquiries to sell my company because I simply hadn't enough money to continue. I had used up practically all of my investors' money. It was either get these products to market now or close the shop. Ronnie and his crew worked tirelessly without any need for supervision. I was very proud of their efforts, but the clock had ticked long enough, and I reckoned I was at most a month away from closing down.

I had just about given up on the whole idea when one morning, very early, around 6:30, I arrived at work to find Ronnie standing outside the front door with the silliest grin you're likely to see in a long time, and I knew he had cracked it. He had bloody well cracked it. I parked my car, got out, walked past him without a word, then turned around and said, "About fucking time" and gave him the biggest hug imaginable. He showed me his work, and the whole team were delighted. It was better than we'd hoped. It was going to rock. I wriggled my cash around to gain us more time. We took another six months to perfect it, tested it until it was bulletproof. It was like when you know you have a royal flush filled on the last card and the others have put in all of their money against you. You knew you had to win. That's how I felt that day, the day my guys had cracked it. It was powerful.

We launched our new products later that year to a royal fanfare, blew the competition apart with our offerings both here in Ireland and of course the UK. We were climbing up the charts in a very short time, and some of the very big boys began to take notice. But for now I was happy to enjoy the fruits of actually making consistent profits for the first time since I had started the company. I could finally sleep!

I worked tirelessly to broadcast our products around the UK and Ireland as fast as I could, and it paid off. Soon our old customers were coming back to us in droves, fed up with the inferior service they had been getting from their old suppliers. We took them back like the prodigal sons, and soon they were demanding more from us. At one exhibition in London I was focused on these partners from Price Waterhouse, the international accountancy firm, and giving them the royal selling treatment. One of my managers kept trying to get my attention, pointing to some really old guy dressed somewhat shabbily who was in the audience and wanted to talk to me. I ignored him and continued licking up to the partner guys.

After about an hour of presentations I bid the partners adieu and finally turned my attention to the old guy. My manager introduced us and told me that he was retired, that an American friend of his wanted him to look after his bookkeeping requirements. He was looking for some software that would suit his needs. He told me we had a mutual friend who had recommended my products, so I said sure, no problem, and I enquired about his budget. Oh, he said, he expected to pay no more than about a thousand pounds but that if I had anything cheaper, then that would be even better. I had thought it was going to be a huge sale, the way my manager had been trying to get my attention, so I was immediately turned off by the guy. My manager looked at me giving me the slow down and listen signal. He was a nice old man, and he told me that there was a good possibility that his friend would be expanding his operations in the UK and elsewhere, that he would probably need a lot more of my products over time. It appeared that his friend wanted the old guy to start a bookkeeping service for all the restaurants he was opening around the world. This got my attention, and I sat him down. I nonchalantly enquired who his friend was.

"Oh, we've known each other since we were at school," he said, "and he doesn't trust anybody else to look after his finances, so he's asked me to do it. I'll probably need many part-time bookkeepers to help me."

"And what's the name of the restaurant chain?"

"McDonalds. Have you heard of them?"

When they picked me up off the floor, my manager thought I was going to have sex with him there and then. It transpired that McDonalds, of Big Mac fame, wanted this old guy to run the bookkeeping for all of their restaurants, as they had just recently entered the British market. That one contract alone gave us revenues of many thousands of pounds every quarter when it reached its prime many years later. The lesson learned was never take anybody for granted, as I could just as easily have blown it. It was akin to the famous story of how Microsoft got started because some manager from Digital had been out to lunch when the IBM hierarchy came looking for a new operating system, and when they heard the guy wasn't there to meet with them, they decided to check out this guy called Gates. The rest, as they say, is history.

CHAPTER 13

WHEN YOU START A BUSINESS, no matter how well organized you are or how well you planned everything, most of the time you are flying by the seat of your pants, swinging this way, then that way, and just hoping that it all works out. You also have to contend with life's little challenges every now and then. As I said, we had two young kiddies, and my office was only up the road from my house, so I used to go home for lunch and play with the kiddies before heading back to work. One day, Jack, who was only two, was sitting at the end of the stairs playing with something when I bent down to kiss him goodbye. I didn't see that he had a fork in his hand, and as he went to put his arms around me, the fork went straight into my left eye. I was in so much shock that as I stood upright the fork was actually hanging out of my left eye. I reached up and pulled it out, and my screams could be heard across the Irish Sea. The pain was excruciating. Jack started to roar with fright, not knowing why his dad was screaming. Maria nearly fainted when she saw what had happened.

I grabbed a towel and told her to get the car and drive me into the eye and ear hospital as fast as possible. I told her to forget about the speed limit. She took me at my word as the pain rocked through my head and my left eye closed down. Sure enough, a motor bike speed cop started chasing us, and I told Maria to step on it and forget about him, as my pain was now unbearable. The cop pulled up alongside the driver's side, waving us to pull over. He took one look at me, put two and two together, and signaled us to follow him. With sirens blaring, we arrived at the hospital with a full police escort. The cop was great. Maria told him what had happened. I was unable to speak with the pain and the shock. He cringed when she told him.

What is it with hospitals the world over? Can they not prioritize? Jesus, you come in with your two arms missing and blood flowing from every orifice, and they say, "Take a number and fill out this form." Hello? can't they see that the patient has no arms or is bleeding from every orifice and that maybe, just maybe he could be classed as an emergency!?

Well, my day was no different. I arrived in with a huge towel wrapped around my head, and I was told to take a number, so I shouted, "I'm fucking dying here, so get me a fucking doctor now!"

It worked, except hospital staff have contingency measures for people like me, who give them grief and curse at them. They sent out Satan's brother, a bollocks posing as a doctor, with the personality of a dying skunk.

"What seems to be the problem?" he asked. *Oh nothing*, I thought, *it's my foot. I just like visiting hospitals with a towel wrapped around my head, you idiot!* Maria told him what had happened. Then he literally grabbed my left eyelid, which had closed shut with the shock, forced it open with the subtlety of a charging bull, ignoring my screams of agony, and after staring at my eye through his ophthalmoscope, told me I had been very lucky, that I had been the thickness of a hooker's fanny hair away from losing sight in that eye. Then he got up and pissed off as the left eye shut down, followed by the right.

A nurse came over to me and told me to swallow a pill, which happened to be a morphine tablet. The pain disappeared almost immediately, and my right eye opened. God save the guys who invented morphine. The nurse said it should be enough to get me home to bed. I was to take another tablet, which would help me sleep. When I asked her for more tablets she said that she was only allowed to give me two. I offered her a thousand pounds a tablet, but she just smiled and said she would have loved to accommodate me, but she simply couldn't. She told me to rest for a couple of days and it should be okay. We made it home, and just as the pain reappeared I popped the other tablet and just about managed to get to sleep.

It took about a week before I could see properly again, but it was fine. There's still a scar on the pupil to this day. I asked God if he could see his way to ignoring me for a few years as I was having enough trouble with my life as it was. I'm still waiting on a response!

I still had to get back to work. I went from town to village all over Ireland selling my wares. I was like a preacher selling bibles. I brought one of my girls, Carrie, with me on one particular installation as the principal in the firm was the head man in that accountancy body, and I didn't want to screw it up. Carrie was great. We always had great fun together. She was smart, and we shared the same sense of humor.

As an aside I have to mention that I was only as good as the people I employed, and thankfully I had the knack of employing some great fastidious people who jumped through the hoops for me. We were in a small town in the back of beyond, and as we arrived with the computers we saw a large printed sheet on the door saying, "Closed for computer installation. Come back tomorrow." We laughed until we realized they were serious. So we unpacked everything, introduced ourselves, and the principal came in, an old gentleman and one of the nicest men you could meet. I began to go through the basics before handing everything over to Carrie to do the full training. I wasn't sure how long we'd be there, but I assumed we'd start heading back later that afternoon.

I had just begun my dissertation when the old guy said, "That's enough for the moment, Bernie. I think we need to take a break."

I looked at Carrie, and she shrugged her shoulders back at me. I said that would be fine, by all means they could take a break, we'd get back to it when they were ready. The old chap took the two of us downstairs, outside onto the street, and into the building adjoining his, which happened to be a public house. I turned and asked him what the story was, and he said, "Oh, I own this pub, Bernie. Now what would you like to drink?"

Well, Holy God and his angels, if I wasn't in need of resuscitation! I mean, it was barely ten o'clock in the morning, and the owner was offering us alcohol.

"Eh, no, I'm fine. I'll just have a cup of coffee," I said.

"I'll have a pint of Guinness," says Carrie, and she looked at me with a "Why not?" look on her face.

"No, she won't," I said, giving Carrie the evil eye.

"A pint of Guinness it is, then, for Carrie, and Bernie will have an Irish coffee," he said as he disappeared into a back room.

"Holy crap, Carrie, this is totally unprofessional. We'll be drunk by mid-day," I exclaimed.

"Not at all. He's already got us fixed up with accommodation and wants me to stay for a few days," she explained.

"A few days? Are you serious?" I balked.

With that the old guy came back with a pint, an Irish coffee, and a large Jameson for himself.

"Sláinte," he said.

"Oh, sláinte," I said. "Eh, I understand from Carrie that you're expecting us to hang around for a couple of days, is that right?"

"Not at all," he said. "You are a very busy man, Bernie. Carrie can stay and do the installation for us. As you know, I've spent quite a large amount of money on these computers, and I want to make sure it all goes well." So I sat there thinking to myself that he was going about it in a very funny way by getting us both sloshed before we did anything.

"So after you finish that drink," he went on, "you head back to Dublin, and we'll look after Carrie and send her back to you safe and sound." Not wanting to argue with him, I looked over at Carrie, and it was only then I noticed that she was showing way too much cleavage. It dawned on me that maybe he was a horny old man as well.

"You do know I'll have to charge a daily training rate plus traveling expenses?" I asked, thinking that I might as well earn as much money as I could while I was there.

"Of course, I expect that. Now off you go." He more or less pushed me out onto the street.

I got a call three days later from Carrie saying things were a little iffy and that she needed my help because she needed to escape. Apparently the old man was going to propose to her. I kidded with her that it might not be so bad. After all, he was loaded and owned half of the town. She might have six or seven kids with him. But she shouted at me, "Bernie, don't mess around! I'm serious. This old guy is one horny old man."

So I sent one of the young lads down to collect her. We never found out if they ever got around to using the computers, but they never gave us a moment's trouble.

I must have met every accountant in Ireland and England over the years, from the brilliant to the obnoxious, the prejudiced and the downright ignorant. I never met as many characters in one profession as I did with the accountants, and they say they're a dull lot. Absolutely not. One typical example was the English always paid you immediately. The Irish never did. The English were very forgiving when something went wrong. The Irish would drown your mother if they didn't get what they wanted immediately. I had more run-ins with the Irish customers than I did with everyone else, but it hardens you. I always maintained that if you could be successful in a tight little country like Ireland, you could be successful anywhere.

There were times when some customers, regardless of where they came from, stretched my patience to breaking point. One such occasion occurred when my support manager, Margie, came into my office one day in tears. I had never seen her cry before. She told me that she was quitting because some boorish lawyer from Galway had cursed at her over something stupid that he had done.

"Are you saying he swore at you because he had screwed up?" I said.

"Yes," she sobbed.

"Where is he now?"

"He's on line four."

I can't stand bullies. I cannot abide any man that hurts women or children. It incenses me to the point that I could easily lose control, and but for my training as a boxer I would find it impossible to show any restraint. So when some bully attacks one of my staff, and one of my managers at that, its time you left the arena. I told her to take a seat, and the conversation went something like this:

"Hello, this is the owner, Mr. Donnelly. Is that Mr. Total-Prick?"

I'll refer to him as Mr. Total-Prick as that was the only way I pictured him. He started to rant a bit, and I let him rant for about three seconds. I knew how to deal with bullies, and the first rule is always to attack first.

"Now you just shut up, you little prick, and listen to me. If you ever say the things you've said to my manager or any of my staff again, I will personally drive down to your offices, drag you out on to Eyre Square, and beat the crap out of you. On second thought, you can send back our products for a full rebate because I don't want someone like you as a customer. I never want to hear from your firm ever again. And if you don't apologize to Margie now, I'm going to jump in my car and drive over to Galway, and I'll find you, and you will never walk again, you total bollocks!"

There was silence on the other end of the line. Margie looked at me in shock as she had never heard me curse at a customer before, so holding my hand over the mouthpiece I whispered

"Do you think he got the message?" She started to laugh. It was good to see her smiling.

There was a stony silence on the other end of the line, and the next words I heard were, "I'm sorry, I don't know what came over me. I didn't mean to say those things to Margie. I will apologize to her." He then continued to tell me about how rotten his life was, that his marriage was on the rocks, no surprise there, and that he had recently lost one of his biggest clients. I toned things down a bit but never let my advantage slip. I warned him that he was in the last chance saloon and that he'd better shape up or ship out. I handed the phone back to Margie as she mimed a big "Thank you." I believe that guy became one of our nicest customers, as we never heard another squeak out of him. As my Da would have said, always take a bully head-on despite the odds. You might get a bloody nose or even a broken something or other, but they always back down, and you will never have any trouble from them ever again.

There was the time in England when I had to take a train into the countryside to demonstrate to a prospective customer. He had assured me that if I could persuade him to buy my products, he would ensure that all of his clients would also buy the product. Sometimes it is impossible to prequalify a sale, you just have to go with your instincts, and my instincts this time were wrong.

I was picked up at the station by his obnoxious son, who displayed his rude arrogance from the outset. I was more disappointed when I saw that he operated his practice from his house, as I had assumed that he had a large office somewhere in the town. It was obvious that this bloke was a small-timer and nothing like what he had painted himself out to be. I was left waiting on him to finish his phone call and soon found out where his son's bad manners came from. The bloke slammed down the phone and without so much as a hello or a how do you doody, he continued to ignore me. I was having none of his ignorance, so I raised my voice and said, "I'd like a cup of coffee please, as I've travelled a long way," giving him the evil eye that said don't mess with me, dickhead.

"Okay," he said, and then he turned his head and shouted into another room, "Coffee, coffee!" I followed his gaze to see a little old woman come rushing into the room as the bully screamed, "Him, him! Coffee, now!" pointing at me. I couldn't believe the way he spoke to her, and I felt very sorry for the housekeeper as she scurried to the kitchen.

"Who is that?" I asked.

"My pathetic spouse," he scowled as his fat-boy son laughed.

He asked me to start my demonstration, but I was beginning to seethe inside, and as the woman placed my coffee on the desk, I smiled at her and thanked her. His contempt for me continued, and after about fifteen minutes, I blew up. "Listen, you piece of shit, unless you show me one sliver of humanity, I swear to God I'm coming around your desk and I'm going to lay you out, and then I'm coming after you!" I blared as I looked back at his revolting son.

I didn't give a damn how it looked. These people deserved a damned good hiding, and I was prepared to give it to the pair of them. He was speechless as he sat there cowering, knowing somebody had the audacity to stand up to him for probably the first time in his miserable life. I started to wrap up my things. This demonstration was over as far as I was concerned. I turned to his rat-faced son and said, "You, drive me down to the station, now!" he looked over at his alleged father, who nodded.

As I was about to close the front door, his wife came running up to me and said, "Thank you, thank you so much. I've waited all of my life to see him put down like that."

"Stand up to him or leave him, but don't take that shit from anybody," I said to her, giving her a smile.

We drove to the station in silence, and I got out of the car and told the son, "You'd want to get yourself some manners, you little prick," and I slammed his door and never looked back. I stood on the platform and thought to myself, *That was definitely one sale I didn't want.* But I was wrong. When I got back to my office, my secretary told me that the bloke had been looking for me all day. I didn't return any of his calls. He rang me every day for two weeks, so finally I took his call, and he begged me to take him as a customer. I told him when hell had frozen over I might just consider it. He apologized, and I told him he'd need to apologize to his wife before he apologized to me. I said I might consider it when his wife told me that it was okay to do so, but only if I got the okay from her. A few days later, the woman rang and said that he had been nice to her for the first time since they were married, and she begged me to supply him. I thought about it, and I rang him back a few days later.

"This is the deal: I will supply you and all of your clients on one condition and one condition only."

"What's that?" he asked.

"You are never to mistreat anybody, especially your wife, ever again, or I will pull the plug on our support services, and you will never get a software upgrade again. Is that clear?"

"Yes, I promise. I'm sorry," he said.

"Put your wife on the phone."

"Hello?" she said meekly.

"I've just told your husband that I will supply him our products, providing he doesn't mistreat you ever again, so it's up to you to tell me if he ever bullies you. I will cut him off if you tell me. Do you understand?"

"Yes, and thank you so much."

That was how he also became one of our better customers, and I never had to speak to him again.

My contempt for bullies was not limited to the UK or Irish shores. Oh no, I could confront bullies anywhere I met them. The Irish government were great at promoting Irish companies abroad, and I took the opportunity of joining one of their export juntas to Kenya. I chose Kenya not because I had some deep covert plan that Kenya was the place to be, nothing like that. It was because I needed to try out my products in a smaller country before entering the bigger markets, and Kenya had the same accountancy rules as other commonwealth countries. Besides, the weather in Ireland had been miserable for months. I needed to go to a place that had sunshine. I arrived to a blazing sunshine morning and a sea of black faces staring up at this white man who had invaded their shores. I couldn't believe how poor the country was. I had visions of beautiful, wild countryside teeming with exotic animals. Instead I saw roads filled with potholes the size of small craters, people living in hovels all around me, as my proposed agent drove me up to his home in the mountains outside of Nairobi. I looked on the positives: the sun was shining, and this potential agent of mine was very enthusiastic about selling my products in Kenya. He had neglected to tell me that he had not informed his wife that I was arriving. It didn't take long to figure out they were having a domestic, a full-blown argument that was only intensified by my presence. I sat there trying to be sociable, but I was bollocksed from the flight over. I left them to sort things out and went in search of the toilet. I badly needed a crap.

So I dumped my load, so to speak, and pulled the old fashioned chain. Nothing happened. Not a drop of water came forth. So there I am in their house, while they're having a domestic, and I've just left a dry, stinky dump in their toilet. I stood on the seat to look in the cistern, and, wouldn't you know it, not a drop of water and none to wash my hands either. Never being one to beat around the bush, I came out and said, "Excuse me. Look, I don't mean to interrupt, but could you please stop arguing as I won't be staying here. I've booked a hotel downtown. In the meantime, I just had a crap, and there's no water to flush it, so could you tell me what I am supposed to do with the mess?"

I figured if they were ignorant enough to have a slanging match in front of a complete stranger, then they could clean up the crap at the same time. They informed me that they only had an outdoor well and that he would get a few buckets of water to fill the tank.

"Fine. Then you can take me to my hotel," I said in a very matter-of-fact way, staring at the two of them, leaving them in no doubt as to exactly what I thought of the pair of them.

It obviously did the trick because I think they may have felt just a little bit guilty after my outburst. They invited me to experience a typical Kenyan barbecue before my flight to London. After we had spent the next couple of days completing our various business meetings with prospective customers, I checked out of my hotel, and they brought me into the bush, to an open-air restaurant. On the menu were all the things that David Attenborough used to glorify. There were giraffe, rhino, buffalo, elk, and all the other exotic jungle creatures, all being barbecued.

Now, I have to explain, as it was explained to me, that these creatures about to be fried were a long time dead, from natural or unnatural causes, and had possibly been frozen for years, as well as their bacteria. I have to say I didn't find any difference between any of the tastes. It was meat, like any other meat, and nothing of distinction. They drove me to the airport, and I said my goodbyes, forever.

I waited at the boarding gate, and after about forty minutes I felt this horrendous pain in my belly just as they announced the final boarding call. I struggled to the gate with my trousers opened and a look of extreme anguish on my face, similar to the look on the flight attendant's face. I told the startled flight attendant that I wasn't feeling at all well, but she just wanted me on board, now. I struggled with my pain until the captain finally turned off the fasten seat belts sign, and I dashed into the tiny cubicle. I stayed there for the ten-hour journey, helped by a very understanding flight attendant who handed me water and aspirin for the entire flight. What a nightmare. I think the couple brought me to that God-forsaken jungle restaurant on purpose. I had no intentions of ever going back to Kenya again, and the rest of the African continent was now under serious review.

On another arranged trip, this time to Australia, I decided to bring Ted, my newly promoted general manager who had replaced Des, my long time right hand man who decided he'd had enough of my industry and wanted to try something new. Neither Ted or I had ever been down under before. We were really looking forward to the trip as we had received good vibes from potential customers about our products. Ted had as much a fear of flying as I had for water, so we made a pretty pair. The flight from Hong Kong was bumpy, and as we flew into Hong Kong the pilot decided to rev up the engines and take off again. Now all of us had assumed that when the pilot put the wheels down that he intended to land the thing, so everybody, especially Ted, farted themselves to death as the pilot announced, "Now, now, everything's okay. I just didn't like the fact that another airplane was due to take off close to our landing strip, so I decided to go around again. This is why they pay me."

After we checked into our hotel, I rang one of our potential customers and asked him to meet up with us at a nearby pub. We all played pool together, but before long I was knackered and decided to go to bed, but not before warning Ted, who was a lot younger than me, to make sure he got enough sleep as we had an early start by train the next morning. I needed him to be alert and ready for many technical questions. He assured me that everything would be fine, and off I went to bed.

I awoke early the next morning around six, had a swim and some breakfast, got myself dolled up, and went looking for Ted. I knocked on his door and heard not a sound. Then I went to the gym and the pool; not a sign of him. So I searched the hotel top to bottom, and, getting frantic, I went over to the concierge and explained my plight.

"I'm waiting for one of my managers, and he's not answering his room. I've tried ringing his room, but there's no answer. Can you help?"

"Sure, let me get my keys, and we'll try his room again," said the concierge. Off we go upstairs to Ted's floor, and at this stage I was running late and ready to kill him. In fact, I thought that if was dead it mightn't be a bad thing because it would save me the trouble. When we arrived at his room, we knocked, then knocked louder. There was no response.

I looked at the concierge, who looked at me saying, "I guess there's nothing for it except to open the door." The door opened, and we looked down to find Ted spread-eagled on the floor, bollock naked, with a hard on reaching up to the ceiling, and the stink of booze throughout the room. Now, when I say a hard on, I can only describe it as the nearest thing to a fully grown hairy turnip I had ever seen.

The concierge turned to me and said, "Well, at least we know he's not dead. I'll be leaving that one to you then, mate!"

As we took one more look at the specimen before us, I nodded and said, "I'm not touching him." I closed the door, leaving him in his state of oblivion.

I had to wing my way through the two meetings, and my demonstrations didn't go too well. I explained my poor showing on the jet-lag and asked them would they mind if I came back to make the presentation again. They said it was not a problem. When I got back to the hotel, Ted was dressed impeccably, wondered why I had left without him. He didn't remember anything about anything. I told him to ask the concierge to explain that morning's events, as I was trying to forget the ugly vision I had of him. I told him that I didn't think I could ever look at him again in the same way. We had a good laugh with the concierge, who corroborated my story, and I rearranged our demonstrations, which fortunately went better the next time.

We appointed a number of dealers to sell our products, and we did well out of that trip, despite everything that went on.

CHAPTER 14

THEN THERE WERE THE MANUFACTURERS and distributors, a breed unto themselves. I was always invited to the Chairman's Dinner by IBM because I was the one with the stories and could keep you entertained, but there's a limit to the power of entertaining. If you don't get any assistance (it's called conversation!) from your audience, you get knackered, give up, and retire to the bar. This happened one year when I was invited by IBM to their annual din-dins. They had put me at the top table, sitting beside the chairman no less. I had never met the chairman and really didn't want to be there, but they insisted. So there I was, plonked in between eight other IBM heads who had as much personality as dead rats.

Chairman John introduced himself, and I started with some small talk. The conversation went something like this:

"So John, have you been Chairman for long?" I asked.

"I'm in my second year," he said.

"Do you go to many of these shindigs?"

"Too many."

So I'm thinking he's a nice bloke, a little bit quiet, but perhaps he would loosen up. I delved a little deeper.

"Tell me, John, do you watch the rugby?"

"No, I don't," he said. Damn, everybody in Irish business watched the rugby. Where have you been John, I thought to myself?

"How about soccer?"

"No interest in soccer, I'm afraid." This was the era of Saint Jackie Charlton, who was about to be canonized for having brought Ireland to the final stages of the World Cup, and John didn't know the first thing about it!

"Hurling, GAA, tennis, or boxing?"

"No, none of those." Sport is obviously not one of John's strong suits. One last try. It was time to play an ace. I mean, everybody plays golf!

"What's your handicap?" I asked.

"I don't play any golf." That completed my little game show, *A Question of Sport*. Result: zero!

"Do you like watching movies?" I asked, searching for my rosary beads, knowing I could talk until the cows came home about movies.

"My wife and I never watch them."

"Theatre?" I enquired. At this stage the entire table was wondering what I was going to do as I looked around for an escape route. Now I took a chance on the theatre thingy, hoping he didn't have any interest because I knew nothing whatsoever about the theatre, and sure enough he didn't disappoint.

I looked around the table, looked at the chairman, and said, "Now John, I'm not giving up on this, but there has to be something you're interested in."

"I suppose it does seem that I live a boring life."

"No, no, no, not at all," I lied, thinking that we were only ten minutes into the dinner and I was due to spend at least two hours with this gobshite!

"What about food?" I asked. "You do eat food John, I suppose?" At this stage the other managers were knocking back the whiskies.

"Yes, we like our food," he said. Hallelujah, success at last!

"Anything of the abnormal variety? Something that could turn this into some sort of a conversation?" At this stage I had given up and couldn't give a bollocks if he had eaten Snow White and all the seven dwarfs.

"My wife and I rather like seafood, especially sushi," he said. Now sushi was a totally unknown factor in Ireland in those days. People could hardly spell it, let alone eat the stuff.

"What about sex, John? Do you and your wife ever have any sex?"

His team of managers turned a whiter shade of yellow. At this stage I didn't care about being an IBM dealer ever again. Well, holy God and his mother if he didn't break down laughing on the spot.

"You know, Bernie, I never really realized how boring I was until tonight," he said.

John resigned that year and took early retirement. I met him once or twice down the harbor in Dun-Laoghaire while he was out walking with his wife. He'd always shout over to me, "I'm still boring!"

"Have a great day!" I'd shout back, not wanting to agree with him.

I was always inclined to get myself into embarrassing situations, primarily because I have little inhibition about saying what I see. There was a classic case in point when my imagination got the better of me and blew right up in my face. Let me digress to give you some of the background to my story.

There was an accountant, we'll call him Mick because that was his name. Mick was a strange sort of bloke. Some people absolutely hated him while others who knew him had no problem with him at all. I was in the latter camp. He had bought quite a bit of equipment from me and had recommended me to a number of his clients, so in my book he was okay. I'd heard he had recently fired one of his staff because she had bad breath. Mick was like that when he was having a good day.

I was due to meet with him about some problem he was having with our software, so I wasn't looking forward to it because Mick would let you have it with both barrels. As I entered his office, I handed him a present, two tickets for something or other that I didn't want. I was generous like that and immediately segued into a subject he liked before he laid into me.

"So Mick, that's a powerful tan you have there," I said.

"Aw, Bernie," he said "I'm just back from the greatest holiday I've ever had."

"Where was that, Mick?"

"Ghana, west Africa."

"Tell me all about it, Mick," I said, hoping he'd forget the reason I was there in the first place.

"The wife wanted to do something a bit different for the holidays, so I booked this African holiday, arranged by my travel agent, and we stayed in a jungle hotel built amongst the trees with all the mod cons, servants, running water, great food, the works. Then one morning at the crack of dawn we were taken on a balloon safari, photographing all the animals from a great height. Absolutely marvelous."

As Mick told the story, I was there, I was in that balloon traveling over the elephants and the giraffes. It was far from balloon safaris I was reared. I thought it was amazing.

"So how did you manage to book something like that?" I asked.

"Ah, there's this big fat bitch that owns a travel agency down in Rathfarnham. She's great at getting these unusual things."

Big fat bitch, I thought. *Jesus Mick, I wouldn't be applying for that job with the United Nations just yet, if I was you.* Mick finished the story and continued to chew the bollocks off me. They don't forget for too long, do they?

Fast forward to my real story. I was invited to the launch of some new computer or other by one of the major distributors at a very upmarket restaurant on St. Stephens Green. Now, as an aficionado of human nature, I knew that every half-baked dealer in the country would be accepting that invitation to sample all the great food and the ambiance of the restaurant because none of us ever had a hope of spending our money in a place like that. Of course it was sold out, and we all packed into a downstairs room and pretended to be transfixed by the technological offerings being pitched to us. Then the bell went for lunch, and we all scrambled upstairs to the main dining room. We had each been assigned table placings. There were free cigars (you could smoke anywhere in those days), the best of wine, and basically no expense was being spared to get us to buy their crap.

I took my spot at a table for eight people, introduced myself to the assembled crowd, and noticed that the seat to my right was vacant. I did my usual and tried to see what the company was like, and of course I was among a group of non-speaking Russians. Well, they might as well have been from Russia because none of them had a word to say. What is it with people? Are we surrounded by taciturn people today or people who are just incapable of engaging in conversation? If people would just ask one question and pretend they're interested, it would make such a difference! In fact, a friend of mine told me that I was to blame because he noticed that whenever there's a group gathering, I tend to burst into the room and join the first group I see, whereas he told he that he stands at the end of a room, surveying the proceedings, before deciding who he wants to join. He maintains that is the reason I gather boring people around me. Boring people magnetize themselves to me, thinking, "I'll have some fun with that bloke!"

Did you ever have that experience where you meet someone for the first time and you know you don't like one another? Well, in walked my experience in the form of a tall, dour-looking woman that you just knew was not someone you'd mess with. Or if, God forbid, you ever married such a creature, you would never return home and tell her you lost your wages. Her name was Sandra. I knew this because she came to the table and announced loudly, "Hi, my name is Sandra!" as she perused the taciturn, the sheepish, the pretty, and the ugly ones. Then she looked down at me.

"Hi, I'm Bernie!" I proffered my hand as she sat in the chair next to me, completely ignoring me and my hand. I guess she had the same feelings about me.

I tried to talk to the bloke on my left, and as I was getting nowhere fast, I decided to engage Sandra, aka Frau Kaiser, on my right.

"Tell me, what do you do?" I said, giving her my best dazzling smile combined with my oozing charm, a totally deadly combination.

"I run my own computer consultancy," she replied disdainfully as if somebody had left a cockroach on the side of her plate.

Trudging on, I asked her what type of computer consultancy she owned. That was a mistake because that allowed her to blow her own trumpet, telling the assembled crowd how wonderful and intelligent she was and to imply that she shouldn't have to mix with the dregs of society like the present company. We had absolutely nothing in common, and even armed with my IBM experience with the chairman, I couldn't break down any barriers to entry, as they say, so I changed the subject.

"Did you manage to take any holidays this year?" I enquired.

"Yes," she said, "in fact, I'm just back from two marvelous weeks in Tierra del Fuego. We skied, climbed the mountains. It was just glorious," she pouted. I looked around the table, and I guessed I wasn't the only one who hadn't a clue where the Tierra del Fuego was, but I was damned if I was going to let on to Frau Kaiser.

Then she asked, knowing that I probably spent my two weeks holidays in either Tierra Del Anywhere or Costa del Nothing, "So where did you go?"

"Well," I said, "it so happens I'm just back from a balloon safari in Ghana actually. My girlfriend and I were staying in a five-star hotel, uniquely built into the jungle canopy." That got the table's attention, I can tell you. Suddenly Frau Kaiser deigned to look begrudgingly and admiringly in my direction, obviously thinking that I'd robbed some bank somewhere to get to Africa. Rising to the occasion, my imagination in overdrive, I painted all of them a glorious picture of an early rising sun as we flipped over the heads of every animal they'd ever seen in the zoo, in our multicolored balloon, laced with a tale of how we witnessed a lion kill just below us, which was a rather rare sight indeed at such an early hour of the morning, but we were accompanied by an expert guide—

"How did you come across a vacation like that?" Frau Kaiser interrupts, and of course just like an albatross in flight which should never be interrupted, I relayed Mick's line without thinking.

"Some fat bitch in a travel agency in Rathfarnham organized it."

Whereupon, and you are not going to believe this, she looked at me with the killer looks that only the Kaiser himself could have ordered.

"That fat bitch happens to be my sister," she spat.

Oh screw me pink with a blue stiletto, I thought as the bloke on my left doubled in two with the laughter and the rest of the table looked stunned. I dropped my face to the table, held it there for a few seconds, stood up, looked at Frau Kaiser, and said, "Aw bollocks, and screw you and your sister!" With that I left the room without having had even a bowl of soup.

I walked out, and, would you believe it, it was lashing rain. I crossed the Green and started laughing so hard, thinking, *How do I always get myself into those precarious positions? Why can't I just be boring like everybody else?* Passersby thought I was a drunk, a well-dressed drunk, mind you.

CHAPTER 15

Our products were superior to anything else that was on offer in the UK, but it's never easy trying to break into a foreign market. Granted both countries had the same language and similar company legislation, which was a huge bonus. The usual route for exporting your products was to try to find a distributor. You can have the greatest product in the world and still watch it die a death in the hands of an amateur. I had tried to do this a number of times with other products I had produced, but what happens is that you are effectively at their mercy. If they don't put in the effort and perform the way they said they would, then you will find that you have wasted a lot of precious time, sometimes years, that you can never recover. Of course you can try to set up your own subsidiary, which will give you all the control but also all the costs, which can be considerable. You will need to have an office in a good location, usually in a city center, which means high rents. Then you will need to hire the best salespeople, which are almost impossible to find, as the best ones are always fully employed at high salaries. What I needed to do was to find a company that was on its knees, that had an existing company structure and a reasonable user base. My idea was to try to inveigle my way into such a company somehow, with a view to buying them.

I had identified a Manchester firm in the same market as us who had been around for what seemed like forever. I couldn't understand how they were still in business because we hardly ever came across them in the field. Thinking that there might be an opportunity there, I rang the owner, Ken, suggesting to him that we should form some sort of a partnership, whereby we could both sell one another's products in each of our respective countries. I knew that nobody in Ireland would want to buy his products, and I figured that maybe he might be having problems with his customer base and looking for some sort of a solution. I knew our products could replace his, giving us a firm foothold in the UK in the shortest amount of time. After a number of calls, he finally relented to having a meeting to discuss it, so off I went to Manchester to meet him.

He had a great infrastructure. His company had been one of the first to enter my market, and he had been very successful initially but had failed to keep his products upgraded to meet the ever-changing technology. As a result his customers were leaving him by the dozen every month. I always could recognize when something wasn't quite right, and I had that feeling that day he showed me around. There was an ominous atmosphere among his staff as I went from floor to floor. There was no joviality. It appeared to me that the staff had a fear of Ken, which is always a bad sign. I had always kept my distance from my staff, but I knew them inside and out at the same time. They trusted me, they knew I was approachable, and they gave me their loyalty in return.

I suggested to Ken that he should allow me to assist his marketing department by offering him my services free of charge. He agreed, as he saw the benefits of having me organize his sales staff, something he was not good at. It gave me the foothold I needed to get to know his company from the inside while at the same time not incurring any of the major costs, other than renting a nearby apartment.

It wasn't long before I realized how dogmatic Ken was. Everything with him was either his way or the highway. I started to get to know all the main people in his company, and it didn't take me long to realize that this was a golden opportunity for me. I needed to buy this company, but I didn't know how I was going to pull it off.

I knew his sales people were very excited about the possibility of selling our products, which were so superior to the ones they had been trying to sell. I also knew that their customers were complaining a lot. They hadn't sold anything to anybody in quite a while, and when I asked their accountant how come they were still in business, he explained that they never sold their software, instead they leased it. He showed me that on the first of every month he simply pressed a button on his computer and all the standing orders came flowing into their bank account. I was really impressed. My company, like every other company, simply sold their products, combined with the relevant hardware as a one-off sale. The only recurring income was the annual maintenance. In fairness to Ken, he had devised this leasing system whereby the customer never owned the products but Ken owned the customers. It was brilliant. Running such a business model took guts. After all, you needed a lot of customers if you were going to rent your products while still incurring the high overheads, producing the products, and supporting the customers. Your initial cash requirements would be huge, only reducing the longer you managed to stay in business. Ken had managed it, and it was this model that was keeping the company afloat all these years.

The only problem for Ken, and the great opportunity for me, was that Ken hadn't a clue how to run his business, as borne out by the fact that he was hemorrhaging customers by the dozen every month while I had the products that they needed. The sales guys and I got on great. I was one of them. I spoke their language and understood what they needed in the marketplace. It wasn't long, about three months, before we had successfully integrated our products across their range of products. My new fully trained sales teams couldn't wait to get out into the marketplace with their new systems. They were good. They were very good because they could do in an instance what would have taken me years to achieve. They knew their market. They knew their customers. They had an affinity with their customer base built up over the years, and their customers trusted them to look after them.

I also trained them how to sell because I was good, and I believed that I was the best in my business. I knew what they needed to know, and they needed to know their products backwards, so we set about a boot camp training program that was continuous. When they came back into the office after a demonstration, I wanted to know if they got the order. If they hadn't got the order, I wanted to know why. If they didn't give me a satisfactory answer, then I told them to demonstrate the product to me the way they had just demonstrated it to the potential customer. I was ruthless in my tenacity to bring them over the line of success, and within a very short time they started to win, and win big-time. They couldn't wait to come into work in the morning because they knew that finally they had somebody that would give them the freedom to sell decent products. They were making money at last.

However, my biggest problem was trying to handle Ken, trying to keep him out of the mix, keep him from dealing with "my" staff. I arranged for both the production and sales staff to detail the plans they would like to see implemented to make their company successful. They had come up with some brilliant suggestions. I had informed Ken that we would like to present our new plans to him. I told the managers to let me run the meeting, that I would give each of them plenty of time to explain what they had in mind, and they were all excited to do so.

In walked Ken, glum as usual. he could never inspire you. If you saw Ken in a whorehouse, you'd actually go home to your wife. He just had that particular way of spreading doom and gloom. I started the meeting, and I was very pleased with the way "my guys" presented themselves and their plans because for the first time they could talk without fearing their boss. When they had completed their presentation, I turned to Ken and said, "Well, Ken, what do you think of the plans?"

"I don't like them," was all he said.

I looked at him, waiting for him to give his reasons, and when nothing was forthcoming I said, "What do you mean you don't like them? What do you not like?"

"I don't like any of it" he said. He said that he had made his own plans. Then he opened his file and continued to tell everybody in the room how his plans were going to work. I couldn't believe what I was seeing. I couldn't understand how somebody could be that contemptible. The guys had put in a huge amount of effort into their presentations. They had honestly believed that they would be taken seriously. Instead Ken had ignored everything they said, completely disregarding their suggestions. After about twenty minutes he got up and left, leaving a room full of disenchanted individuals who had just had the stuffing beaten out of them. The sales manager said to me that he hadn't expected anything else, that Ken was always that way, that he never listened to them. I told them to stick to their plans, that they were to give me a week, and that they would get what they wanted. They looked at me in disbelief and left the room totally deflated. It was time to get rid of Ken.

I flew back to Dublin and got to work on my plan. I was going to buy that company in Manchester. I arranged a meeting with my investors, and I told them of my plans, that I wanted to buy Ken's company. After I had made my presentation to them explaining all the reasons why it was a perfect fit for me, they asked me how much. I said I would need two million sterling. They didn't balk too much, and in fairness the bank guy came back very quickly and gave me the nod. Now all I had to do was persuade Ken to take it. I got on the phone only forty-eight hours after my last visit, and it went something like this:

"Ken, how goes it? Listen, how would you like to retire?" Having got to know Ken over the past year I knew he didn't like to beat around the bush where money was concerned. I also knew that he had become disillusioned with the software business, having become so stressed out, particularly these past few years. I also found out that he had his eye on a piece of land in the city that he thought would be just right for development and a far easier way of making a living.

He laughed and said

"What do you mean?"

"I mean that I might be able to raise the necessary finance to allow you to do what you told me you'd love to do

"I'm interested in selling the company". Ken also knew I was interested in buying his company, so I said,

"Ken, I can get you a million sterling." There was a definite pause which told me that he was at least interested in pursuing the conversation.

"Where are you getting that sort of money?" he said, knowing that mine was only a young company and that I didn't have any money personally.

"Besides, I'd want a lot more than that."

So I knew I had him. It was just a question of the number. I asked him to sleep on it and to ring me the next day with his number, his valuation on what he thought his company was worth.

I didn't know what figure he had in mind, but he rang me the next day and said, "I want two million," just like that.

"Done," I said, and I told him I'd complete the deal with him by the end of the month. It took a bit longer, but then it was bye-bye Ken.

The staff were flummoxed. They couldn't believe it. I had got rid of Ken, and I was their new boss. I always acted fast, maybe a bit too impetuously for many people, but it suited me, and that was the way that worked for me. I didn't hang about. I already knew what was needed to get things working again, my way, and having had the luxury of getting to know the people and all the main players, I already knew who I wanted in charge. I had ranked them all in my mind, and my ranking didn't match Ken's.

The day I closed the deal with Ken, I brought my new number one, who was Ken's number five, into my office and told him he was the boss. He was a young guy, in his late twenties. I liked him, and I knew he was efficient. I had seen him working, and I liked the way he operated. I then told him who I wanted as my numbers two, three, four, etc., and while he was obviously in shock at his own promotion, I told him I was going to fire Ken's top four guys, which included his original management team. The only one I was keeping was his accountant, whom I rated. I told my new manager that I didn't want an office, a computer, a secretary, or anything else. I didn't want people writing to me. I didn't want to talk to any staff, and I only wanted to hear about problems that he couldn't handle. I also said that I would come and go as I pleased, but I would inform him of my arrivals and departures. I said I was always there for him if he needed me. He could hire and fire anybody he chose as long as he made budget. I would concentrate on making sure he got all the products from Dublin as he needed them, on time and in great working order.

Then I asked him if he had the addresses of the people I was firing. I arranged for us to visit the houses of those people on my first Saturday in charge, as I wanted to surprise them, so that they were unprepared for what we were about to do. We arrived at one guy's house as he was cleaning out his garage, and I told my new manager to walk up his driveway and tell him that he was fired, that he would get his severance pay, and that I would be waiting in the car looking at them. The guy was shocked, looking down at me in the car. I looked nonchalantly into his eyes as if I couldn't give a bollocks. I didn't. That was how we fired all the people we needed to fire, but not without checking first with our legal people about what we were entitled to do. In typical Ken fashion, they had contracts that meant nothing.

By the end of the first week I had placed all the people I wanted into their respective positions, gave them all good salary reviews, and told all of them what I wanted to happen. They were in awe and jumped to it, knowing that all the plans they had discussed at the meeting with Ken could now be put into action, knowing they would sink or swim on their results.

I then went back to Dublin, brought my second in command, Ted, into my office, and told him the same thing, that he was the new managing director, that it was up to him to supply the UK with great products, on time and in great working order. I also told him that I didn't want to deal with staff or customers in the Dublin office anymore, that he was in total charge. I cleared out my office and told him he could have it. I also told him that if he needed me he could contact me by phone because I was going to Manchester to oversee the operation there, and I didn't want to be troubled with problems in Dublin. Now for the tricky bit. It was time to tell my wife.

As I said before, Maria was always very supportive. I told her of my plans to be in Manchester. She said that it wasn't a problem, besides she had enough on her hands with three lively children, Cathy having been born the previous year, and a forth on the way.

I used to travel over on a Sunday night or first thing on a Monday morning, arriving back in Dublin on a Friday, just about in time to be a father to an ever-growing family. Cathy was nearly a year old when you came along, Lora, and it was bedlam. To be honest, I didn't know which way to turn. There were babies everywhere, and I was glad to be able to escape overseas to get some peace. I was not the father I should have been, even at that early age, so the outlook for my future fatherhood was not looking good. I'm not sure I loved the idea of a large family, but it was a bit late now to be thinking that way. Maria was obviously up to her knickers looking after all of you, and her parents were now part of the furniture. I rented a new apartment closer to the office, as the previous one had been too far away and the Manchester traffic was as bad as any city in the world. It was perfect. It had a stand-up piano, something I always had an inkling to learn.

For the next year I let the two managers do their thing with precious little interference from me. To occupy my time, and to give my management teams free rein to prove themselves, I started to take piano lessons. I came from a musical family, my mother loved to play the piano and her brother, my uncle, was very proficient having learned to play the piano by ear. Da was mad about his violin although he wasn't very good. I was intrigued about reading music as it was my first time getting to know this fabulous new language. I would stay in Manchester from Mondays through Fridays traveling back and forth like that for the best part of a year. It wasn't always easy not to interfere so I concentrated on my piano and I became pretty good at it which gave me a lot of satisfaction.

The two companies gelled, grew and prospered. The old customer base loved their new products, and we had worked out a deal that would allow them to pay us more money every month by increasing their direct debits only marginally, giving them all the new products. Everybody was happy. We stopped losing customers almost right away, and our competition not only started to take notice of us, but they were pissed that some Irish company was making big inroads into their customer base. If you want to get noticed, you must attack your opposition in their home territory.

Obviously I was bored much of the time because of my decision not to involve myself in the day-to-day running of the businesses. The strain of traveling back and forth between Dublin and Manchester began to tell and sometimes I woke up not knowing where I was living. I also missed the companionship of my friends in Dublin. I felt that my decision to delegate the running of the companies was the right one. However, my main reason for doing it was not being fulfilled. I had wanted to step back and take a good look at where we were going and make strategic decisions but it never happened. I found it very hard to motivate myself, I needed people interaction. It was something I had to learn and it wasn't easy. It took me a long time to achieve it but I did manage it over time. I found out that once I had a routine to fill in my day I could focus a lot better. My routine was to get up early, usually around six o'clock, something I was used to doing from my early altar boy days. I came from a family that worked by the clock as Da had to obey the time religiously as he worked in the movie house. He had instilled this discipline into us, making sure we were always on time for appointments and we were never late for school, indeed we were never late for anything. After breakfast in a nearby cafe I would then go to the gym and workout for an hour or so. Then a shower and a walk to think about or make new plans. I worked from my apartment and I always made sure to ring my managers in both companies every day at the same time for an update and discuss my ideas. Every month my management teams and I would get together, either in Dublin and Manchester and discuss our overall plans for the company. They enjoyed it as much as I did, as this was their first experience of group company structures. I was able to share my experiences and I know they learned from me. It was great to see their enthusiasm for their work progress and prosper.

It was inevitable that Maria and I began to live decidedly separate lives, although it appeared to me that she never really noticed or cared as she was all consumed raising our family.

There was one time she decided to bring all of you down to her parents' house for the weekend, leaving me by myself as I had given her some excuse for not being able to go. My friend Jimmy had arranged to go out on the town, and we ended up in some pub on a bitterly cold winter's night. Jimmy started chatting up a couple of girls, and I have to say I wasn't in the least bit interested in doing anything. I just wanted to have a few laughs with my friend, but Jimmy said, "Let's all go back to Bernie's house in Dun-Laoghaire and continue the party."

He had told them that of course we were both separated single men. In my alcohol-encouraged stupor, I agreed, and the next thing I knew I was driving home, followed by Jimmy and the two birds. I had told them that I needed to get to my house before them because of the security in the house, but I knew I needed to clear the decks of dozens of toys, diapers, prams, buggies, and everything else that a four-baby house would naturally have. I had just about managed to shove everything into the kitchen before I had to let them in, as they were freezing their nuts off at the front door.

"Sorry about that. Had a bit of trouble with the alarm," I lied.

"No problem," said one of the girls, so I led them into the "good room," having made sure there was no incriminating evidence of children lying around.

"Let's open the champers," said Jimmy as he produced two bottles of the expensive stuff.

"Okay, let me get the glasses," I said as I headed for the kitchen while Jimmy put on the music.

I had to climb over everything: clothes, rattles, buggies, and toys. I got the four glasses and noticed that things were very quiet as I headed back to the party room.

"How come there's no music?" I shouted as I entered the room to find Jimmy stone faced, looking at the beautiful, professionally taken photograph of myself, Maria, and our four gorgeous babies hanging slap bang in the middle of the wall.

I took one look and exclaimed, "Aw yes, that's my twin brother. Remarkable resemblance."

With that the girls leapt up and told Jimmy to drive them home immediately.

"Aw, bollocks," I said and went up to bed with Jimmy saying, "You can't leave me here! Don't leave me alone!" as I laughed myself to sleep. That was the one and last time I'd ever try that lark.

But with no social life in the UK, I found it very easy to get bored, and not interfering with my management was paying large dividends. The opportunities to stray arose every now and then.

I was in Manchester one time absolutely bored out of my tree and decided to look around. I don't know who picked who, but I suspect that I was the one that got picked up. She was great fun, and we agreed a price for the night, but rather than take her back to my place and let her know where I lived, I booked us into a bed and breakfast somewhere in Manchester. She had all the gear with her: nurse's uniform, secretary girl, whips, and all types of bondage equipment.

I paid the landlady with cash, and she gave us her downstairs bedroom, the biggest in the house. During the shenanigans that went on, the bird asked me had I ever had a golden shower. I said I hadn't. She asked me would I like to have one, so thinking it was some kind of yellow liquid you put into the shower head, I said, "Sure, why not?" and off she went into the bathroom.

I was getting really horny waiting on the invitation to join her in the bathroom. The next thing she appeared, dressed in a flimsy negligee. She jumped up on the bed, spread her legs, and said, "Ready?"

"Sure am!" I said, and with that she started peeing all over me.

"Mother of mammies! What in Jesus's name are you doing?" I shouted, only then realizing what a golden shower was. She said that Hitler used to love it when Eva Braun did it to him. That explained a lot, I said. We managed to mess up the bedroom big time, so we planned our escape for the middle of the night before the landlady saw us.

About three months later I saw her picture on the front page of the *News of the World*, a Sunday rag. It appeared she was thrown into jail for bigamy, having obtained a lot of money from foreigners who needed a British spouse to get a green card. I wonder if any of those "spouses' got a golden shower.

This is what happens to me when I get bored. I get dangerous. I knew I had better do something and quickly.

My Indian manager had been pleading with me to come over. Seemingly the local chamber of commerce were delighted with this new Irish technology company choosing Calcutta for their operations. They wanted to present me with an award. I decided to make the journey, much to the delight of my Indian management team and the local chamber of commerce.

I don't know if you've ever been to Calcutta. It wouldn't be exactly the type of place that Trip Advisor would include on their "Best Places to Visit" section. It's a disaster area, extremely poverty stricken, but somehow the locals seem to like it or at least they pretend that they do. I was due to stay for a week, and I brought Ronnie with me. We checked into the only five-star hotel.

I don't know who is in charge of awarding these stars, but somebody in FIFA is getting a lot of money. I picked the highest room while Ronnie got a room on the ground floor. I always found that you got less bugs coming into your room the higher up you went. We had barely checked in when there was this almighty scream coming from the ground floor. I looked over the bannister and saw Ronnie running around like a headless chicken. Apparently he had found a massive snake in his room. He joined me on the higher floors, and neither of us slept a wink.

It was indeed an eye opener, seeing the way things operated in their society. Indian people are very family oriented. They work hard, usually smoke or drink a lot of whiskey, and when they get home they like to go to the theatre or the cinema. Foreigners usually get the Trotsky's very quickly. We were no exception to this rule. The thing I found most disconcerting was the arrangement they have in restaurants about apportioning toilet paper. You have to ask for the number of sheets you think you're going to need, which makes it a very difficult calculation when you don't know how long your Trotsky's will last. They use the tithe system in restaurants. It's a way of creating employment for the billion-plus people that need work. One man takes your order; you will never see him again. Another guy brings you water, another confirms your order, and then a steady stream of waiters bring the food to your table, each one exchanging little pieces of paper, which are then forwarded to the accounting staff, whose numbers I was unable to determine. It appears to work, but don't be in too much of a hurry to leave the restaurant, as the aforementioned Mr. Trotsky is never too far behind, so to speak.

There was one experience I will never forget, and even flying over Mount Everest in a rickety twin propeller plane could not beat this story. Skip had arranged for an air-conditioned car, because without it you would simply melt. No other explanation necessary; you melted. It's so bad in the summer that they leave the dead bodies on the roadway, I kid you not, and a truck goes around during the evening picking them up. I told Skip that I needed to get some cash from an ATM, and seeing there was the grand total of two ATMs in the entire city, we had to travel across the city to find it. As I keyed in my numbers, melting away on the sidewalk, waiting on my cash and Skip puffed away at his cigarette, I turned around to investigate a strange noise behind me. The pavement slab had started to move. As I watched the full-sized slab of concrete rise into the air, I saw what can only be described as the ugliest looking zombie-type animal I had ever seen in my life coming up from beneath the slab. I turned and grabbed Skip's arm and said, "What in Jesus' name is that?"

"Oh my God," he shouted, "I've never seen one that big before. For God's sake, run!"

If ever Ireland needed to enter two people in the Olympic hundred-meter dash, then we would have been contenders. We ran so fast we forgot about the car and only stopped running when we realized we hadn't a clue where we were going. He told me, after we got our breaths back, that the "creature from below" lived on the dead bodies but usually only came out at night. It was India's version of an armadillo, but far uglier. I can tell you I couldn't wait to get back to Dublin.

CHAPTER 16

It was early evening on a weekday night and I was working in my office when one of my staff said that my sister Barbara was downstairs and wanted to talk to me. I was shocked because I only ever saw Barbara sporadically, not like nowadays where we talk every week. I immediately thought that someone had died.

When she came into my office she looked worried, and I asked her what was wrong. She said she was good. She had called in to tell me that she didn't think I looked well. I was really surprised and looked at myself in the office mirror. I knew I had lost weight but I didn't see anything different. I told her that I was fine, that there was nothing to worry about. She had seen me at our mother's house the previous weekend and thought I'd lost a lot of weight and had looked very drawn and pale. I told her I had given up sweets (I have a shocking sweet tooth), that I had been on a diet, and that that was the reason I'd lost the weight. She still didn't accept it and asked me to see a doctor, so I promised her that I would.

My sister is a worrier and always has been, but she loves me to bits, and I love her, just like you should love your brothers and sisters. I shrugged it off, and when I got home that night I told Maria what Barbara had said. I asked her if she thought I looked okay, and she said I looked fine. I thought no more about it.

Then Friday of that same week, just as I finished work, I did my usual and joined my staff for an evening drink in the local pub. I always drink beer, but that night, for some reason, I had a glass of white wine. I didn't finish it.

I said I was tired, and I went home early. When I got home I told Maria I was exhausted, I had been feeling very tired lately, and so I went to bed.

During the middle of that night I was awakened by a shaking frenzy. It's the only way to describe it. It was like a scene from the movie *The Exorcist* in that I could not control the shaking from head to toe. I didn't know what to think as this was a completely new experience for me. I was really scared, and I went downstairs. You were all asleep in bed as I cowered in the corner of the kitchen. The only thing I could think of was to drink some whiskey. It didn't help, and I continued to shake in the corner uncontrollably. I eventually calmed down, and the shaking stopped by itself, so I went back up to bed and asked Maria to hug me. I told her what had happened, but she said nothing. We slept.

The next morning, Saturday, I woke up and felt fine. I lay in bed thinking about the night before and shrugged it off. My body had been screaming at me, telling me something was seriously wrong, and like a typical man I ignored it. Maria, however, had called Ray, our family doctor, and up he came into the bedroom.

Ray had been our doctor for years, and we got along well. I really liked him. I was embarrassed at first, but I got serious when Ray got serious. I didn't know it then, but Maria saved my life by making that call. I have never forgotten that, and I never will.

Ray asked me to go over exactly what had happened to me over the past week. He asked me had I been eating properly, sleeping regularly, all the usual stuff, so I told him about Barbara's visit and that I always seemed to be tired lately. I had been losing weight, but I had been on a diet. And of course I told him all about the previous night. He said he didn't like the sound of it and wanted me to go down to the Blackrock clinic and get some X-rays. I asked him when I should go, and he said right away. At that moment I was taking him very seriously.

I went to the clinic on my own in a total haze. I had the scans, and I waited around for what seemed like hours. I remember wondering why other people were coming and going all day, getting their results, and I was still hanging around waiting. Eventually a nurse told me that there was something wrong with the X-rays and that they'd have to do the tests again. I found out afterwards that they usually say that when they have found something and need to redo the tests to be certain of the results.

They did the scans a second time. This time they said everything was fine. They'd send the results to my doctor, and he would be in touch. The next day, Sunday, I hung around all day, obviously worried and curious what was going on inside my body. On Monday I was in my office when the phone rang around 10:30. It was Ray, and he asked me to drop up to him, that he had the results and he'd like to see me. I asked when, and he said now. I vividly remember walking up Georges Street in Dun-Laoghaire in a worried trance. He led me into his office, and I saw the X-rays pinned to his window.

"I got the results, Bernie," he said as he pointed to my heart.

"Have I got two hearts, or is there something wrong with your X-rays?" I asked him, pointing to a similarly sized shadowy object on the right side of my chest.

"That's cancer, Bernie," he said and looked at me the way a friend would look at you, not as my doctor.

When someone is told they have cancer they spiritually and immediately leave the building. They are not there. They hear nothing other than their own heart beating. I would recommend that when doctors have to discharge such deadly information to a patient, they should leave the room, go off and play a round of golf because the patient is not listening.

"It's one of two things," Ray Said. "It's either leukemia or Hodgkin's disease."

I was desperately trying to focus on what he was saying, and eventually, after a minute or so, I said, "I've heard of leukemia, but what the hell is Hodgkin's disease?"

He explained that it would be better if it were leukemia as there were better treatments and results for that type of disease. If it were Hodgkin's, it was not good as there were very few remedies. However, he said that the good news was that if it was Hodgkin's, it so happened that there was a leading Hodgkin's oncologist who had just set up his practice in Dublin, having just returned from the States. He had already taken the liberty of phoning him.

They were best friends, and the specialist had agreed to see me. I said when; he said today. *Wow, today,* I thought, and he said that I was to go in now.

I left in a complete daze, having asked him to write down how you spelt Hodgkin's. I walked back to the office, told my secretary I had to go into hospital for some tests. I got into my car and went home. When I got home, Maria was sitting at the dinner table having coffee with her friend. I remember looking at them. I walked straight by them without saying a word and went into the library to get the encyclopedia and look up Hodgkin's. It said that Hodgkin's was a fatal disease and that there was no known cure. There was no Google in those days, and the encyclopedia was your first port of call for anything like this.

I came out to them and I told them that I had cancer. They continued talking as if I wasn't there. This was the contradiction that was Maria. First she saves my life by contacting the doctor, but after that she totally abandoned me. I could never explain it. It's like someone who saves a person from a burning building then totally disappears before you have the chance to thank them. The way Maria used go into her shell was infuriating to me. I took a plate and smashed it against the wall, and I said, "I have fucking cancer!" That got their attention all right because the friend got up and said, "I think I should leave," and Maria said nothing.

If we had been a normal couple, she would have shown some emotion, but she said and did nothing, she just stared at me. I was to find out that we would not be going through this together, supporting each other every step of the way, showing one another that each meant everything to the other. I knew I was going to need a lot of love, and I wasn't going to get any from Maria. I think it was at that moment that I knew our marriage was over.

I walked out of the house and drove myself to the Mater Hospital. When I arrived, I wasn't waiting long. I met Des, the oncologist. He told me it was definitely Hodgkin's. He explained the prognosis and went through the treatment. He said that there was a cure, that seemingly some Mafia guy in New York had developed Hodgkin's about six years previously and had given millions to a team of doctors to develop a cure. A rough cure had been found about three years before me getting it. Those doctors had been given an ultimatum by their Mafia boss: "If I die, you all die," which would definitely concentrate the mind.

I asked him how long had I to live, and without any hesitation he said two months. I suddenly became very aware of my fallibility. When God tells you that you have a finite amount of time left on his planet, things take on a whole new meaning. What seemed very important five minutes ago was suddenly totally irrelevant. Suddenly that meeting on Tuesday with the bank manager could wait. And was this really the right time to be thinking of having an affair? Strange thoughts enter your head, everything is suddenly surreal as you realize you are no longer in control of your body. You are absolutely helpless as you now transfer your decaying body over to the medical staff to do with what they can.

Des said he wanted to operate. I asked him when; he said now. Jesus, everything in the past three days had been now, now, now. The hospital had already checked, naturally, to see if I was covered by insurance, and as luck would have it we had only upped our coverage to the top plan some three months previously.

They had asked me if I wanted to contact anybody. I thought about it for a moment or two, and then I rang my secretary. I told her that if anybody was looking for me that I was in hospital getting some tests done and that I would be back later. I decided that Maria didn't give a shit whether I was at home or not and so I never bothered to contact her. I was then taken upstairs, stripped off, and by 4 p.m. that afternoon I was in surgery. I would be there for many hours.

Meanwhile, in the real world, consternation was erupting as my parents found out from my sister, who had found out from my secretary, that Bernie was not good. My secretary took it upon herself to ring Barbara, as she was worried about me. Tommy arrived over into the Mater hospital, went up to reception, and asked to see me, only to be told that he couldn't see me as I was in theatre.

"What's he doing watching movies when he's supposed to be sick?" he asked. Bless him, he could be such an idiot sometimes. When they explained to Tommy that the hospital theatre wasn't your average IMAX, he jumped in his car back to collect Rose and Barbara.

I was seven hours in theatre, and when I awoke I was very groggy and I felt crap. I turned my head to see this guy sitting there, the anesthetist, who asked me if I was okay. I asked for a mirror. I saw all of these tubes sticking out of me and large stitches across my chest, including some stitches in my throat. I asked him why I had these stitches in my throat, to which he responded, "Well, you see, we made a bit of a mistake there. We had misread the charts and thought you were in for a different type of treatment, but fortunately we managed to correct our mistake before we did any real damage, and sure you'll be as right as rain in no time. You won't notice a thing there, you see?"

As I continued to look at myself in the mirror he said, "You're not going to sue us or anything, are you?"

"No, I don't think I'll be suing you, as I've more important things to be thinking about, like living," I said as he scurried off. I lay there in a daze, unable to think straight, drifting in and out of sleep.

About an hour later this doctor guy came in, and I asked him was I okay, did everything go okay.

"No, you're definitely not okay. We found massive cancer in your chest, but we managed to cut most of it out." I asked him what the prognosis was, and he said I had a fifty-fifty chance of survival, that I was going to be very sick, and that I would lose all of my hair. With that, Mr. Happy exited, leaving me in sheer terror.

I jumped out of bed and started pacing the room, pushing the IV tree and cursing out loud. I remember vividly seeing my patience wearing wings and flying out of the window of my room, never to return. My self-control was replaced by a newfound anger with the world and all who were in it. I would never be that happy, easy-going person ever again. All the usual melodramas came into play, such as "Why couldn't my bollocks of a so-called brother get it?" I knew of at least a million people that deserved this crisis in their miserable lives far more than me.

I lay there transfixed and feeling terrified. It had all happened so quickly. Then Des came in and told me that he was happy that he had got all the cancer in my chest. I told him what the other doctor had said, and he said that wasn't the case, that, as I was young and in good health, I could withstand the treatment better than most. Most importantly, he said, it had been discovered just in time. Another two weeks and it was bye-bye Bernie. He said that I had an 80% chance of survival. Yes, I would be sick from the treatment, but I might not lose all my hair.

I felt relieved. I could work with eighty-twenty. I then wondered if this was their good cop, bad cop routine. Then he said that he was more worried about the cancer in my spine. I nearly collapsed, and he said that when he could he would investigate but that it would have to wait until he was happy that the Hodgkin's in my chest was cured. He said it looked like it was just starting in my spine, that it was a very difficult thing to diagnose, and that he hoped it might just be benign.

I fell asleep, and when I awoke I found my sister Barbara and both of my parents at my bedside, white as sheets and Barbara crying. I tried to rise in the bed to tell them that I was okay, but I just fell back down. I had absolutely no energy whatsoever. I asked them how they had found out about me, and they told me about my secretary contacting them. Then Tommy said that he had rung Maria before they left their house, and when she answered the phone it went something like this:

"Do you know that you husband is dying of cancer and is at this very moment under the knife in the Mater Hospital?" said Tommy in his usual break-it-to-them-gently type of way.

Maria didn't answer because they found out afterwards that she had fainted.

I was heavily sedated and unable to speak, just mumbling, and they said they'd see me tomorrow. They still couldn't display any emotion, no hugs or kisses except from Barbara, but I knew they loved me. Tactility could wait.

The next day I awoke early feeling totally crap. I remember thinking about a number of things, but I wasn't morbid. I was going to beat this thing. I was not going nowhere without a damn good fight. I was thirty six, and I had a lot to do.

I never once thought about God, other than to call him all the names under the sun. I would get back to him later. It was funny because I had been so holy and devout as a young boy that at one stage I thought of entering the priesthood (lucky for them), yet at this stage of my life I had abandoned God and religion completely. I never thought about Maria either, which wasn't completely strange, when you think about it. We didn't have a marriage or any real relationship. We simply didn't care about each other. When her father heard that I was dying, his only comment was, "What about the children? What's to happen to the children?" Yes, I love you too I don't think.

Maria and I never spoke about my sickness, never discussed what we should do if this happened or that happened. It never arose. Maria would bring you kids in to see me just the once. You were only babies really, and hospitals were no fun, but if Maria came to see me three times that was about it during all the time that I spent in there. Not once did she hug me and tell me that she loved me. Despite all of this it seemed to make me more resilient. I had my family who loved me, and they would always be there for me. But as for having a loving wife, the answer to that was no.

The first week went by, and I was under the full chemotherapy treatment. There were seven injections a day together with nineteen different kind of pills. The chemo was awful, in its infancy and very raw. Over the years it has improved greatly, and they have perfected the drugs, but then it was raw.

There was one particular drug they injected that I could only describe as the death wish drug because you wanted to die when it got inside of you. It ran immediately to your bum, where it seemed to dance around your arse and asked your stomach to join it in a full-blown Riverdance! The nurses used to joke about it and would ask you if you wanted them to shuffle the pack so that you didn't know when it was coming at you or if you wanted it first, second, or when? I used get them to shuffle it. I hated that injection, and even today relating the story still makes me nauseous. A week went by, and I was visited daily by my sister and my auntie, who used to ride in to see me on her old bike. She was in her late seventies.

One day I awoke to find my beloved brother standing at the end of the room, leaning against the wall. I thought there and then that I must have died.

"Joe, what are you doing here?" I asked.

"Eh, Bernie, I heard you had cancer."

"Yeah, that's right, but you needn't worry, Joe, as it's not contagious."

"Oh, great. Well, see you."

And off he went.

That was the depth of our conversation, not a "Can we sit down and discuss what a prick I've been to you all of your life?" or "I want to tell you I'm here for you and if there is anything I can do for you, then all you have to do is depend on your brother Joe." My arse.

The Mater Hospital and staff were outstanding. They fed me five-star food in amazing surroundings. I told them that I apologized for cursing at them all the time, and they just pooh-poohed it away, saying that they had an eighty-year-old nun on the same floor who would put Satan himself to shame. Apparently once these drugs went inside you they took control of everything, including your free speech. I was embarrassed how many times I told everybody to go fuck themselves, and that was for bringing me my meals!

The doctors monitored me constantly. They said that the chemo was going well and that my body was not rejecting it. They also said that the main reason people die was that (a) they didn't get seen on time and (b) they weren't strong enough to handle the drugs, as it was the treatment that killed most people. I'd been extremely lucky about getting seen on time, and thankfully I always kept myself reasonably fit and strong. My only physical negative was that I still smoked, and I liked them. Then, unbelievably nowadays, you could still smoke in the hospital, even at the patient's bedside, blowing rings of smoke into the guy's face as he faced an operation for lung cancer!

I remember that I had one cigarette left, and I was dying for it. I also knew that Des was totally antismoking. I waited until I heard nothing, and I was just about to light up when Des appeared. He looked really angry, and he told me if he ever saw me smoking he would stop my treatment, period. He also said that my chances of getting other cancers were 100%. I stopped smoking immediately and packed them in for good.

About three weeks later, it was a Saturday morning, I was lying in my bed reading the newspaper, and for the first time in what seemed a lifetime I was feeling pretty good. I didn't feel sick, and I'd just enjoyed my breakfast for the first time in forever. I was looking out of my window when the door opened and in walked little Mary, all five feet nothing and one of my regular nurses. She came over to my left side, took my hand, and said that this doctor was going to take a sample of my spine using what she called a lumbar puncture. I looked to my right to see what I can only describe as a guy with an AK47 submachine gun. This doctor looked at me with real fear in his face. I looked at Mary. Mary looked at me, then the doctor, and Mary's quiet voice said to me, "You are going to absolutely hate this, and I am going to hate it too because you have to hold my hand while he shoves this into your spine, and there's no anesthetic. Don't ask me why there's no anesthetic, but that's just the way it's going to be. So let's get it over with because I'm due to go home in fifteen minutes."

I looked at the doctor and asked him in a rather high-pitched voice, "What are you planning to do with that machine gun?"

"Now don't worry about this at all," he said. "It only takes a few seconds, and your oncologist needs it done to examine the possible cancer in your spine." He told me to hold Nurse Mary's hand and turn around. Now, when somebody tells you to turn your arse towards the ceiling while he does something terrible to you from behind, I have to say that you will feel more than a little vulnerable. I imagine it would be like having to spend your first night in a maximum security prison cell, six feet by four, sharing said cell with a Mr. I-haven't-had-sex-with-anybody-in-four-years-and-tonight's-your-lucky-night-and-did-you-bring-the-butter?

I have only ever met one person since then who was a member of the Lumbar Puncture Club. I cannot describe the pain. I grabbed Nurse Mary's hand and simply crushed it. She was crying for me to release her as she fell to the ground. I called that doctor every expletive imaginable as I nearly passed out. I told him I would kill his family, dig them up, and kill them again. I lost pounds in perspiration as he rammed his oversized needle straight into my spine to get a sample of my spinal fluid.

I have to say, the doctor was sweating from every pore as well, and poor little Mary was nowhere to be seen. They did it without warning, and when I saw the amount of a sample they had taken, I couldn't believe they couldn't get it some other way. I never relaxed in that bed again. I was constantly at DEFCON One, always watching the door.

Mary announced that she didn't want to be a nurse anymore, and I didn't blame her. I apologized for nearly breaking her hand, and she smiled and told me she had another one. It transpired that, yes, the cancer was in my spine, but it was benign, and we were pretty pleased about that, none more so than me.

When I was released from hospital I got a taxi home as Maria, by this time, had more or less abandoned me. I had resigned myself to a life of trying to survive and exist. Survive because I knew I had to fight this thing alone, doing what the doctors told me to do. Existing because I was all alone. The children didn't know what was going on outside of their own little lives, as far as they were concerned, dad was just sick. Maria was cold towards me and non-compassionate. I found solace in going to work every day and the staff were delighted to see me back. They were the only ones who had been worried about me, the only ones who cared, I felt secure being around them. I couldn't understand how my in-laws never showed much compassion or support for my situation, it was as if they were afraid to come near me. I did overhear my father-in-law say to maria in the kitchen one day

"What about the children when Bernie dies?"

I was taken aback as I had never once thought about dying and it told me what people were thinking. But this sort of comment made me ever more resilient. I had always been like that, if someone told me I couldn't so something, then I would do my damnedest to prove them wrong.

The next three or four months were spent getting drugs every other day. Sometimes they were too much on my body, and so the doctor gave me a reprieve every now and again. There was one day I was in the office, and I just threw up all over the prospective customer. I'm not entirely positive, but I don't think he was too pleased about that. I told my secretary to drive me into the hospital, and I ran up the stairs, threw open the secretary's door, saying nothing, and walked straight into Des's office as he held a patient's breasts. I ignored the sight and told him I needed to be taken off the medication.

"Would you mind giving me a moment please?" he said to me.

I looked at the woman, then her breasts, then the doctor and figured maybe I should leave. He gave me an immediate reprieve from taking any further drugs for two weeks. It was heaven, but the two weeks flew by, and I had to resume the onslaught. I puked everywhere. I was in bed most of the time. I lost weight, lots of it. People said I looked like Christopher Lee in Dracula.

I found the only way to forget about it was to immerse myself in my work, and so I did. I told the staff not to tell the customers that I was sick as otherwise we might lose them. Customers depended on our continuity, so if my competition found out that I had cancer they'd use that information against me in the marketplace, saying, "Oh, Bernie's dying; you shouldn't buy from him."

It was very difficult. The doctors told me to take it easy while the banks said they needed more repayments. The banks won. Having cancer during those days was like having AIDS when AIDS first appeared. People were afraid of you. They were afraid to touch you or shake your hand in case they got it too. People stayed away from me. I was the walking dead, and they didn't want to be around me. Most of my staff were young, and so they were fine about it. As far as they were concerned, Bernie was Bernie and he was back to being his normal self—apart from the weight loss, the puking, the impatience, and the temper tantrums. I used to bang down the phones if someone pissed me off. They bought me a plastic rock that made a crashing noise whenever you threw it against the wall. I had to buy extra batteries. My life was a total mess. Things were about to get worse.

CHAPTER 17

It was going to be the year from hell, and I was totally screwed up. I was becoming a different person, someone who didn't care about anything anymore.

In June of that year we were all down in Rosslare for a weekend break when I got a call from Barbara.

"Bernard, Da's dead," she said. Just like that: "Da's dead."

It was the furthest thing from my mind. I couldn't believe it. I sat down on the bed and, with Barbara roaring crying, tried to fathom what was happening. There had been no warning, no temporary sickness or period where he had been unwell. He had just collapsed and died. He was only sixty-five. Maria came running into the room when she heard the news. She looked sympathetic. That's about all I can remember.

I drove up to Dublin on my own in total shock. I arrived at my aunt's house, and I found my mother and sister in tears and totally bewildered. We comforted each other as best we could. My brother Joe arrived, I hadn't seen him in years. We nodded to one another but that was all the warmth that we showed one another. He seemed emotionless and never comforted my mother, it seemed like an inconvenience to him, having to be there.

Seemingly, Tommy and Rose had been invited to dinner at my aunties, and as Tommy loved a flutter on the horses—or anything else for that matter—he had done his favorite bet, called a Yankie, which basically means you pick four of anything to win, and if they do then you stand to win a lot of money. Having noted that three horses with the word *Red* in their names were running at the same race track and that the his favorite football team, Liverpool, the real reds, were playing in the F.A. Cup final that same day, he decided that he had the winning combination that would end all of his financial woes. It was a highly technical computation that was typically Tommy. Liverpool duly beat their rivals Everton to win the Cup, and two of the horses had romped home to win their races, so he was desperately excited to find out if his final selection had also won.

He told Rose that he was going down to the bookie's office about a mile downtown to get the result. It was a beautiful evening, and, remembering that Tommy was not the fittest man on the planet, for him to even consider walking a mile was an event in itself. He never arrived home. He had collapsed outside the bookie's shop and had been taken to Beaumont Hospital as a John Doe as he had no identification on him. He was pronounced dead on arrival.

My mother and my aunt had searched for him for over twenty-four hours. They had gone around looking for him on their bikes. They had gone into the local police station. They had stayed up all night filled with terror because they knew this wasn't like Tommy, and then the cops rang to say there was a John Doe in Beaumont hospital. They were then taken by the police down to the hospital to identify him, it must have been traumatizing for them!

I drove my mother, Barbara and my brother Joe over to the hospital to see Tommy and when they wheeled him in on the gurney, I fell down crying. I kept saying it can't be true as I looked at his little face with his special grin. The tears rolled down my face as I held my Mum and Barbara, who were now in the middle of a nightmare. I looked at his dead body, and I swore to him that if I ever got the chance to escape from this rat race that I would leave skid marks. There was no way I was going to end up like Tommy. He was only sixty five, one month into his retirement and his life was over. I was going to do everything in life that he hadn't done.. He wanted to take boats, planes and trains everywhere he could and I told him that I would finance everything for him as I wanted him to always be happy. I swore to myself that I would never let it happen to me. I was going to make sure I got healthy and I was going to stay healthy all of my life. Whatever I wanted, I was going to do it all.

The post mortem revealed a body that had simply shut down. The arteries were totally blocked. He had had no chance. The coroner said he wouldn't have known what hit him, it was that sudden. Therefore he had experienced no pain. All the things I had planned to do with him were consigned to the grave. I had organized a surprise vacation for both of them on the Orient Express for later that year, now he'd never even know about it. He had been looking forward to his retirement for so long as he wanted to see the world for the first time in his life. He had never flown in an airplane and he wanted to visit California as he had seen a movie about it when he was young and he had dreamed about it all of his life. I had planned to organize a surprise trip for him and my ma to spend a week in San Francisco and another week on a cruise up the west coast. I had even arranged to have them chauffeur driven knowing how bad a driver he was. It was all for nothing, Da was gone.

The Catholic church in Monkstown was packed with people. When I got up to make a reading I could hear people audibly shocked at my appearance. Most of them knew I had cancer, but very few had seen me. It was tough for Barbara and me making the readings, impossible not to cry. After the ceremony it was customary to bring people for a drink, so I had arranged for everybody to go across to the local pub, and when I walked in about a hundred or so people suddenly fell silent. I asked a friend what was wrong with them, and she said, "Bernie, they think you'll be the next to go."

"Drinks are on the house," I shouted. It was the first time I had realized what people had been thinking. I suppose I couldn't really blame them for being less than subtle. After all, I did look like somebody who had just arose from the dead. I had probably lost half of my weight at that time. None of my clothes fitted me, and I was a ghastly pale color.

Da was gone, and the only thing left to do in his memory was to see if he had the winning ticket on that damned horse. He had the ticket on him when he died. I went to the local bookmakers, and while the Ma waited outside in the car, I found out that the horse had lost, so he had won very little from his Yankee bet. Maybe the shock of it losing was what killed him. We'll never know.

I went outside and said to the Ma, "Would you believe it, the bloody horse won!"

"I knew it!" she said. "I just knew that's what killed him. How much did he win?"

"Five hundred."

She told me to split the winnings between Barbara and myself.

I miss him.

More bad news was to follow as later that year my manager Fred told me that his wife had delivered a baby after many years of trying. They were a bit old, but they were obviously delighted. A couple of days after the birth, my secretary drove me up to the hospital to see the baby. When we arrived with flowers and chocolates in hand and entered the room, we saw that the mother was holding the baby in her arms, but the baby was dead.

I had never seen a dead baby before, and I never want to see one again. The baby had been stillborn, and I didn't know what to say, as Fred had not told us anything other than it had been born. I had to sit down, as I felt faint, and when the nurse came in and asked the mother if she was okay, I raised my hand and said I wasn't feeling good at all.

My secretary explained about my cancer and the chemotherapy I was undergoing, so they rushed me into the adjoining bedroom and attached all sorts of measuring devices to me. While they were doing so, Fred passed by on his way to see his wife. He saw me in the bed and asked me what the hell was going on. He couldn't stop laughing when he heard what had happened. It was a macabre situation, him coming to console his wife and seeing his boss in bed in the adjoining room at a maternity hospital!

My cancer treatment continued all of that year, and I was in and out of hospital every week. I cannot remember having one heart-to-heart conversation with Maria during 1989 or thereafter. I had made my decision. I was going to leave Maria. I had no idea how to approach her, and every time I tried I just couldn't bring myself around to telling her. I was afraid. I was terrified of having to tell my children. I didn't know how. There was nobody who could advise me. If I had gone to a priest, he would have said don't even think about it, as I'd be condemned to hell for eternity. Therapists, as I've already said, didn't exist, at least not the type that could handle my situation in Holy

Catholic Ireland. I couldn't tell my friends, as I didn't know how they would react. I couldn't tell my family because I didn't want to upset them. Nobody had a clue about my intentions.

The more I thought about it, the worse I felt. How could a married man abandon his wife and four young babies? What sort of animal would do that? I was not going to get any help or sympathy for my plight from anybody.

Then one day, on a London to Dublin flight, I saw a man reading the *Sunday Times* and a big headline article entitled "If You Have to Leave Your Children, Then the Earlier the Better." I ran to the newsagent upon landing, and it was like it had been written for me. It said that while there is no right time to leave your children, if there is no other option, then do so when they are young, the younger the better, because human beings are hardy. They can forget. They will survive. It also said that the longer you leave it and the more of a relationship you have developed with your children, the harder it will be for them.

I decided to try one last thing. I asked Maria to go to a marriage counsellor with me. She was opposed to it at first, but, prompted by her mother, she reluctantly agreed. She was her usual nervous wreck as we sat in the counsellor's office. It was a female counsellor, and she was not a happy bunny with me. She directed all the blame and her venom towards me. She never once looked at Maria, and I felt like I was in school being berated by the teacher for being a bold boy.

We went back a couple of times, but it was useless. It was exactly as I thought it would be. It was over between us.

During the rest of that year and through most of 1990, when you were three, May, Jack and Cathy were seven, six and four respectively, we tried to carry on ignoring the inevitable. I think Maria thought everything was fine, that it had just been a bad period in our marriage and that everything would work itself out. I knew that, had I stayed, it would just have been a matter of time, with lots of anguish for everybody in the long run, giving the same result but with a lot more acrimony. It wasn't going to work. We had been together for eleven years, and the past seven or so hadn't existed for us as a couple.

I met a friend for lunch, to test run my speech. He knew Maria very well. When I told him I was leaving Maria, he dropped his soup on his suit, went white, and couldn't believe it. Okay, he knew things were lousy in my marriage, but he never expected it. You see, I didn't plan it. I hadn't had some long-term goal to leave my children or my marriage, but I knew I couldn't foresee my life going on the way it was going. I wasn't worried about my business. I knew I was very capable and would somehow get it back on track, but my marriage, now that was something that had died a long time ago.

So the time came when I approached Maria in the kitchen, and I told her that I was leaving, that I couldn't go on. I told her I had rented an apartment in town and I was going to live there. Her immediate reaction was that I was to be the one to tell the children, that I was to tell them there and then before I left the house. She had an angry look about her. It wasn't pleasant, and she didn't want to discuss it.

On that fateful day we brought all of you into the living room, and I'll never forget it as I told all of you that Daddy was leaving. It was, you, Lora who walked over to me and uttered those fateful words, "Does this mean you will be gone forever?" You were only three years of age, and yet you were imagining your life without your dad. I looked at you with your beautiful eyes looking at me, and I said yes, but that I'd still be around, that I would always be your dad, and that I'd always be close by. Maria sat motionless as she listened to me, watching the tears well up in my eyes. Finally I couldn't stop crying as I left the house, leaving the four of you sitting side by side on the sofa, four little children who looked so lost and bewildered. I remember leaving in a haze, in shock obviously at what I had just done. I felt very sad and very alone.

I awoke the next morning, having hardly slept, and I felt totally strange, in a trance almost, as if someone had clicked a switch at the back of my neck and released me of all strain. I had mixed feelings as the days wore on. I missed the hustle and bustle of home, the noise of my children running around, the sitting down for meals, and the general innocuous but important chatter as everybody did their thing. Strangely, I never missed Maria. I never thought about her for one second. I had absolutely no feelings towards her whatsoever, good or bad. It was as if she had never existed. How weird was that? You could spend eleven years of your life with somebody, sleep with them, and share all of your life's secrets and yet never miss them.

My business was just about hanging together. I had been away for so long getting treatment that, even though the businesses were being managed properly, they still needed my input to drive them forward. I was concerned that if I didn't make the break with Maria now I might not be able to afford to support her and the children. I also knew that her five-year sabbatical from her employment was almost over. I didn't want her to lose her income or her pension, so the timing had to be now. If I had left it any longer, she would have been in financial difficulties, and who knows what would have happened.

So it was time for the lawyers, and boy did I get hammered. Maria hired the best lawyer in town, a stalwart lawyer for women only, and it was a case of no contest when pitted against my lot. She wiped the floor with them. To be honest, I didn't care. I just wanted to make sure that Maria and all you children were looked after. I was left with my car and my clothes, which didn't fit me anymore. I signed the biggest alimony payment in Irish history then. I was also left with a business that was anything but healthy. She didn't want any part of that. Maria got the house, the money, the insurance, everything. I didn't contest anything other than my visitation rights to my children. We had it all signed by the judge, and that was it.

Of course I saw my children every week, usually at the weekends, but there was no greeting and no civility shown to me by Maria whenever I called down to collect you. It was hard for you guys. You were all so young. You didn't understand what was happening, and I couldn't explain it to you the way I can explain it all to you now. It wasn't any fun, and I felt it too. Maria made absolutely no effort to make the transition easy. Instead, she put obstacles in my way at every opportunity. After some time I began to make things work between my children and myself, even through very difficult circumstances.

One day Maria arranged to meet me in Wynn's hotel during her lunch break. I was worried that something was wrong with one of you, as she wouldn't say over the phone why she wanted to meet with me. I knew I had been late one month with the alimony and had asked her for a two week extension as a one-off. She refused, and I was never late with a payment after that. So I knew it wasn't a money problem.

She was nervous, as only Maria can be nervous. Her hands were shaking, so I knew it was not going to be good. She came straight out and said that the children didn't want to see me anymore, that I was not to call down to the house, and that she'd appreciate it if I didn't cause any trouble and let them get on with their lives. I was stunned, shocked beyond words. I asked her if you had all of said that. She said yes. She had nothing more to say to me and told me to adhere to her wishes and the children's wishes.

I left the hotel in a daze. Maria never spoke to me again after that. I tried ringing, but she never took my calls. When I wrote to her, I received a lawyer's letter telling me that all future communications were to be directed through their offices. I was barred from seeing any of you again. So here we are, all these years later, never having been together or sharing anything. I've missed every important event in each of your lives.

People have asked me why I didn't contest it in the courts, but there were a number of reasons. The most important one was that I didn't want to be the one to upset you guys any more than I already had. You needed to settle down after the trauma. You were still babies, going to school and needing total care and attention, and I didn't want your mother running around lawyers' offices. I was also broke, and there was also the matter of my cancer treatment. Another thing that shouldn't be overlooked, and it's something that I learned much later, I was traumatized too, but nobody gave a crap about me. I needed therapy more than anyone, but I never realized I needed it at the time. I thought I was fine, but how could I have been after everything I had been through? There were no therapists worth their salt in Ireland at that time that could handle my situation.

I think I should stop there because I don't know if I've said too much or not enough. So let me answer your question about why I left you. The answer will disappoint you because I'm not going to say that I didn't leave you, or that it was your mum that I left, or that it was Maria's fault, or that it was solely my fault.

I left you and your siblings because it suited me. It suited me that Maria barred me from seeing you. I didn't fight it because I didn't want to fight it. Then I didn't want to be with any of you. I wanted to be free to live my life on my own. I was totally selfish, and everything was a hassle to me, so the fact that I didn't have to call down and see all of you suited me. To my total shame I say that. These are things I've learned about myself over the years. To my shame I've missed everything about you growing up, and I will never be able to replicate it. The more the years went by, the more difficult it became to try to reach any of you because I felt that I was no longer a part of any of your lives, which I wasn't, apart from the financial support. But I've known for quite some time that I do love all of you, that I do miss you all very painfully. I have done so for many years. I couldn't find a way back to you until I received your email. The door always seemed closed to me, and I didn't blame you if you kept that door closed. I deserved to be in isolation from you. I deserved the pain and the loneliness. I thought all of you hated me.

So, Lora, I've given you the complete story of how I got to that point in my life where I left you. I have been as honest in my writings to you as my memory recalls. There have been no embellishments or acrimony in my portrayals. Everything happened that way.

So will you let me know what you think now?

I do want one thing from you. If you can see your way to forgiving me, then that would make me so happy. I need your forgiveness. If you can open the door just a little bit, then I'll do the rest.

Can you tell me how you feel and what you would like to happen between us?

I love you, Lora. I always have, and I always will,

Your Dad

CHAPTER 18

SHE DIDN'T RESPOND.

I'm always like this when I don't get an immediate response, no patience whatsoever. My wife is always telling me to slow down, that people are not like me, that they will respond in their own way in their own time, but I can't change no matter how hard I try. I was always impatient to close a sale, and the last bit of patience seemed to disappear that day in the hospital room. I was like that all the time at work. I had to make sure that all queries from our customers were responded to by the end of each day. I had drummed that work ethic into my staff and management, and it paid off. Customers knew we gave a great service besides great products. I moped around for days waiting for Lora to respond, kicking anything that stood in my way, berating myself for being too bloody honest. I'd blown it. Another week went past, and finally a response:

> Hi Dad,
>
> I've been working over my response, trying to be as honest as possible because you were so honest with me. I read everything twice or three times in some cases, mulling over the pages and rereading them. Your life was sometimes difficult for me to comprehend. Please keep in mind that I am not in any way angry or resentful. In fact, I hope that once you've read my response we can put the past behind us and move on.

You were always praised in our house. I never heard a bad word about you. Everyone who knew you in my family always spoke very highly of you, even though you felt you never really got along with them. You were our dad. There was always a photo of you on the mantelpiece in the dining room. That's my image of you. You were in your early thirties with dark black hair.

But I didn't want to just know you from hearsay and from what I read. I think you are ambitious, hardworking, and apparently a very charming man. I admire your gumption and determination to succeed, and I appreciate that I will never understand the struggles you faced. I have had so few worries in my life, and now, as an adult, I can really appreciate how fortunate I am and was. I thank you for giving me that start in life. As for what my life was/is like, if you still want to get to know me after reading this, I'd be happy to get to know you too.

I tried to put myself in your position, dealing with the weight and the stigma of divorce, but judging you by your business accomplishments, your tenacity from a young age, and your determination and ambition to realize your dream. You are a man who goes after what he wants and does not let anyone stop him. You started from nowhere, dominated in your chosen field, beat a terminal illness in the face of overwhelming odds.

So knowing this about you, I can only conclude that if you wanted to be a father, then nothing could have stood in your way. I do not intend to diminish the obstacles that would have been in your path. It would not have been easy, but in my opinion, you made your choice, and I am glad that you have come to that conclusion too. I know it's not easy to admit one's failings. You have taken it on the chin, and I appreciate it hugely. I'm more than glad that you can admit your faults and your failings. That means a lot to me.

In many ways, I am quite like you. I am determined to the point of stubbornness, and more than that, I know what I want. So if you wanted me in your life, you would have found a way. I don't feel angry or upset about you leaving me. I used to, but not for almost ten years. If you need forgiveness, you have it from me. You see, I know who I am, and I love the person I have become. I wouldn't be this person if my past had been different. I had a parent, an incredible force of love and support, who made me know that no matter what, I was never alone. I was loved, and I was cared for. That is what a parent is. This may sound cliché, but clichés do not fall from the sky. Clichés are hyperbolical truths. All I needed as a child was for someone to be there, and I had that. Financially you supported me, and that is something that I was brought up to appreciate. Please do not think I overlook your financial sacrifices. I always knew how much you gave, and you will never know how much I appreciate what you did for me.

But when I think of a parent, I have only one. A parent is someone who brings you up and cares for you as a child. I am no longer a child, and the time for parenting me is over. I don't foresee that kind of relationship for us. I don't know how you will feel when you read this, but if you want to be a friend, for us to have some sort of relationship going forward, it is up to you. I hope you are well.

Lots of love,

Lora

I was so overwhelmed at her response I could barely take it in. I reread her letter a dozen times. It made so happy. I had to think long and hard about my response to her. She had been so mature to accept and realize that I had been telling her the truth, that my ramblings didn't upset her like I feared they might. And above all else she had forgiven me. She had also called me Dad, and she had sent me her love. I was overjoyed.

I decided to ring her. We exchanged our contact information, and I made the call. It was great. It was easier than my first call to Jack because Lora had made things easier for both of us. She told me about how she had taken up teaching, how she spoke German, Spanish, French, and some Korean, that she was teaching in a German university, and that she was moving back to Dublin as she had been offered a teaching position at a college in the city. She was looking forward to returning home as she would be near her two sisters, her nephews, and her Mum. I told her that writing to her and revealing all to her had been good therapy for me also, that I felt a lot better about myself and that I had come to realize a lot of home truths about myself. It had been a good confession for me, and I was glad to have her as my priest. I told her I felt embarrassed having to disclose some of the things a father should never tell his daughter, but she disagreed. She felt that every father and mother should tell their children about their lives, their backgrounds, and how things came together when they decided to start their families. She said that if they had reared their children correctly, then they would be more than capable of handling the truth that their parents disclosed. She felt she knew me a lot better than she had thought, that my writings cleared her images of me, that she now knew the truth about me. She asked me to continue telling her my stories about how life unfolded for me after I had gone from their lives, and I said that I would be happy to do it. She felt that as I had only covered the period up to the time I had left them and that it was equally important to tell her about the intervening twenty-five years. She had no doubt that only then would she truly know everything there was to know about me. I was glad she wanted me to do this, happy that she felt my life was interesting enough for her to take the time to read about it. I was happy to continue.

CHAPTER 19

THAT FINAL YEAR THAT MARIA and I spent together, before the separation agreement, was horrible for both of us. Like any relationship that goes sour, it's never easy, and in our case it was made much worse because we never confronted the issues that created our problems in the first place. So it dragged on and on until the inevitable split. While we were torturing ourselves by trying to live together, I was also going through the full stages of chemotherapy, and it was not pleasant. I am sure it must have been equally crazy for Maria, not knowing what to do and seeing the man she once knew change into something she didn't recognize. I couldn't have been easy to live with. I was moody and trying hard not to get depressed, to not think about dying. The doctors could only tell me that the treatment was going well, but they couldn't say how much more I needed or what the result would be. I am not saying that I wasn't responsible for all of my actions, but some of the things I did were not Bernie, not the person that I recognized.

I desperately needed a lot of love at that time, and our marriage was not accommodating. So now I knew that my marriage was finally over, I simply didn't care about anyone or anything, including myself. I had lost my dad, and I had so looked forward to spending real time with him and showing him and my ma the world they hadn't seen, letting them have fun and sharing some of that fun with both of them. I knew I was about to lose my family, the four beautiful children whose lives, through no fault of their own, were about to be shattered.

I knew Maria would be okay. She was a great fighter, and she would have a great home, a very valuable property with a small mortgage. She had two adoring parents, grandparents who would help out in every way. She was clever, had a great government job that was permanent and pensionable with a great salary, and above all she wouldn't miss having me around. I had no idea how much it would cost me financially, and I didn't care about that. Whatever I had I would give it to her, to ensure that she had more than enough to support all of you.

I also lost all of my friends. Not one of them helped me or counseled me. I was told by one of them that he was sorry he couldn't hang around with me anymore because his wife had told him not to associate with me, otherwise he would be in trouble himself at home. It appeared that the wives were disgusted with the fact that I had abandoned my wife and four babies. As far as they were concerned, I was a pariah, a leper, and they didn't want their families to catch anything from me. There was one exception from one of Maria's family who rang me to say that, while he didn't agree with me divorcing my family, he did feel sorry for my personal situation. I appreciated it. I was the loneliest man on the planet then.

I wasn't feeling good one day, and I was forced to stay in bed on my own in my new apartment. I had been puking most of the night as the drugs did their thing. The phone rang, and it was Bill, one of my oldest customers who owned a medium-sized accountancy firm. He wanted to know how I was feeling. He had been looking for me at my office and had heard I wasn't at work. The reason he was concerned for me was because I had befriended his only son David, who had also developed Hodgkin's disease. David was only 21, and I saw him many times at the hospital where we were both being treated by the same specialist. He had been diagnosed with Hodgkin's following an accident at home when he had been fixing his car and something had fallen on him. They had taken X-rays and found the cancer. It was too late; the cancer was well established, so he was bedridden. It's horrible to see anybody in an emaciated state, withering before your very eyes, but it's magnified when the person is so young. Somedays he looked good, but when they'd pull back the sheets to bathe him and you saw his skeletal legs, you knew things were not good. I tried my best to comfort his mum and dad as I knew both of them were devastated at what was happening to their son. But nothing could stop the inevitable, and David died at the tender age of only 21. So it was that Bill and I kept in touch. He used ring me at work for no other reason than to talk to me, as I reminded him of David.

This particular day I had to ask him to hold on as I needed to run to the bathroom to puke my ring up. I puked for over three hours, nonstop into the toilet bowl, and when eventually I returned to bed, I picked up the phone and Bill was still there. He asked me if I was okay. He had been listening for three whole hours to my vomiting. When you get sick from a bad night of overindulging on the town or maybe some food poisoning, you feel a lot better once it's over with, but retching is different, and retching for hours is painful. Your stomach churns, and your throat burns. You don't throw anything up, only bile. You keep asking God to let it be over, but it's relentless as your body fights the battle of battles against the powerful drugs sweeping through your system. The doctors know that the patients who survive are the ones who can beat the treatment.

My own understanding of cancer is a fairly nonscientific one, but nobody has disagreed with my assessment when I've said to them that I believed all cancers were caused and advanced because of stress. Why else would a dormant gene suddenly spring to life? If a gene is in a family's lineage, why does it come to life in certain people but not the entire family? In my case, nobody could remember anybody in my family ever dying of any disease other than heart problems and perhaps the flu. The unknown quantity is that nobody knows, even today, some twenty-five years later, despite all the advances in medical science, what kick-starts cancer, and what stops it from advancing is a complete mystery. They do know how to treat it. They know if the treatment is going to work and if the patient has any chance of survival. The drugs are wonderful and getting better every year. Doctors know that catching cancer genes at the early stages is vital to having any hope of success. They simply don't know what makes it start to grow again. Stress was a major factor in my case, and I have to say that when I suggested this to the medics when I was first diagnosed, they all scoffed at the suggestion, but I can tell you that they are now convinced that stress is a major factor.

I was in that oncologist's waiting room so often that I had reread every one of the magazines, and one day I saw a beautiful young blonde girl run past me. She had just found out she was dying. The doctor said it was too late. She was only twenty-two, she was beautiful, and she was going to be dead within three months. My oncologist, one of the finest in the country, used get really pissed off when he was helpless. It angered him that people ignored the signs, the fact that maybe you are getting tired a lot lately, or you are losing weight too quickly (a big sign), or you don't look well. There are always signs flashing like beacons, and yet we ignore them all. We will take our cars for regular servicing to ensure that everything is working correctly, we have the engineer check out a strange sound in the engine, yet we ignore the most vital thing of all, ourselves! I was no different until my sister Barbara brought it to my attention and I happened to have that night where my body shook like hell, ringing the alarm bells.

I also felt then how important it was to get proper counseling, to have someone to talk to on a professional basis that could guide me through the stages of my disease. I needed to talk to other sufferers, to find out how they were managing, what they did to reduce the pain, the puking, the mental anguish. I wanted to know how they handled difficult situations, what stage they were at, giving me some hope as I lived from day to day. In Ireland then there was nothing, no facilities other than a small house across the road from the hospital where you could go and rest for a while, but that was it. During my cancer term there were no group meetings like there are nowadays. I made myself available to the Irish Cancer Society to see if I could help in any way, but all they made me do was welcome visitors and make them some tea.

I did meet one woman, whose son had exactly the same level of Hodgkin's as me, and she begged me to call her son, who owned a well-known motor dealership in Dublin. She explained that he had become reclusive and withdrawn and she was very worried, so I rang him and left one message after another until finally he picked up my call. I told him who I was, that I wasn't some quack evangelist trying to save his soul but just another businessperson exactly like him who had contracted the same disease and was making great progress. I also told him that I was willing to share my experiences with him and that I could help him, but he was very distant with me. I couldn't break down his barriers, barriers that he had obviously constructed against all comers. He had given up, plain and simple. It was the Dalai Lama a couple of years ago who, when asked what disappoints him most about humankind, he replied that man spends all of his health trying to make his wealth, and if he succeeds in attaining that wealth, he then proceeds to spend all of that wealth trying to get his health back. A very smart man, that Dalai Lama. The answer is plain and simple: don't ignore the signs, get checked out if you have any concerns whatsoever, and, as my father always said, "Don't be always worrying."

I badly needed to get back in harness in my company as things were not good. Sure, we were making some money, but not nearly enough to meet my development costs. Even though we had launched our new products, there was still a huge amount of further development required to complete them. We were also under a lot of pressure from customers to produce add-on products to meet their client's needs, and we were far away from accomplishing that. There was also the continuing problem of keeping up with the legal compliance issues of our products. Our products were used by practicing accountants who had to adhere to "the Companies Acts" so that they could report on behalf of their clients according to the law, and our products had to provide that facility automatically. My sales force were performing, but they needed help. They needed exhibitions and seminars to promote the products so that they could bring in new business. And all the while our opposition were not standing idly by. In addition, I was constantly fighting my cancer. It was relentless, but that didn't matter to the banks. They needed constant feeding.

CHAPTER 20

So what would any person do when confronted with the following facts: that he was broke; separated; the father of four children he couldn't or didn't want to see; someone who happened to be in the mid-stages of level-four cancer and who was now abandoned by all of his friends, former family friends, and acquaintances, who basically suggested that he should do everybody a big favor and just die? What would any partly sane person do? They would lick their wounds, dust themselves off, take a full stock of their life, and get some order into it. That would be the sensible thing to do. Of course what did Bernie do? He only went and bought himself an eighteen-room Gothic-style mansion with nine acres of land in the beautiful Vale of Avoca nestled in the rolling Wicklow hills in the garden of Ireland. Of course he did!

Don't ask me to try to explain the whys and why nots, but you have to understand my state of mind then. I didn't have one!

I had loved the house I had bought at that auction, the one I had just given to Maria as part of the separation agreement. It was spacious and private in a terrific location. I hated my new apartment life with all of its lifeless emptiness and cold. Physically, it was a lovely apartment, but the life that came with it sucked, and I had found that I would do anything but go home to it, which was ironic because I didn't want to go home to the big house when I lived at home with Maria and you guys. I decided I needed my own place and not an apartment.

I scoured the property pages until one day it jumped out at me, this property in Avoca village, about an hour from my office, a village I knew rather well. This was the place my parents brought us to on our summer holidays, not to your normal five-star hotel but to a broken-down caravan in an open field, and I loved it. We had spent many a summer there with other families in their recreational vehicles. It was our first introduction to the countryside, the smells, the animals, and the beautiful scenery. Tommy loved it too; the Ma not so much. There was no running water; everything came from the well in buckets. There was no electricity; we played board games using kerosene lamps. No flushing toilets; instead you did your business in larger buckets using a chemical to kill the stink and a coloring liquid to avoid having to look at floaters.

I loved it all, and I couldn't wait every year for our annual vacation. It was these memories that came flooding back to me as I looked at the advertisement, so I made an appointment to see this amazing property. I had no intention of ever owning it. Besides, I was broke.

I arrived on a beautiful summer's day. The birds were chirping their song, "Oh What an Idiot We Have Here." At least that what it sounded like. The gardens were in immaculate shape, in an obviously pristinely managed estate. It had everything but my name on the front gates. As I parked the car at the fountain and headed up to the amazing church-like front door, I was greeted by the hopeful sellers and a greasy-looking estate agent. It was indeed beautiful, from the two California redwoods at the front of the house down to the rippling Avoca River that passed through the end of the estate, ideal for that lazy picnic on a hot summer's afternoon. The only neighbor was the local rector, and the entire estate was perched on high, overlooking the sleepy village, which consisted of two public houses, two shops that sold everything, together with the village cop shop. It was a typical Irish village scenario. I was hooked there and then. Without a penny to my name, but I was hooked. I reasoned that my life was in ruins, and nothing good had happened to me in a long time, so why not imagine that I was the country squire, lording it over all and sundry? I had never been one to worry too much about money. After all, I never had any in the first place, and as I owed so much I reasoned that it was not my problem, it was the bank's problem. I had never allowed money to interfere with my progress. If I needed it, I would always find it somewhere.

I was never a person who dreamed of owning any chattels, paintings, horses, boats, or whatever. My policy had always been if I couldn't afford it, then I didn't want it. This was to be my first exception to my mantra.

I asked the agent about the asking price, and he said two hundred and seventy grand in real Irish pounds, that's about a million dollars in today's terms. I nearly shit myself. I told him I couldn't afford that sort of money, and I said my farewells to the owners. He said he'd have a word with the seller and get back to me. The weeks passed, and I had forgotten all about my sojourn into the fantasy land of house buying, when one day I was in my office selling anything I could, whipping my sales guys, and basically distracting myself from any reality that resembled my life when the phone rang and my secretary told me that some guy was on the phone and she thought that he wanted to buy something.

He never introduced himself. Instead, he said that the price of two hundred and fifty was acceptable to his client and could I do the deal? I hadn't a bog's notion what he was talking about as I frantically flicked through my potential sales file, looking for the potential order he was referring to. Rather than delay things any further, I said absolutely, that he should tell his client that the deal was done and to send me the relevant documents. He was delighted, and I thought it was strange that a guy could get so excited about a trivial item that cost only two hundred and fifty pounds.

I didn't give it any further thought until a few days later I received a bunch of papers informing me that I was about to become the proud owner of an estate in County Wicklow. It was only then that I managed to put two and two together. Of course I laughed at the farce of the whole thing, and I could have easily said there had been a big mistake, but something inside me said that this was the right thing to do, something that spoke to me in angelic tones with backing music. This something should have had his testicles removed without an anesthetic!

Off I went in search of a mortgage. Now, I wouldn't have classified myself as being the ideal candidate for obtaining a loan, and neither did any of the financial institutions. I couldn't say I blamed them as I was stony broke. I tried all the usual suspects, anybody I knew in the loan business, but when they heard that I wanted a one-hundred-percent loan and that my security was a three-inch disk of software code, I was told to take a hike. Banks were only interested in bricks and mortar as security. Nothing else would suffice. They were not interested in any security they could not physically feel. They didn't understand it.

As luck would have it, I received a call from one of the insurance companies, and I knew the guy who rang me. After we exchanged pleasantries and a few stories—we had always got along well—he told me that my application had come across his desk because he handled all large loan applications, and as he was about to shred it he noticed my name, so he decided to give me a call. He had opened with the line, "I bet you are glad you never called me a fat bollocks?" and it was only then that I realized who he was. He was a bit heavy, but he was also a very smart guy, and I liked him.

After he heard the details about the house I wanted to buy, he asked me one thing. "If I sanction this loan, I don't want to see it coming across my desk as a bad debt, is that clear?"

I told him that I had never reneged on a debt in my life and that I wouldn't let him down. He approved it. I was ecstatic, and that was how I became the new Squire of Avoca. There's one born every minute, so they say! I was still in shock when they handed me the keys, and the previous owners looked very happy as they sped away.

I toured my property. It was beautiful and frightening at the same time, considering my predicaments, but I was never one to shy away from a challenge. And boy was this a challenge! My mother was in shock when I told her about it, and when I showed her around the property she nearly had to be resuscitated. My sister was speechless, but I suppose they were more concerned about my physical state rather than my mental one, whereas I didn't care about either of my states.

The house consisted of two stories over a basement, built in the gothic style some two hundred years previously. It had been beautifully restored by the previous owner, who had invested a huge amount of money to get it looking like it did. There were eighteen rooms, including a massive living room with a glorious, huge marble mantelpiece and a large window with separate access out to the gardens. The dining room had a table large enough to seat ten people. There was a separate television room annexed to a large kitchen and a further dining area on the other side. There were five rooms in the basement, all with separate access to the gardens, which could be used as bedrooms or games rooms, depending on your requirements. There was a separate bathroom area too, and another guest bedroom on the split floor leading up to the master bedroom, which was huge, with large bay windows looking over the estate. The bathroom was just as big, with a huge step-up bath in the middle of the room. There was a full-sized tennis court and adjoining outhouses for housing equipment or animals. The grounds were teeming with plants of every description, the grass was as green as you could get, the views were wonderful, and the privacy was surreal.

The Avoca River flowed through the end of the grounds, and this is where I found myself at the end of that perfect summer's day, listening to its rush as it meandered under the hanging trees on its journey to the Irish Sea. I looked back up at the house, and I said to myself, "What have you done, Bernie? What have you done?"

I made the journey up and down to work every day. It took less than an hour. That was until winter arrived, when it took an hour and a half along badly surfaced roads, but I wasn't going to admit that to anybody. As far as anybody was concerned, it was not a problem.

I was concerned about the security. It was quite isolated, and although the local guard assured me that there had never been any trouble up to now, I decided it was time to buy a dog. After all, what self-respecting squire didn't have a dog? That was when Max came into my life.

Max was a beautiful rough collie, in the Lassie style, and I loved looking after him. I had wondered what Tommy would have said now that I finally had my dog. The first thing I needed to do was fence him in, which was a little tricky when you have nine acres to fence, so I decided against that and tied him up to a massively long rope when I went to work. I had a gardener, Paddy, who came with the property, and he looked after Max during the day.

What I hadn't realized was that the postman who delivered my mail every day had been tormenting little Max with an electric pole, driving the poor animal wild with terror. As a result he ended up hating men for evermore, especially postmen or anybody in a green van.

I started to turn the business around again for the better now that I was giving it my full attention. I also started to make new friends, all of whom I met through the business. One of the guys heard about my health problems and rang me one Monday morning saying he was sending over the keys to his apartment in the Canaries and that I was to go over there anytime I wanted. Never one to miss an opportunity, I immediately looked out the window to see it was still raining and booked myself a flight.

I bought Bob Dylan's new album at the time, called *Oh Mercy*. I have bought several copies over the years as they got worn out from overplaying. It always gives me a good feeling. Dylan encapsulated my mood perfectly for that time with the dark "The Man in the Long Black Coat" to the angry "Ring them Bells" reaching out to me as I slumped my way around the hot Canary islands and tried to enjoy the warm sands. Whenever I would feel down I would reach for that album.

When I arrived at my friend's place I found it not up to my standards. The place was filthy, and so I spent the entire week cleaning it. I didn't mind so much, as it gave me something to do, and I was grateful for the opportunity to lie in the sun, as I was still very sick from the treatment. When he saw what I had done, he told me the place had never looked better and that I could visit anytime.

This was also the time that the whole country was going mad about Jack Charlton and the Irish football adventures with Italia '90. I embraced the atmosphere with gusto like everybody else. It was electric. A group of us decided we were going to follow the team, and all twenty-four of us headed to mainland Europe as Ireland went in search of glory among the footballing elite. I was also celebrating the news that my doctor said I could stop taking the chemotherapy, needles, and pills as he thought the treatment was going better than expected and he wanted my body to take a break.

It was great to be having fun at last, and the lads didn't disappoint as we caroused around the cities and the towns, following the contingent of Irish supporters. One of the more memorable moments involved a situation I found myself in with Eamonn, one of the many characters on board. We had been out on the town and got back to the hotel around midnight to find a typical Italian wedding in full swing. Not being people who would miss a party, we gatecrashed our way up to the top table, where there was one guy sitting on his own. In next to no time, Eamonn and I are singing all the Irish songs while the Italian guy joined in the revelry as a lot of heavy looking bodyguard types looked on disapprovingly.

After a couple of hours I decided I'd had enough and made my way to bed. Just as I arose, the Italian said, "Where you go, Irish?" pointing to my chair and telling me to remain seated as Eamonn belted out verse twenty-four of "My Wild Irish Rose." I suddenly got a little concerned with his attitude, and then it dawned on me that the Italian was really an Italian, the genuine Mafia type, and those big blokes were indeed his bodyguards. It was time to plan our escape, but Eamonn was having none of it as he ignored my gestures to do a runner.

With the wine flowing and the band still playing, I asked permission to go to the bathroom. It was granted, and as I made my way slowly across the floor I looked back to see Eamonn looking after me like somebody about to be sent to the gas chambers as he sang, "Don't leave me this way! / I can't survive, / can't stay alive. / Don't leave me this way!"

The last note I noticed was a little out of key. It was then that I noticed that most of the guests had disappeared, leaving Eamonn with the Italian and his henchmen. I rammed a chair up against my bedroom door and couldn't sleep properly as I kept waking up, looking under the sheets for a horse's head.

The next morning I made my way downstairs for breakfast, and I found the rest of the lads eating away. I asked them had they seen Eamonn. With that they pointed in the direction of the ballroom, where Eamonn was now dancing with the Italian as the band still played on. He looked over at me, pleading with me to rescue him from certain death. He had been up all night and hadn't even been allowed to use the bathroom. All the lads went over and rescued him. The Italian finally disappeared, and Eamonn collapsed. Any time after that night I went to the bathroom, Eamonn followed close behind. He was not taking his eye off me for the rest of the trip.

Of course we had to go to the local knocking shop downtown, which was a state-run brothel. I had seen some knocking shops over the years, but nothing like that one. It was organized methodically: entrance this way, wheelchairs that way. You paid a small entrance fee, and then you made your way into an enormous arena, some twenty-thousand square feet of floor space with many bars and the ceilings full of hanging televisions showing every type of pornography. None of us had ever seen anything like it. In typical Irish style when confronted by such terror, we formed a circle and headed for the bar. There were girls of every shape, color, and creed. Big ones, small ones, wide ones, but every one of them was gorgeous and very sexy as they paraded around the floor, dressed in skimpy negligees and G-strings leaving very little to the imagination. Nobody in our group was going first. We glanced at one another as we drank our beers, fearful of being picked from the herd as the lions circled around us. One of the more Catholic guys among us said that he would definitely not be indulging in the debauchery and, in fact, wanted to go home. I have to say it looked a bit intimidating to say the least, even for me. There were hundreds of other guys there from all over Europe—Dutch, English, Germans, and ourselves—so the girls were very busy.

As we huddled together just like the King Penguins do in the Antarctic to keep themselves warm, into our midst appeared the most delectable little Asian girl you'd ever set eyes upon, who was obviously highly educated because her first words were "Fucky fucky? Who wants fucky fucky?"

Now you didn't need to be a Joycean scholar to figure that one out, and so somebody mumbled, "How much?"

That girl was very commercially minded because instantly she explained our options, starting with prices for one at a time, a sandwich—being two or more at the same time—and of course a menu of offerings ranging from harmless fun to the sadistic. We informed the young lady that we needed a few moments to discuss things, and as she hovered around advertising her wares we did a few sums and we figured that it wasn't bad value for money, all things considered. So we decided to have another round of drinks to discuss said options. Well, wouldn't you know it, the guy that was on his way home earlier announced, "I'm weakening, boys," to the cackle of laughter from the group. He then said that he had brought no money, and he asked for a loan from the assembly, who willingly obliged, dying to see him be the first to lose his virginity. Off he went with the little pixie across the floor to the roars of "Ole, Ole, Ole," the raucous shouts of encouragement from the Irish contingent, and the general boos and hisses from the other Europeans.

We huddled some more as we discussed how proud we were that one of our own had taken the leap of faith, when no more than two minutes later he returned, crestfallen and embarrassed, as his pixie moved around the other guests, drumming up more business. It seemed that the pixie was an expert in her craft and had obviously sucked him dry before he could take his trousers off. The other Europeans bellowed with joy and laughter at our ignominy, crying, "One nil, one nil, one nil!" So it was imperative that we send in our center forwards to rescue the game or at least come out with a draw.

We had just qualified for the quarter finals of the championship in Rome, so a lot of celebrating and recuperation took place. We all hooked up at a massive outdoor bar and restaurant the day before our next football match. It was a glorious day, filled with sunshine, and there must have been some seven thousand people there from all the countries of Europe.

A group of Dutch lads joined us. These lads were something special. They were all in uniform, and it transpired that they were a fighter bomber squadron from the Dutch Airforce. Boy did they look the part. The commander would have put George Clooney to shame, he was that good looking, and the rest of his lads were no slouches either. They were great fun and of course they enjoyed nothing more than the company of the Irish. They were stationed down the road and due to fly home early the next morning.

My friend Keith and I were asking them loads of questions about their F16s—where they operated, what action they'd seen—when a sudden quiet came over the entire bar. The reason was obvious. All eyes centered on the most amazingly beautiful blond haired girl that anybody had ever seen. She glided past everybody towards an empty table at the front of the bar where she ordered a drink, totally oblivious to the seven thousand pair of admiring eyes ogling her. Even the women were staring at her, she was that drop-dead gorgeous. I said to Commander George and my friend Keith that we were going on a mission. We were going over to Aphrodite, sit down at her table, and Keith and I were going to give her the full unexpurgated best of Irish bullshit to seduce her and successfully take her back to our castle and have our wicked way with her, obviously.

I made a few rules, one being that Commander George was to sit there and say nothing at all. He was only to speak when she spoke to him, if she spoke to him at all. So with a deep breath, and downing our beers for encouragement, we arose and made our way in single file towards Aphrodite's table. I have to say that she took it all in her stride with an equally breathtaking smile as we sat down. Keith sat to her left, me on her right, and commander Clooney sitting opposite her. I started off by introducing myself and Keith, completely ignoring our Dutch friend as if he didn't exist. He played it totally deadpan.

I attempted to impress her by announcing that I was the president of IBM, had my yacht down at the harbor, while Keith interjected by telling her he was an international banker and he had his jet in the adjacent field. The bullshit continued for over fifteen minutes, and when we took a pause for breath, trying to figure out what to say next, Aphrodite casually turned to George and asked, "And what do you do?"

"I'm an F16 fighter bomber commander with the Royal Dutch Airforce," he replied.

How can you possibly compete with that? Apart from the fact that he was much better looking than us, he blew us straight out of the skies, and she visibly melted. It was time for Keith and me to make our exit but not before George and his new girlfriend joined us at our table and we spent the rest of the day imbibing and laughing heartily.

But the story doesn't end there. I asked George if he would do me a great favor and fly over our hotel the next morning on their way home. I gave him the hotel name, and after a short discussion with his fellow pilots he said he'd see what he could do. He couldn't promise anything as they would need permission to alter their flightpath, but he told me to be outside at the pool at precisely 6:03 because at 6:03 and a half they'd be flying over Bulgaria or somewhere like that. These guys didn't mess about.

We arrived back at the hotel around four in the morning, and I told the lads to stay up for the flyover. They all scoffed, saying not to be an idiot, that of course the fly boys had no intention of ever flying over our hotel, and off they all went to bed. I got hold of the giant Irish tricolor flag we had brought with us, and I spread it across the swimming pool. It looked great, and I sat by the pool like a little kid waiting on Santa Claus to arrive. I then thought that maybe I had misread them and felt a little let down when suddenly there was a slight murmur overhead, which gradually got louder and louder. Within seconds an almighty roar shook the buildings as five F16s blasted across the sky in majestic formation, flying so low that they witnessed a screaming Irishman below them, whooping and a hollering with the excitement. They were gone in seconds, but not before giving me their salute by waving their wings. I thought to myself at that very moment, *Lord, you can take me now. I have seen the light, and the light has set me free!* I sat there mesmerized by what would be an everlasting memory, a feeling like no other. I felt like a king who had just received the royal salute.

The other boys came down to the pool in total shock as they had missed the event of the century, a private one-hundred-million-dollar air show arranged by yours truly. They never doubted me after that.

CHAPTER 21

It was very lonely in Avoca, even with the big house and the lavish surroundings. At times I loved it, and at other times I felt very isolated. I was also desperate for some female companionship, and I found it in the most unlikely circumstances. I happened to be in the UK visiting some customers. I mentioned about Avoca and where I lived when one of the senior partners said he knew Avoca very well as he had a good friend living around that area, and my ears popped up when he said that his friend was a woman. I told him it was hard to meet anybody, and he said he would have a word with his friend and introduce us.

Sure enough and true to his word, I was at home one day when the phone rang and Kathleen introduced herself and invited me around to a party at her house the following Saturday. I was delighted. She sounded great, but I had no clue what was in store. Saturday night duly arrived, and I managed to find the house okay. Kathleen was a decent-looking woman who introduced me to her husband. *Bollocks!* I thought to myself, so Kathleen was not on the menu. She took me into her living room and introduced me to Claudia.

Claudia was a big tall woman, not fat, but big in the bust area and German to boot, as they say. What I didn't know was that word had spread around the area that some guy known as the squire was new in town and more importantly he was available and he was loaded. Now I wanted to disperse a couple of inaccuracies about the gossip, particularly the bit about being loaded, but then again I was never one to spoil a party. Claudia was on to me like a loaded gun, and my gun was already loaded for quite some time, so I figured why the hell not, she was a sexy woman, a bit dour and serious, with that typical North European flavor. We chatted amiably for most of the evening as we enjoyed our supper. She then announced that she was having a party at her house the following Friday and we were all invited. She neglected to tell me that I was on the menu.

This was great, a bit of action at last, so off I went in search of her house the following Friday night, and holy crap-a-rooskey it was twice as big as my place and purposefully built by the good lady herself, who was obviously not short of a few shekels. I was greeted by two enormous dogs outside who looked like they could play with you before devouring you, but this particular night they looked timid enough and on their best behavior. The house was alive with lots of people. Claudia grabbed me, gave me a quick tour of the house, and then sat me down at the dinner table with her German friends, who all seemed pleasant enough, except they all spoke German for some reason! I sat opposite Claudia, who was sitting beside another girl, and I was left trying to make small talk with a German bloke beside me who was well on his way to being fully loaded.

I didn't want to make a show of myself on our first unofficial date, so I sipped the wine and daintily ate some food, taking in all the action happening around me. There was plenty going on, and the noise levels of all the guests told me that everybody was having a good time. With that the girl opposite grabbed Claudia in a wild embrace and started kissing her there and then at the table. I looked beyond them into the kitchen, and there was a couple going at it hammer and tongs on the table, bollock naked. Then a sort of conga dance started as a group of them started chasing one another around the room, grabbing each other's privates and anything else that their groping hands could touch.

I turned to the bloke beside me and said as nonchalantly as I could, "Quiet sort of night, huh?"

"Dis is de sort of ting dat goes on every party time," he said in his best German English.

"Oh, then this is a regular sort of event then?" I mildly enquired, noticing that my "date" was now in a full wrestling match on the carpet and appeared to be under a lot of pressure.

Things were definitely on the up and up in sleepy Avoca, I thought to myself. The only trouble was I wasn't a lesbian, and I didn't speak any German. But, never one to shy away from a challenge, I reckoned that I'd catch on to the lesbian thing pretty quickly and a six-month correspondence course should put paid to the language problem.

As I contemplated my plans, Claudia jumped up and announced to everybody that the party was over and that everybody should go home. Holy crap, things moved very fast with the Germans! I grabbed my jacket and bid my goodbyes to Claudia, thanking her for the evening.

"Not you," she said. "You stay."

She led me into another room. Soon everybody had been thrown out, and she came into the room as if she had just attended a church prayer meeting.

"What would you like to drink?" she asked. Damn, this lady was something else. Minutes before she had been wrestling with some bird on the floor while her guests were banging one another on her kitchen table as the rest of the guests did the conga around her living room, then she coolly asked me what I'd like to drink! This was not a lady to be messed with.

"I'd love a brandy," I said as quick as you like. She handed me a Hennessy brandy in a beautiful Waterford Crystal snifter together with a selection of chocolates.

Not knowing where to begin the conversation, I said, "You throw a great party."

"Oh I hope you were not shocked by my friends. They are a lively lot, but things always get out of hand," she said rather nonchalantly.

"Not at all. I loved it," I said, not wanting to screw anything up. I believe in live and let live, and I was thinking to myself that if she wanted to re-enact the old lesbian scene again, then wheel them in because I was more than willing to engage. "Tell me Claudia, what's the situation with the girl kissing you?"

"Oh, she's always doing that. I am not lesbian, but she has always fancied me. I hope it doesn't bother you because she is a good friend."

"Not in the slightest. I am a very broadminded person, and, as they say, variety is the spice of life!" I said, wondering where this was leading. I decided to change the subject because at this stage I wanted to know everything about our Claudia. This was a lady who was definitely passionate and very willing, and I was a man who was very willing to be passionate.

So we talked about our businesses. She was very impressed that I had my own software business that extended to three countries, and I have to say I was very impressed myself when I heard what I had to say. I was nearly thinking of dating myself! Then it was her turn to tell me about her business interests, and boy she did not disappoint. She told me that she ran her father's lumber businesses in four countries since he retired, that she was an only child and was due to inherit everything when her parents passed away. *Pass on*, I thought to myself, *and where would you like to get married?* Before I could enquire what sort of wedding cake she'd prefer, the next thing I knew we were upstairs in the sack and purring like little kittens all night long.

This, as Humphrey Bogart said, was the start of a beautiful relationship that would last about—three weeks. The following Monday I was in my office when my secretary announced that somebody was in reception and wanted to see me. Now, I hated when a customer arrived unannounced because it always meant trouble, but this time I was met by Claudia.

"Is everything okay?" I asked, and she said she was just passing and wanted to ask me something. *Holy crap*, I thought, *she couldn't be pregnant already?*

"Would you like to come to a party with me tonight?" she asked.

I looked at my calendar, and I saw that I was free for the rest of that year and beyond. "Sure, tonight is fine," I said, thinking there's never a dull moment when Claudia is around.

"Great!" she said before pointing out that the party was in Austria. A good friend of hers had invited her weeks ago, but as she had nobody to escort her at the time, and seeing we were now an item, she had accepted the invitation. Of course she had already booked the flights and organized the accommodation.

"Wow, that's a bit sudden," I said, looking a bit taken aback to say the least as I usually kept all overseas parties for the weekends. So I looked out the window, saw the low grey skies overhead, turned and looked at her ample bosom, and said, "Absolutely, Count me in! I need to drop back home though and grab some clothes, organize a few things—"

"Don't worry about that. We will be back in two days. I can find you an outfit for the party over there. It's a costume party, and we can buy anything else we need on the way."

Boy, no wonder these Germans nearly won the bleeding war! She was one hell of an organizer. I rang Paddy down at the house and told him to look after Max, that I'd be back in a couple of days. I also told him not to forget to feed the very expensive fish in my aquarium, which I had inherited with the house, a one-hundred-gallon tank with a variety of exotic fish. Off we popped in her car to Dublin Airport, grabbed the plane, and we arrived in Vienna where she had her MG Midget waiting, as you do.

We drove for hours over the Austrian Alps, arriving at what I can only describe as a castle in the sky, one enormous castle owned by some duke friend or other, and I was shown into a room with lots of costumes while the duke whisked Claudia away. I decided against the Napoleon outfit, as it was a little small for me, and opted instead for the gorilla costume in case I ran into somebody I knew. No fear of that, says you, as nobody spoke any English and I never saw Claudia the entire evening, so I lodged myself by the bar. What a disaster! Did you hear the one about this gorilla at the bar while his bird was being hammered upstairs by a duke?

I have no idea what went on in the castle that night, but nothing was happening to yours truly, and that was for sure. She arrived back at some hour of the early morning without so much as a how do you do and told me to get into the car as we were going to Stuttgart to see her parents. I was quickly turning off the great Claudia until she told me she was worth about twenty-five million euro, and, as I already knew how much I was worth, I decided to put any ungracious thoughts to the side, helped by an image of my bank manager and my destitute children versus the possibility of a life on easy street for all.

We arrived at the parents apartment—seemingly most Germans rent apartments rather than own houses—to find Herr and Frau Gunther. I cannot remember their names, so Herr Gunther will suffice, who was a little bit standoffish as Claudia introduced me. It didn't take long to work out that the Gunthers weren't getting along together—they pointed out their separate bedrooms—so I anchored myself to the old man, as he seemed the friendlier of the two, while Claudia made her exit to complete her business.

"So what do you do, Bernie?" asked Gunther.

I told him quickly about how successful and wonderful I was and turned the conversation to him and how he got to where he was. He told me that he had started his lumber business in England, then had opened a processing plant near Waterford in Ireland, and retired a few years ago, knowing that Claudia was more than capable of running the show. He then showed me his photo album of his children. *Oh crap,* I thought, *there are more siblings!* But his children were photos of cows, yes cows. Not your ordinary McDonald cows but Charolaise cows, the expensive kind.

Now I know nothing about cows udder than—I threw that one in—you can eat them in McDonalds or drink their milk, but he was ecstatic about his little old cows, and I was impressed when I heard how much the entire herd was worth. Holy crap, we were talking very serious money here. I decided I'd better do something to impress them, so I told them I needed to go downtown and get something, and off I went in search of a jeweler's shop. It was time to buy Claudia something.

I decided on a watch, a decent watch mind you, one that would look good and that would be below my credit limit at the end of the month. I opted for a Movado—cost eight hundred euro, credit card available balance nine hundred euro, leaving things a little tight, but as this was an investment in my future I figured it was worth it. When Claudia returned, I made a little drama out of my presentation, which she thanked me for and threw the Movado on the table, never to be seen again. I made sure Gunther got a good look at the watch, and he knowingly approved.

After we got back to Ireland I was delighted that Max was good, but the same couldn't be said for my fish. Paddy had forgotten to feed them, and as a result half of the aquarium had been cannibalized. The larger fish had eaten the smaller ones as they were starving. It was time to get a load of goldfish.

I had been ignoring Claudia's calls. I had decided I'd had enough, that the great Claudia was not for me despite her twenty-five big ones. I reckoned I was better off on my own, so I was a bit afraid of confronting Claudia because she wasn't a woman you'd want to mess with, hence the ignoring of said many phone calls. I rang her one night and asked her could I come over as I needed to talk to her, so I arrived over to be met by the two lions masquerading as dogs parading the driveway. I had barely taken my coat off, telling her gently that I had met an old flame of mine and that I wanted to be honest with her and break it off.

"Out! Get out!" she screamed as she pushed me outside and banged the front door.

"Eh, any chance I could have my coat?" I enquired to no response, only some mad rantings emanating on the other side of the door.

I turned around to see the two lions were looking up at me, and they were not at all happy, hearing their mistress was in distress, and started to growl at me. I can tell you I walked very gingerly over to my car saying, "Who's a good boy? Who's a good boy?" and made it to my car jacketless. I got home and poured myself a brandy, thinking that I had indeed made the right decision as a first wedding anniversary was not something that would have happened. In fairness, she did ring me a few days later and apologize for throwing me out. She thanked me for being honest with her and said I could collect my coat anytime.

"Eh, you couldn't just FedEx that for me Claudia, could you?" I enquired.

Now, it wasn't a total lie when I told her that I had met someone else. I had received an invitation from my bank to attend their annual shindig dinner, and they wanted the name of my partner for the table placements. I gave them my secretary's name, but she refused to go with me. Then two other girls declined my invitations as well, so I asked one of my managers if he looked good in a dress. He told me that his sister-in-law was arriving home form Europe, that she was great fun and would be delighted to go with me.

That was how I had met Angie, and when we sat down at the table the place card said "Bernie & Friend." Angie was eventually to become my second wife. Sort of.

CHAPTER 22

I DID TRY TO SNEAK times to see you kids whenever I could. I would get information from people telling me if you were playing sports, and one day I went to see Jack playing soccer. He was in goals, and he saw me and seemed pleased to see me. I had brought a little Brownie camera to take a few photos, and as I was doing that I was confronted by a group of women who appeared from nowhere and wanted to know what I was doing taking photos. I told them that my son was in goals, and they shouted over to Jack, asking him if I was his father. Things had changed over the past few years, and they thought that I was some kind of pervert.

It was also around this time that my back started to act up big time, sometimes for only a matter of a few hours, other times for weeks. I was in Avoca one time, playing with Max, when I hit the floor and conked out. I was out for over twenty-four hours, remembering nothing, and when I opened my eyes, I saw Max lying down, wondering what time he was due to have his dinner. He didn't like this new game that we were playing. I still couldn't move a muscle. The pain was excruciating. I lay there for another few hours and was getting very worried and very hungry when luckily Paddy, my local handyman, peered through the window and saw me lying there. He rang for a doctor, who gave me a shot of morphine, which got me back on my feet. I told him that I wanted to go see my back guy up in Dublin. I also forgave Paddy for the fish episode, as I don't know what would have happened had he not turned up. I was in the doctor's surgery, surrounded by every Tom, Dick and Mary coughing and spewing their guts up when Ray opened the door. He took one look at all the people waiting, saw me, and announced, "Bernie, you're next," when I was at least fortieth in line.

He told me that he loves seeing me in his surgery because it's never anything ordinary, always some tropical disease or unknown sickness that gets his adrenaline pumping as it might be his ticket to a worldwide cure and his fortune. But this time it was "only" my back. Now, he did admit it looked really bad and recommended a back specialist to me. He gave me a prescription for a lot of morphine tablets, and I said I'd let him know how I got on. The next day I was in my office and dying to have a movement otherwise known as a crap, so I plonked myself at the ceramic altar. What doc neglected to tell me was that morphine tablets tend to block the passages. To put it another way, it was like trying to pass a bowling ball. I didn't know whether to push or suck, and when it was neither halfway out nor halfway in, I just wanted to die. The agony was something else.

Then somebody came in wanting to use the toilet and, not knowing it was me, he asked, "What are you doing in there? Will you hurry up?"

To which I replied, "This is your boss speaking. I'm having a bit of a problem here, so would you go somewhere else?"

"Eh, sorry boss," he said as he ran out.

As the sweat poured down my brow, I decided I had to do something, but the bad angel—clever bloke, that—said, "Let's hang around and see what happens. Why go through that misery?" The good angel said, "It's time to either blow a gasket, lose about ten pounds, or evaporate." The good angel won. I couldn't sit down for a week after that.

It was time to ring the specialist. Trying to get a specialist in those days was hard enough, but trying to get him to perform back surgery was even harder as none of them wanted to operate due to the insurance companies' litigation experiences. I told the back surgeon that I couldn't go on like this, never knowing when my back would break down. I said that recently I had had to stand the entire flight home from New York to Dublin and that I couldn't sit at the movies. I gave him every example I could. He showed me the scans and explained that the disks were just like a burst tube in a tire. The tube part rested up against the spinal cord, resulting in excruciating pain. I think he realized that I was not bullshitting him, so he decided to book me in for surgery.

Of course having the surgery is one thing, but it's the recuperation that takes the longest time and is probably the most important part of getting better. Little did I know that it would take a recuperation period of over twenty years and many chiropractors, Chinese doctors, witches, and every other indigent that you could lay your hands on before I could finally announce that I was totally cured. That was after popping God knows how many pain killers.

One of the chiropractors I met in Portugal asked me had I been a breech birth as there was evidence that breeched babies were very prone to having back problems. I said I didn't remember because I was only nine months old at the time! I did ask my mother, and she was shocked and asked me how I had found out. It appeared that having a breech birth in my day was tantamount to having an exorcism as it was frowned upon, especially by the nuns, who said you must have been a bad mother to have an upside down baby. I was told that when they used to send in the forceps to turn the baby around in those days the baby got such a fright seeing this monster appearing in the tunnel that he had to go through that he would recoil and probably damage his back. Nowadays, of course, the mother has a caesarean, which is always successful and a whole lot easier on the baby.

Maria did contact me once, telling me that the kids wanted to see me, and I couldn't have been happier, except I was bed ridden with my back at the time when you all arrived down to Avoca. All of you were nervous, seeing me like that, and I was disappointed I couldn't show you around. You didn't stay very long, and we never saw one another after that.

While the business was doing okay, it wasn't going to set the world on fire in its present state, and any preconceptions I had about possibly selling the business in the future had very little foundation. I needed to take stock and make a definite plan. Apart from my back problems there was the ever-present cancer. I decided I couldn't let it rule my life. The doctors had taken me off all treatment, saying that I had responded as well as could be expected. It was up to me to keep myself fit and healthy, and everything should be fine. I just had to lead a normal life. When I asked them if they thought the cancer would come back, they told me that there were no guarantees but that every year that goes by my body would get stronger. When I pressed them they said that if I survived the next ten years, then I should be out of the woods.

Okay, I reasoned, ten years to go before I can finally stop thinking about dying. In the meantime I was going to pretend that the ten years had passed because what was the point of continually worrying about the damned thing? If it gets me, then it's over. If I can manage to live not thinking about it, then at least I can give myself a life. Anyway, that was the thinking, and in hindsight it was the correct attitude to take.

So cancer was now finally off the table. My separation was final and complete. I was not thinking about divorce because this was divorce Irish style, and I definitely had no intentions of ever marrying again. I knew that Maria wouldn't contemplate divorce in any circumstances because she was a devout Catholic. The kids were all doing as well as one could expect. They had each other, they had their schools, they had a great house and fabulous grandparents who were around all the time. They had a dedicated mother, and they were well provided for financially as long as I kept up the payments. The fact that their father wasn't around didn't seem to be a major issue, and there was no point in delving into any psychological aspects as none existed then. So that left the business as being patient number one, who had just been released from intensive care, was in the remedial ward, and needed some stimulants.

There was a software convention in New York, and I needed to update myself on what was on offer, technology wise, so I took Ronnie with me, business class all the way, as there was no way I could sit in coach for such a long journey with my precarious back, and I didn't think Ronnie would have appreciated me sitting up front in a lounge chair while he had to mix it with the poor sods back in coach fighting over a packet of peanuts. The great thing about business class in those days was that flight attendants really meant it when they said welcome aboard, as they presented you with their fine bone china and crystal with their great food and decent wines. Today the airlines' attitude is that they don't give a crap if you are aboard or not, you'd be lucky to get a sandwich that wasn't solidified. They throw you some made-up food tray that's supposed to be either curry or chicken, but they both taste the same, and you are constantly under orders to do this, put your tray up your bottom, etc. Those were the days when airline travel was a joyous experience, and Ronnie and I lay back and took it all in.

Ronnie eats up all that techie stuff, while it sends me asleep, so while he went to lap it all up I decided, having become totally disinterested in the convention proceedings, and as we were staying in a five-star hotel, that I would have my first massage. I made a reservation and, not having a clue what was about to happen, I was hoping the masseuse was going to be one of those full-breasted, long-legged blondes, preferably from Sweden, and I wasn't that fussy if she couldn't speak any English. I was shown into a very large cubicle by the attendant, was told to undress and put on the robe. She told me that my masseuse was called Wendy and that she would be with me momentarily. Now, any girl called Wendy has got a lot going for her. It oozed of sex, and my imagination took flight. In the middle of the room was a bed like a hospital gurney, with a hole at one end, so I pondered the design, wondering which way I was supposed to lie down and what I was supposed to do with the hole. Now, in case it has escaped your attention, I am a reasonably intelligent human being, but sometimes my imagination gets in the way of common sense. I hopped up on the table and put my arse in the hole, thinking that this was the only part of my anatomy that would fit. I sat there thinking that this was most uncomfortable, and I wondered how Wendy was supposed to massage me. As I sat there, hoping that this wasn't going to take too long, as my arse was developing a large, numbed circle, Wendy appeared from behind the curtain. The Wendy that stood in front of me with her mouth wide open was not the same Wendy that was jumping overboard in my mind at the same time. This Wendy was definitely in her seventies, was about four feet six, and looked very shocked and appalled at what confronted her because she said, "What are you doing?"

I immediately had visions of my mother saying the same thing when she caught me wanking in the shed at the rear of our house. I didn't feel good then, and I certainly didn't feel great now. I tried to explain that in Ireland we always sat in the hole, but she was having none of it. I can honestly say it was one of the few times in my life I actually felt embarrassed. She told me to get off the gurney and lie down, putting my face in the hole. *My face, of course, how bleeding obvious was that!* I thought as I looked down at the floor, hoping that there would soon be an earthquake and that I'd never see the great Wendy again. If there had been a mirror underneath my face you would have seen me say words like, "You absolute plonker! You dickhead!" and then you would have seen me laugh my bollocks off as I usually do in circumstances like that. My erection, by the way, had long ago flown the coup in shame.

I picked up Ronnie at the conference center during a coffee break, and I was listening in on a conversation of a group of young geeks who were saying things like, "That bozo should get off the stage," referring to some guy who had just given a lecture. The "bozo," it transpired, was a highly qualified individual that probably invented the Enigma machine, so when I heard these guys being disrespectful it got my back up. I turned to one guy, and I asked him how old he was. He told me that he was twenty-one, so I asked him did he think he was qualified to desecrate a person's character when that person was obviously an expert in his field? He looked pretty sheepish then, and I wanted to clock him one. Just then Ronnie interrupted, knowing where it was leading, and suggested that we should go for a pint. He knows my weakness.

It was time for my first helicopter ride. Ronnie had never been on one either, and so we took ourselves off downtown to the Hudson River, but not before I had knocked back a few pints to give me the courage to take the trip. Ronnie was younger and a lot braver than me, and he hadn't had all the near-death experiences that I had, so I needed the beer more than he did. In no time at all we were about to board the helicopter. Now, when you see a helicopter in the flesh, so to speak, you realize how small and tinny they really are and how much of an idiot you are for even considering getting into one of them. My remaining angel had a word in my ear and so I decided to abandon ship, but Ronnie pointed out that we had already gone through the drill and that I had paid in full and any rebates would be out of the question. I also did some research, and the only thing keeping me up there was a thing called a Jesus bolt. If it broke, it would be bye-bye Bernie. I told my remaining angel to shut up and use any remaining powers he had to get us up and down safely, so we crammed into the back seat, all four of us—myself and Ronnie, a young kid, and some fat bird—so I made sure I was in the middle, away from any window, and took out my rosary beads. Into the cockpit stepped a twelve year old, at least that's what he looked like.

"Eh, how old are you son?" I enquired.

"I'm twenty-one, sir," he replied.

Now, I like the way the Americans say "sir," I find it very respectful, and so I said, "Eh, well would you move over there sonny, because 'sir' is getting out!"

As I unbuckled my seatbelt, he said, "Sir, I am a fully qualified pilot. You have absolutely nothing to worry about," as he pulled a lever and off we shot vertically into the sky like a rocket. Now there was nothing in the instructions I read anywhere that said anything about leaving your stomach on the ground, but I definitely saw mine waving up to me from down below as I dug my fingers into my legs. I peered to my left and saw Ronnie practically hanging out of his window in sheer ecstasy at the wonders below him. The kid beside me was staring at me, not having seen somebody with a look of sheer terror on their face before. I then looked at the fat bird on my right, who was roaring crying and saying things like, "Oh my God, look!" I thought, *This is it! We're going down!* Except she was getting overemotional, as most Americans do, at the sight of the Statue of Liberty below us. To me it was like someone has just thrown you off a cliff. There's nothing under your feet but air, and you are waiting to hit the ground. I hated it. I never saw a blessed thing, but I pretended that I loved it and raved about it to anybody who would listen to me in the pub afterwards.

The final night I told Ronnie that we'd better have a look at the twin towers because, as sure as eggs are eggs, people back home are going to ask, "Did you see the twin towers?" I thought it would be nice to have a burger for dinner and a few pints and take in the sights, which was the reason I only brought a hundred bucks with me. We never carried credit cards with us in those days, probably because we never had any credit. I have to say that the towers were very impressive, especially when you compared them to Liberty Hall in Dublin, our largest skyscraper, which could possibly have reached the fourth floor of the twin towers.

We zipped up to the top floor in the fastest elevator I'd ever been on to the Windows of the World restaurant, which I thought would be a great place to have an old burger. We were shown to a table, but not before the waiter insisted on the two of us wearing one of their jacket and ties. It was one of those "up your hole" type restaurants where they have a waiter for every procedure, where they charge you a fortune for a bottle of water, and where you have a hard time finding the food on a plate. I figured that asking for two burgers and two glasses of water were out of the question. The waiter hovered around us like a vulture around a dying carcass. I looked at the menu, and it got a lot worse. It was also one of those restaurants where they don't put the prices on the menu, sort of like when you go to the pharmacy with your doctor's prescription, hoping to Jesus you don't need a mortgage to pay for your prescription. I told Ronnie that we were both ordering the lamb chops, no veggies, no spuds, no nothing else, just the lamb chops and definitely no booze because I was not at all sure that my hundred bucks was enough to cover the lamb chops, let alone anything else. Vulture waiter wings back with his notebook and pen, ready to write his memoirs, when I said with my most endearing smile, "Eh, we're in a bit of a hurry, so we'll both be having the lamb chops."

"Would sir like vegetables or our chef's speciality tonight?" he begged to enquire.

"No, sir and his friend are on a diet," I said, as he was really beginning to piss me off. With the look of a Stalag commander about to shoot a thousand peasants, he handed me the wine list, which I rebuked.

"Neither of us drink alcohol, and we'll just have your tap water," I said, waiting and hoping he was going to throw a punch so we'd get thrown out of there. He whipped away the menus, and I said to Ronnie, "That's grand, Ronnie. Now don't be tempted to order any dessert," but he had already figured that one out. The lamb chops arrived, and I swear to God you wouldn't have given them to a beggar, they were that small.

"We're going to have a hard time making a long conversation out of this meal," I said to Ronnie, to which he nodded, scarfed whatever meat was hanging on the bone, and never touched his knife or fork, straight from the hands as it was the only way you could get the meat off the damned thing. I told Ronnie that when I got the bill I was going to put the cash on the plate and when I gave him the nod we were both going to do a runner.

Vulture arrived with the bill. Ninety-seven dollars versus my hundred equals no tip! Welcome to New York! I couldn't believe the price. There was definitely going to be trouble afoot. I kept looking at the waiter as he was keeping his beady eyes on me, and when I saw a gap, I said, "Now Ronnie, run!"

So we whipped off the jacket and ties and ran towards the elevator, only to be met by a long line of people waiting to go down. We both looked back, waiting for the waiter to come looking for us. The doors opened, we jumped in, and just as the doors were about to close the waiter wedged his foot in the doors screaming at us, "You never left a tip! You never left a tip!" so we just stared at him as if he was accusing the wrong people, not wanting to be embarrassed in front of all the other people.

"You Scottish are mean pigs!" he said.

So as not to disappoint him I said, "Och aye, laddie, Scotland the brave it is," as there was no point in getting the Irish into trouble, and I knew our cousins from Scotland wouldn't mind in the least being praised for their shrewd handling of money. With that the doors closed. I often wondered if that waiter was working on the day the towers collapsed. I hope he was okay!

CHAPTER 23

It was 1995 and the Italia '90 lads decided that they wanted to go to South Africa because they'd heard the golf was great and they also knew some former heavyweight rugby guys down there who had extended an invitation. You never offer an invitation to an Irishman if you don't want him to appear because he will appear, and he won't disappear too quickly either, so you'd want to be careful in that regard. Now, I know nothing about rugby, or many sports for that matter. In fact, I'm not a very sporty person at all except I do follow golf and the premiership, but that's about it. So when they asked me to join them, I jumped at the opportunity. I knew we'd have great fun and the additional benefit of sunshine did not go unnoticed. What a trip it turned out to be. We had all the usual suspects, including Eamonn "there will be a price to pay," F16 Keith, and a whole host of characters, some twenty-four in all, that would execute any dull moment that raised its ugly head. South Africa is huge, nine times the size of Britain, and we arrived just one year before Nelson Mandela was due to be released. Whoever organized things did a great job, as we had top-of-the-range accommodation overlooking the ocean, the skies were a pristine blue the likes of which I hadn't seen before, and the golf clubs were beckoning.

Now, I must fill you in on my golfing prowess. It didn't exist then. I was definitely a novice, and I had only played about two games in my life. Some of the guys lived for the game while the rest could basically belt it about the place without causing too much damage. We arrived at one of the super golf clubs they have in abundance down there, and we teed up to cheers and jeers on the first tee. It came to my turn, and what scared me the most was not the jeering,

I was well used to that, but the fact that some little black kid had to hold the tee on the ground with my golf ball balanced on top because the ground was too hard to plug in the tee. I told the little fella to leave the ball on the ground, but he said he would lose his job if he didn't hold the tee.

I don't know who was the more nervous. The young lad under me didn't look the best as a bead of sweat crept down his face. I don't know how I managed it, but the kid was still alive as I made my swipe at the ball and the ball went straight into the bush. Now, another rule I learned was that the guests were not allowed to search for their balls. That was a job for the young black lads because there were dangerous creatures in those bushes that go burp in the night and guests were precious, whereas the young lads could be replaced.

After about an hour of slashing my ball around the course under the baking hot sun, Eamonn decided that he'd had enough of watching me attempt to play the game, so he told me, didn't suggest, mind you, but told me to only use the five iron for everything. So on the tee, par five, no problem, five iron please, and off we went. Approach shot, five iron. Chipping, five iron. I used the five iron for everything except the putting, and, you know what? It worked in so far as we managed to get into the clubhouse before the monsoon rains arrived in November, but at least we made it back.

South Africa was something else. The mix of the agony and the ecstasy, agony for black people, ecstasy for everybody else. The population was a mix of Dutch, Afrikaners, British, Asians, and the Zulu. They all had one thing in common: they all hated black people. I couldn't understand it myself but that's what we were told. Now my understanding of the way it worked back then was that the Indians ran the financial side of things, the British handled the commercial side, the Dutch or Afrikaners ran the police and the military and the blacks ran nothing and basically did nothing either. There was a lot of hatred amongst all of the tribes, regardless of color, and you got the feeling that it was a society living on a powder keg.

We met some of the expats who now lived there, and they were held in high esteem by the local and national press. They advised us not to bring up the apartheid subject while we there as things were already tense now that Nelson Mandela was in charge So one of the nights we were in a fabulous restaurant in Cape Town, and we had a system for paying. Rather than try to collect from everybody for their meals and all the hassle that comes with it, three people were picked each night to pay for the meal, then three more the next night, and so on. So we made sure that McDonalds was off the list for everybody. I was on duty that night, and so I left the standard fifteen-percent tip, only to be chased by the manager who insisted on giving me back my tip, as it was more than a month's wages for the waiter guys and he didn't want to start a precedent.

Even though you were out to have a good time, the politics of South Africa jumped out at you from everywhere, so you couldn't ignore it. I made my acquaintance with a beautiful black girl down on the beach, as you do, and we hit it off big time, so much so that she invited me along to her place for dinner that night, which I gladly accepted. The rest of the lads were busy doing their thing, so off I went to meet my girl who lived in a modern apartment block.

On the way up in the elevator a girl walked in dressed in the tightest, shortest, leopard skin hot pants you'd ever seen in your life that must have stopped her circulation. That combined with the two bazookas of breasts that could slam you up against the wall and take your two eyes out of your head made me guess that perhaps she wasn't on her way to evening prayer! She looked at me and not wanting to be unsociable I asked her how much, and she said seven pounds so out we got and into her room where business, as they say, was transacted. About ten minutes later, we both climbed back into the elevator and it so happened that she was going to the same floor as me, and of course wouldn't you know it, she was also going to the same room as me because of course her best friend happened to be my date for the evening. She looked at me as her friend with the beaming smile opened her door, then back at me basically telling me without words "Get your ass out of here, I will count to three then my friend and I together with some jungle creatures are going to rip you to shreds" Yes I think that was what she said, I'm not entirely sure because I was out of there quicker than Flash Gordon on speed never to return.

We had been invited to the Ascot of South Africa, the annual "no blacks allowed" horse racing event, and we were the welcome guests of somebody rich who had his own private marque, or tent as we call them in Ireland, loaded with every conceivable alcoholic drink you could name and a few more besides, together with a lavish display of food. We dived in, taking in the ambiance and watching all of the talent, which abounded, women who oozed class, sex and money. The only rule we were given was we were not under any circumstances to ogle, chat up, or stare at any of the ladies. You could look, but that was about it. Otherwise we would not be seen again and a lot of hungry lions would not be hungry for a while. We got the message and duly got blotto, as you might say.

One by one we managed to struggle out to the various Land Rovers that awaited us and piled in on top of one another, completely drunk, and left in the hands of our hosts, who were free to do with us as they pleased. The next thing I knew I awoke as if I was going through a hurricane. I was banged here, there and everywhere around the Land Rover. I was in the back seat, and I saw my friend Eamonn in the front seat, completely out of it, also being thrown about.

Our driver said, "Hey, you're alive! What a day! Did you enjoy yourselves?"

"Eh, yeah. The name's Bernie. What's yours?"

"Norman's the name, and drinking's my game!"

"Eh, Norman, I hope you don't mind me asking, but where are we, and where are we going?"

"I'm bringing you to my house, mate. We are on my land, and when we get there the party resumes. A hey!" he shouted.

Obviously Norman enjoyed a good party, so I'm thinking we're on his land so not far to go then. That's good, that's very good. Wonder when he's going to kill us?

"Eh, where are the rest of the lads, Norman?" I asked.

"Oh, they're in the other cars. They should be there shortly as they left before us."

"Tell me, Norman, how far have we to go to your house?"

"About another," he thought about it, "I'd say another hundred miles."

"Holy Mother!" I said. "Eamonn, wake up! Eamonn, wake up!" I shouted, trying not to show too much fear in my voice and managed to eventually revive him. After I explained in hushed tones and a few Irish words thrown in to confuse our Norman, I realized that Eamonn was now completely sober. When you realize you're about to die, it's amazing how quickly you sober up. We were not traveling on a nicely surfaced road here. We were in the bleeding jungle, where there are things that eat you if you get a breakdown, many things that eat you. I know because I'd seen it on the Animal Channel and various Tarzan movies.

"So Norman," I said, hoping that he and I could be best friends and then he would kill Eamonn first and maybe I'd find a way to escape—sorry Eamonn, but every man for himself, as they say, "How much land do you own?" I kept talking, hoping that he would slow down and maybe we could jump out.

"Oh, I don't know," he said, "probably about nine thousand acres or so."

Nine thousand! I thought. *That puts my little nine acres in Avoca into perspective.*

"And what do you produce here?" I asked as we rocked our way through trees and God knows what.

"I have horses, cattle, and a number of vineyards," he said, opening up to me as he was obviously very proud of his achievements.

"You must have many people working for you."

"Yis," he said in his best Afrikaans, "I have a lot of blicks working for me."

No, that's not a typo. He did say "blicks" because I asked Eamonn, "Did he say 'blacks' or 'blicks'?"

"Blicks," says Eamonn, now looking at me, telling me in silence that he didn't want to die out here in the jungle.

"Oh," I said enquiringly, "and what do they work at?" as twenty more miles elapsed.

He told us that he had about five thousand "blicks" working for him, he wasn't exactly sure. I told him that was perfectly understandable and to please continue as I checked the locks on the doors, but figured I was actually safer dying in the Land Rover. It appeared that they all worked mainly on the land, producing wine, and as payment for their labors they got free lodgings, which consisted of three-bedroom mud huts with adjoining bathrooms. They were also allowed to farm the land for their families to produce enough vegetables to keep them alive so that they could continue working. In addition, they had the added benefit of free medical care from the local witch doctor. He also informed us that they had very short life spans as they were allowed to make their own wine for their own consumption but apparently filled fertilizer bags with grapes then buried them for about three or four months and drank the contents, which was way too soon to consume, and as a result they all died pretty quickly. This didn't seem to bother our Norman in the slightest as he said there were plenty more "blicks" where they came from. Generally I thought it was a great deal all around with permanent and pensionable employment and all the benefits, and I relayed my thoughts to Norman, who nodded approvingly that I had approved. *Whew!* I thought. *That just might save me. Sorry, Eamonn, you're screwed.*

Eamonn was no slouch and could see from past experiences what I was up to, so, trying to inveigle himself into my little bit of espionage, he asked Norman, "What do you think of the great Nelson Mandela?" looking back at me with an obvious smirk on his face.

"Dat big blick bastard, he has caused nothin' but trouble. He is the cause of this great country being in the state it's in. I'd shoot him in the morning. Let me tell you that before he arrived on the scene I could be driving along my road on my estate and you could kill a blick in your car and there would be no trouble, no hassle. Now because of him you have to get the blick's name and address!"

You could say there was a stunned silence from the two Irishmen in that car. You could say that we were lost for words. You could say all of that except one of the aforesaid Irish people—and I was not the one—started to cry and said he hated Mandela too and anybody else that Norman hated, so I leaned forward and said to Eamonn, "Would you like salt and pepper in your pot, or will we let the slow heat bring out the natural flavors?"

We finally arrived at Norman's place at some ungodly hour in the morning, and we kissed the ground when we got out of the car. Eamonn and I hugged each other. I have to say I was very disappointed with Norman's house as it was not what I had expected for such a wealthy landowner. It was your basic common or garden bungalow built during the sixties with no mod cons. He brought us into the house around the back, and we found all the rest of the lads getting arsed-about-face drinking vodka. They had taken bets that we wouldn't make it because apparently Norman was totally and utterly insane. *That's nice*, I thought, *we had to get the insane one!*

We needed encouragement, and so we imbibed, a lot. When we awoke the next morning I was bollock naked, yes, double check that, answer correct, bollock naked, and as I looked around the room I counted eight other blokes in the same position, also bollock naked. *That's it*, I thought, *Norman is at this moment stoking the fire and putting us in one at a time.* But when I looked around I found all of my clothes neatly stacked and ironed. It appears that this was the done thing in Norman's home. When the guests went to sleep one or two of the housekeepers took our clothes, cleaned them if necessary, and ironed them.

We eventually all made our way into the kitchen, but instead of breakfast, insane Norman produced at least three bottles of vodka and continued to down one himself. Now, our boys are strictly beer boys, with one or two exceptions, and they found it impossible to keep up with him. When I asked him how he handled security all the way out here in the bush, he said that it wasn't a problem because he had many guns and the blicks had none, and when he wasn't home he used a security firm with very specialist skills, as Liam Neeson might have said, which involved placing twenty-four poisonous snakes in the house to roam free and putting up appropriate signs about the place, informing any would-be intruders of the situation. It seemed the "blicks" hated snakes, and I have to say I'm in the same camp there. Only one problem with that: snakes tend to have many babies, and there could be an extra one or two in the house when the security firm comes to collect them. They never know if the babies arrived or not. Then he informed us that at the moment there were one or two loose ones in his house, which was our cue to announce that we had to catch a flight to anywhere, and so we hurriedly made our exit, paying one of the drivers to drive us in his van.

Question: How do you fit twenty-four Irish blokes in a fifteen-seater van in a big hurry?

Answer: Tell them there are snakes in the house.

Next stop, Johannesburg and Sun City. Bye, Norman, forever.

We arrived in Joburg refreshed and raring to go. Sun City is about a two-hour drive away, and it's like Las Vegas in the desert, a million miles away from civilization. It's a tremendous feat of design and engineering to have so much water and electricity in such a dead zone, but the guy whose idea it was, Sol Kerzner, deserves a lot of credit for doing something as ballsy as this.

We settled in very easily, enjoying all the trappings of the wave pool, the casinos, and the shows, which were terrific. After a couple of days I began to make some noises about going on a safari. After all, I explained, this is Africa, where all the animals come from, where everything you've ever wanted to see as a kid is right in front of you, the things that David Attenborough had been going on about on the BBC since you were born. It was like throwing pearls before swine. Unless I could guarantee them girls—preferably half-naked—booze, and five-star comfort, they were going nowhere.

Eventually I had convinced twelve of them that they should go, so my twelve apostles and I waited on our bus one beautiful morning as dawn was breaking. The excitement was palpable as I gazed upon the raggedy band of geniuses who were still in the deep throws of sleep and hungover to boot. The first problem arrived in the form of a non-air-conditioned bus, but I managed to get the driver to shut up about it as otherwise we'd never get them on board. Anyway it was still cool, and it wouldn't get really hot until around midday. By then my apostles would be in raptures, having experienced what other people only dream about. I tried my very best to keep them all interested, but when you've been driving along rickety roads for about two hours and all you've seen are wildebeest and more wildebeest, the natives tend to get a bit restless.

So I mentioned to the driver of the alleged travel company, who excelled in African Safari trips, "Eh, if you happen to see any animals doing anything, it might not be a bad idea. Otherwise there are a few animals on board who might just decide to do their own safari hunting with you and me as the game."

I think he got the picture because when he turned around he saw twelve very restless and increasingly irate Irishmen looking in one direction, and that was straight at us.

"Any sign of any animals, Bernie?" they enquired.

"Well lads, you can't just click your fingers and the animals come dancing now can you?" I retorted, taking none of their crap.

"Well, I don't give a crap. I'm throwing you and the driver off this bus, and I'm going back to the hotel," said a three-hundred-pound former rugby player, and with that the driver made a call and reported a major kill very near the entrance to the national park. So they all agreed that the three-hundred-pound rugby player should take his seat and give us one more chance. I looked at the driver, and he appeared confident. I enquired where the nearest airport was just in case. Well, hang out the flags, there they were, a whole pride no less of savage-looking lions gorging themselves on some poor animal, and we all hoped it was one of those wildebeest. It was a major triumph, and the driver and I were more than happy that we would live to see another day. Apparently the park does this anytime there might be a problem. They throw a dead sheep by the entrance gate, and the lions are never too far away from an easy meal, but of course we never mentioned any of this to the lads.

After we made it back to the hotel I decided that was enough of trying to recommend anything cultural to the lads, so I did what I always did, I did a runner. Now, doing a runner wouldn't be exactly the correct term to use in these type of cases as there is nobody chasing me. It's just the way I've always acted whenever I got bored. I like to go walkabouts, as the Australians say. I like to do my own thing. It's probably where I get all of my stories because, as I've said before, I am a great believer in human nature.

I went backstage at one of the shows and found a bevy of beautiful girls all half-naked as I made my way through their dressing room. They were the dance troupe that had just finished their performance. I've always found I get away with things when I'm on my own. I don't have that lecherous look that other guys have because I'm not the lecherous type. Therefore I'm not intimidating to women, so they are not threatened by me.

I sat down with one of the girls and asked her what was happening partywise tonight, and she told me that the girls who just finished the show were free for the weekend and were heading back to Joburg for their usual weekend of partying. Her name was Misty, and what a gorgeous girl she was. Within two shakes I was on board the hotel coach and on my way to Joburg with Misty by my side as I led the girls and one other bloke in renditions of every Irish song they had heard, which made the two-hour bus ride pass quickly.

In no time Misty had got me through all the security so that I was well known in each of the events we visited. There was the fancy dress party, no gorilla costumes this time, where all the girls dressed semi-naked, which was very nice indeed, and the blokes had to wear uniforms, animal costumes, and the like. I grabbed myself a superman outfit, and it looked great. The only rule was no cameras, as they didn't want any newspapers getting hold of their photographs and threatening their livelihoods. These girls made a lot of money dancing and didn't have to sell themselves.

We then went to party number two, which was a rave, and we danced crazily for what seemed like hours, the sweat pouring off us. Around four we were still going strong, and I was amazed at my stamina because usually about now I would be horizontal.

I awoke next day around midday, surrounded by beautiful naked girls in a fabulous hotel complex, and thought I had died and gone to heaven. Felt good in the head too and probably lost about ten pounds.

I asked Misty to show me around, and I particularly wanted to see the non-touristy spots of Joburg, so she did so. She pointed out the shanty towns. Now, if you want to witness poverty and deprivation, you should visit the shanty towns of Joburg or any country in Africa. They are everywhere, and how people manage to eke out an existence beggars belief. That sight certainly sobered me up.

Misty asked me if I'd stay the night and offered to drive us both back to Sun City, the next day being Sunday. I was a bit concerned that I'd already been away for nearly two nights, and I expected the guys were wondering where I'd been, so I took the company bus back that evening with a view to seeing Misty the following evening.

The next evening I went looking for Misty only to be told by one of the girls that Misty had been killed in a car accident that morning. Some trucker had skidded off the road straight into her car. She died instantly. I was devastated, as were the whole troupe. I had only known her for two days, and she was dead. I arranged to attend her funeral, and the entire cast turned out. It had turned great memories into ones of sadness. Thoughts of Misty overshadowed the fact that I should have been in that car with her.

CHAPTER 24

THE YEARS ROLLED BY, AND Angie and I started to date seriously at that stage. She was a very pretty woman with long blonde hair. She worked as a flight attendant with one of the Irish airlines and had recently returned from Greece, where she had ended a relationship. She hadn't any real intentions of entering into another one until she met me. We got along just great. She was my partner at any of the work functions. We partied with her friends from work and generally had a fun time. One of the party nights involved going to one of the male flight attendant's houses in North Dublin. He was as gay as gay could be, as most male attendants were, and he was great fun.

When I first dated Angie we arranged to meet at one of the Dublin pubs, and when I arrived the girls were in full swing, as were the guys. It was a gay pub. Feeling somewhat uneasy, as this was my first gay association, I made my way over to the bar, as you do, and promptly ordered myself a Guinness. I don't normally drink Guinness, but I felt that it was the best macho drink in the circumstances as I didn't want to be taken for gay. There was another bloke at the bar drinking Guinness as well. I sidled up to him all macho like, and it transpired that he was married to another of Angie's friends. He was decidedly not gay, so we ended up covering each other's backs, so to speak, and relaxed a bit. In no time the "boys" came over and, after a few drinks, I asked one of them if he thought I was gay.

"Oh darling, you couldn't be anymore *un*gay if you tried, sweetheart," he said, which was music to my ears, and in no time at all I was in among them, joining in all the songs we could think of. I've had a load of gay friends since then. It's crazy to think that we have such insecurities about our fellow men.

Any time I had to fly to the UK I'd make sure that I was on Angie's flight, as the other girls would make a big fuss of me and hand me bottles of champagne, extra sausages, all the goodies. It was great. It wasn't long before Angie and I got serious, so serious in fact that she decided she was going to move in with me in Avoca. I was delighted because I really liked her and wanted to share my big house with her. We settled in quickly, although it was hard getting to know the natives, as they were a reclusive lot. So we made our own company, with friends calling in if they were in the neighborhood. We would go to the local town for nights out or Angie would cook. She was a good cook whereas I was hopeless, couldn't cook an egg, as they say.

Christmases were probably the loneliest times because nobody was down our way, but we'd buy the big tree and do all the decorations, take Max for his walks, and generally life was working out good for a change.

Now one of the things you definitely have to do when you are a squire of anything is buy yourself a gun. You need this when all the other squires go hunting, and you especially need one if you've never hunted before like me. But it wasn't easy getting my hands on one. Paddy, my gardener, had also told me that he thought he had seen somebody snooping around the house when I was away, so that made my mind up for me. I had also asked a detective friend of mine what I should do if I was confronted by a burglar in the house, and he told me that I shoot the bollocks dead then shoot a second round into the ceiling. That way I could always say that I gave him a warning shot. Sound advice, that!

I had made all the necessary enquiries about buying a gun, but with all the IRA stuff that had gone on down the years it was a pretty exclusive club. It wasn't like America where you went into your local Wal-Mart and said you'd have an AK47, enquiring whether they took coupons. I was at home one day when there was a knock at the door, and who should be there but Malachy, the local Garda sergeant. I never understood why every Garda station in every Irish village had to have a sergeant. No ordinary police officers, only sergeants. It was as if you had the choice of doing the ordinary police exam or the sergeant's exam when you wanted to join the police force. If you happened to know the local parish priest then you automatically qualified for the sergeant's position. So I looked at Malachy, wondering what I'd done wrong to warrant his visit. I had met him a few times in the village.

"How can I help you, Malachy?"

"I heard you'd be needin' a gun."

"I would, but I can't get a license because I'm not a farmer and I never owned one before."

"Have you bought a gun?"

"No, I haven't. Sure that would be illegal," I said, wondering where this was leading.

"Would you be interested in buying this gun?" he said as he produced a mother of a shotgun, something that you'd see in a cowboy movie.

"I don't know. How much is it?"

"It's four hundred pounds."

"But where would I get a license?"

"If you buy this gun, you won't have any problem getting a license."

"Four hundred it is," I said, and I told him that I would drop the money down to the station in the morning.

"Cash, if you don't mind, Mr. Donnelly."

"Cash it is," I said as he informed me that I was now the proud owner of a Beretta five-shot repeater, which meant that you could shoot five bullets before you had to reload, which would be very handy if you were about to rob the local bank.

"Would you mind showing me how it worked, Malachy?"

"You'll figure it out yourself without any problem," he said and drove off as quick as you like. I paraded around my estate with my Beretta five-shot repeater and decided to have a go at shooting it just as Angie arrived home. I told her the story of the gun, and when she asked me had I had any experience of using one I told her I hadn't a bogs notion but that I was just about to try it out.

I loaded it and aimed it into the sky and pulled the trigger. With that a pigeon fell from the sky right at our feet, dead! I couldn't believe it. I never saw the damned thing. I imagined how the pigeon probably said to his missus that he was just going out to the end of the branch to check the weather and that he'd be back in a jiffy when some bloke blew him out of the sky, and his missus will never know the truth! I never shot another thing after that as I felt sorry for the old pigeon. And even when I did go on a shoot I ended up missing everything anyway. I was a terrible shot.

There was one event that took place at Christmas when Angie and I had one or four too many drinks and were making our way home through the back roads to our house. Now, drinking and driving in Ireland was a non-event then, and all of the previous times for that matter, but they had recently introduced drunk driving laws, and as we came around the bend at the local hotel we nearly crashed into Malachy the police officer.

"Jesus, Malachy, what the fuck are you doing in the middle of the road?" I blurted out. I had nearly driven over him. "I could have killed you there!"

Angie suddenly reminded me that we were well over the limit, but I always found that if you're in a sticky situation, then your best bet is to run with it. Don't retreat or you're dead.

"Jesus," I said, "you'd want to move your road block up the road a few hundred feet or someone is going to run over you, Malachy."

"Do you think so, Mr. Donnelly?" he said. "You know, I'm only here because of all this new drunk driving business. I mean, I don't mind a fella having ten or eleven pints, you know, as long as he's careful like."

So I knew I was definitely okay because I had no more than five pints.

"Quite right there, Malachy. Anyway, I'd better be going. Look after yourself! All the best!" I said as I scampered down the road. *Only in Ireland,* I thought to myself. *Only in Ireland.*

Which reminded me of a story I had heard only a week before this event when a friend of mine was well over the drink driving limit but had reasoned in his own mind, whatever few brain cells that were alive at that particular time, that he was fine for driving as he was just one final roundabout from home. As he approached his exit off the roundabout he missed it, and instead of continuing on and catching it the next time around, he slammed on the brakes and was about to reverse his car when some poor unfortunate devil crashed into him. My friend got out of his car feeling pretty shook up. He took one look at the other guy in his car only to realize that he was even drunker than he was. The police arrived very quickly, and, as there were no injuries, they took my friend's license and insurance details and told him to report to the Garda station on the following Monday. Then they arrested the other guy.

My friend spent an anxious weekend wondering what would happen when he reported to the police station on Monday, so he dressed in his finest suit and presented the outstanding information to the desk sergeant. As the sergeant perused the documents my friend nonchalantly enquired about the other driver. "Oh him," said the guard. "You wouldn't believe it, but he swears that you reversed into him!"

"Go away!" said my friend, looking incredulous, and deftly made his exit, feeling very grateful to the other bloke. You wouldn't get away with it nowadays.

Max became a big part of our lives down in Avoca, and I told you before how he hated men, especially postmen, but he adored women, and they loved our Max. Anytime a man would come to the house I had to make doubly sure that Max was locked away because he had nipped a number of guys already, never seriously, thankfully. One day I totally forgot about him when the new postman arrived down, and, not knowing anything about our dog, he got out of his van and rang the doorbell as he needed us to sign for a registered package. When I opened the door I barely had said my hellos when out of the corner of my eye I saw Max making a bee line for the guy, and he was on him like a great white shark gobbles a seal. The guy had no chance. I screamed at Max to let the postman go, but the postman's pants were already ripped and blood was streaming down his leg. This was not good. I finally managed to grab Max around the neck and pin him down while the poor postman eventually made it back to his van and safety. I dragged Max around to one of the outhouses and locked him in, as he was still going ballistic. I'd never seen anything like this from him before.

When I got back to the postman he had already vanished. He was gone, out of there like a bat from hell. I said to myself that this was the end for Max. There was no way he was getting a reprieve from this attack because if it had been me that he attacked like that, I would have shot him with my gun. I probably would have missed!

I brought Max out of his prison cell, and he had calmed down. He knew he was in big trouble. I looked at him, and he looked at me. He said, in his way, "I'm in big trouble?"

I said to him, "Max, I cannot mince my words. There's nothing I can do for you. You are totally screwed."

I always had conversations with Max. I believe he understood every word I said. After an hour or so I decided to take him to the vet and have him put down. I put Max in the back of the estate car, and he looked like a condemned man going up to the gallows. I swear to God he knew it. I went up to the gate, and I looked in my rearview mirror. He was looking back at me all very quiet, so I looked at him and I looked straight ahead. Left turn was the gallows, right turn was a final attempt at salvation. The only hope he might have was to ask the postman himself to give his verdict of guilty or not guilty.

I turned the car right towards the sorting office. I arrived down to the sorting office, and I rang the bell for service. When the girl opened the little shutters I told her why I was here, that my dog had attacked one of her postmen and I was wondering if he was okay because I was going to have the dog put down.

"Put down!" she exclaimed. "Don't do that! That was Mick that got bitten. Sure he's always getting bitten by dogs. He's terrified of them."

With that a second girl arrived at the window, and when she heard the story about me going to put my dog down and that he was in the back of my car they told me to show them the dog. So I led them outside to my car, and when I opened the trunk and they saw my Max in all of his glory, well the only two words that sprung to my mind were "Academy Award." Max was amazing. He looked the way only he could look with his magnificent Lassie brown coat, his gorgeous eyes, and the look of a host of angels that cried out, "Who me? Sacrebleu!"

"You are not going to have that gorgeous dog put down. We'll put Mick down before we'd put him down," they said as Max reveled in the limelight.

"Do you think so?" I asked, fully knowing the answer, but rather than let Max off the hook completely I figured I owed it to Mick the postman to at least give him a say. So the girls told me that Mick had taken the rest of the day off, having visited the hospital for a tetanus shot. They gave me his home address. I assured them that I wouldn't have Max put down, and off I went in search of Mick. I swear when I looked at Max he was purring at his performance and was just short of manicuring his nails in triumph. I said to him not to get too cocky, that the postman was going to have the final say. I decided to buy a bottle of Paddy whiskey to soften him up. I arrived at his house, and out he came to the front door, limping with his leg all bandaged up.

"Hi Mick, do you remember me?" I asked.

"Indeed I do. You're the man with the dog," he replied, and he invited me inside. I told him that I was sorry about what happened, poured him a big glass of whiskey, and toasted him.

"Sláinte," I said. "Are you okay, Mick?"

"Yeah, the doc said I'll be fine."

When I asked him did he want me to put the dog down, he said, "No, no there's no need to do that. I hate all the bleeding dogs. Never liked them, and they never liked me. I was thinking of giving this job up anyway, so leave him be." With that I got back in the car, took one look at Max, who was staring at me apprehensively, waiting on the verdict. I said to him, "You are one lucky little bollocks, Max, one very lucky bollocks." He would have said, "I know, Bernie, don't I fucking know it!"

CHAPTER 25

ANGIE AND I WERE GETTING on really well. We were having a great time, and life was good. We were doing normal things, and I was living a "normal" life, which made a great change. We had been living together going on three years, and we felt very comfortable in each other's company. She was a single girl with no complications, unlike me, so it was inevitable that the subject of marriage would come up eventually. She needed to know where our lives were going. Were we going to commit to each other? We were both fully aware of the complications involved in trying to get married as the laws of the land were construed towards married couples, and even though Ireland had introduced divorce in 1995 it was still an Irish divorce law for an Irish people, meaning it wasn't worth a damn. Maria was never going to agree to a divorce when the Catholic Church decreed against it.

I took my problem to a firm of lawyers, who came up with the Haiti solution. It appeared that we could go to Haiti and apply for a foreign divorce and get married in the States. Haiti was the only country that allowed you to do this, and it was the only answer for Angie and myself. At least she could call herself Mrs. Donnelly.

We decided to do it, so I got in touch with a travel agent, Thomas Cook in London, who asked me why I wanted to go to Haiti. This was the first time I'd ever been asked by a travel agent why I wanted to go to a place, so I told them that we wanted the sun. They sort of said, "Yes, sure," and booked me flights from London to Miami, staying two days in Miami and a week in Haiti.

Off we went, and, oh my God, what a dive! We stood waiting for our bags at Port au Prince Airport with disbelief written across our faces as we surveyed the hundred-plus brown faces staring up at two Caucasians staring back at them. Somebody tapped me on my shoulder, and I turned around to see this white guy asking me if I was with the United Nations. I said I wasn't, that we were here on vacation, and he told me in disbelief that nobody comes to Haiti on vacation, that the only whites here on the island worked with the UN. I began to get a nasty feeling in my loins, and we nearly crapped ourselves when we saw the state of the place. Our taxi was riddled with bullet holes. I looked out one window while Angie looked out the other window. We both had our mouths open in disbelief.

The brochure had assured me that the hotel was Haiti's answer to the Waldorf Astoria. It wasn't. We dumped our cases in our room and ran to the bar for courage, only to be told that they only had enough gin for one round. They had no beer, not even bottles of beer, and the kitchens were closed. This was turning into a nightmare before it began, so we knocked back our drinks and retired for the night, but not before we jammed a chair up against the bedroom door and locked all the windows. Next thing we knew, the electricity went down, so we managed to find some candles, and I told Angie that I'd take the first shift and wake her up in four hours. There was no way we were both going to sleep in that place at the same time.

The next day I was due to meet Jacques, our French-speaking lawyer, who was to arrange the paperwork for the courts. Jacques was as slimy as they come, and I didn't trust him at all. I left Angie at the swimming pool at the hotel, and she begged me not to leave her alone for too long. Jacques and I made our way down to the courts through the typical third-world traffic of a million bicycles, war-torn Toyota trucks, and battered cars, staring at the poverty-stricken natives and the broken-down shacks that represented their Rodeo Drive. I should have known better than to go to Haiti, having been to other God-forsaken places like it all over Africa, but we were excited about this Caribbean Island in the sun and about our impending marriage. I signed many forms at the courts, and we were told to come back again the next day when the judges would be in session. Jacques dropped me back to the hotel, where I found Angie lying near the pool, crying.

When I asked her what was wrong she just pleaded with me to get her out of there. She couldn't stand it as she spent most of the day fending off the natives, who had been hassling her. There had been no food, as the kitchens never opened, and there was no alcohol, so I promised her that I'd have her out of there the next day and that she wouldn't have to spend another night. How I was going to do it? It was time to use my mother again!

I met Jacques the next day, and I told him that I needed two tickets to Miami immediately as I'd had a phone call during the night from my sister in Ireland saying that my mother had just died. I had used the "my mother has died" trick whenever I was confronted by a dire situation that needed a miraculous escape. Sometimes it was "my mother was taken to hospital" when I wasn't satisfied with my accommodation or I needed an upgrade. If I arrived home early from rotten vacations, my mother would ask, "Well, son, did I die again?"

"You did, Ma."

"And what country is it this time I'm barred from?"

"Portugal, Ma," I'd tell her as she added it to her list, which included Spain, England, Malta, and now Haiti.

"That is terrible news," said Jacques, "I will get on to it right away." He pondered my sincere look of devastation. "Were you close?"

"We're talking about my mother here, Jacques. And we all have only one mother. We might have many fathers, but we only have one mother, Jacques."

"Very true."

Sure enough, Jacques came through and had managed to get me two tickets on the six o'clock flight to Miami that very same day, but we had to make sure we got what we came for first. Sorting out the foreign divorce was not going to be easy. It was like watching grass growing the way those courts operated. There were three judges in attendance, and when my case came up they went through my documents with a fine-toothed comb. After many hours listening to them conducting their proceedings in French, I finally jumped up and told them in English about my dead mother, and after it was translated, things seemed to move a lot quicker. With only a couple of hours before our flight, we finally managed to get the stamped official documents telling me that my divorce was granted. We screeched to a halt at the hotel. I found Angie and told her about the urgency of the situation, and with obvious delight she was packed and in the back seat of the car faster than the great Houdini. We were on board the airplane with about ten minutes to spare. As the plane took to the skies, we bid our adieus to Jacques and his screwed up little island, which was about to get even more screwed up when the earthquake came through in another few years. I hope those judges were okay!

We were back on American soil, and boy did it feel great ordering large gin and tonics at the poolside, being waited upon, and charging it to our room. Traveling the world really opens your eyes. After a few days rest we were more than ready to start our vacation, and we hired a car and made our way up the East coast of Florida, passing all of those towns we had only ever seen at the movies or on television from Miami through Palm Beach to Cocoa Beach, ending up at Cape Canaveral.

We went in search of our "Church of the Divine Whatevers," where we were due to get married. Angie had found the place. How she did I have no idea. It made me laugh anytime I had rung them from Ireland to ask them a question, their answering machine would say, "Welcome and please leave your message after the beep, and remember a winner never quits and a quitter never wins." I love that crap. Only in America!

They had been expecting us, and in no time the service got under way. Angie looked great in her new dress that she had bought for the occasion, and I didn't look half bad either in my new suit. It was a woman minister, and within twenty minutes we were anointed. It was great, and Angie looked radiant.

I was really looking forward to the honeymoon because, as luck would have it, there was a rocket launch that very same afternoon from Cape Canaveral, which was only up the road. It was to be our first rocket launch ever. There was a big crowd there when we arrived, and I set up my new camera, aiming it straight at the amazing rocket ready to blast off into outer space, to infinity and beyond. It was all very exciting. Angie could take it or leave it, but I was over the moon, so to speak. When the countdown started, I turned on my camera. I had a great view. Then I heard the engines roar, and the people shouting and whooping, as Americans do, but my rocket was still on the ground and there was no smoke, not a whiff. I was looking at the wrong bleeding rocket. There had been two rockets, and I picked the wrong one. I had missed the whole thing. Jesus! Then everybody laughed when they realized what I'd done. I guess that job as a NASA flight navigator was off limits for me.

We still had a great time, though, even without the rocket launch, but we arrived home a week later to our beautiful house in Avoca and trouble. Someone had moved into the ever-vacant cottage at the entrance to our driveway, and they were about to be responsible for starting World War III. It was a small cottage of the non-distinct variety that was plonked at the entrance gate to my property, and it looked like three old people had taken up residence there. So Angie, looking a little agitated, asked me to go up to them and find out what was happening. The person in charge was an old Scottish woman who together with her even older husband and mother, who had to be in her nineties at least, had bought the place and intended to live there. I introduced myself and gave them a bit of a background to my house. They seemed pleasant enough, so I told them if I could do anything for them that they were to let me know, and I left it at that.

I relayed all of this to Angie, who seemed placated enough, and we had dinner. The next day as I drove up my driveway on my way to work, who should be strolling down the drive but the old woman with her even older mother. So I just waved at them and continued on. It was four that afternoon. I remember the time very well because I took Angie's phone call, and she was perplexed to say the least. I couldn't understand what was wrong, so I told her that I was on my way home. When I got home I found her in a rage, a steaming rage, blathering on about the people in the cottage encroaching on our land, taking a liberty with our property without even asking permission. So to calm things down I said that I would go up and speak to them, and off I went.

To be honest, I had no idea why Angie was so agitated, as I didn't have any problem with somebody going for a walk on my property. Okay, they should ask for permission, but it was no big deal. Rather than start out on the wrong foot, I told them that it was dangerous to be using the driveway as visitors wouldn't be expecting to see anybody if they drove down the hill, so I advised them to seek alternative recreational paths. They said they understood and that they'd go somewhere else.

They didn't, and they began to piss me off when they continued using my property over the coming months. Some people are born to be a pain in the ass. Why can't they just follow the rules like everybody else? I eventually had to get the lawyers involved, sending them warning letters only to be told that the new residents had every right to walk on my land as it was some sort of designated open path available to all the community according to the land registry. *Oh, bollocks to that!* I thought.

And so the saga continued for over a year with Angie getting more perplexed. I decided that it was time to plan our exit from Avoca as those people probably existed to make other people's lives miserable. It wasn't the main reason for wanting to leave as I had also become tired of the road journey, especially during the winters, and in addition it had become very lonely as we realized we had become very isolated. It took another year, but eventually we found somebody who fell in love with the place the same way that I had all those years ago, and we decided to buy a new house in a lovely little spot in Greystones, a small town about an hour from the city center. It was a nice little three-bedroom house, one of a hundred or so houses that were just being built in a small housing estate.

We said our goodbyes to Avoca and those nice Scottish neighbors. I hope they were okay! We then said our hellos to the town of Greystones as Angie announced she was pregnant and we were about to welcome our son Billy into this amazing world.

CHAPTER 26

BILLY WAS BORN IN 1998 and he was a healthy nine pounder. We were both over the moon and i was so thrilled for Angie as she had been through a lotto hassle when we dealing with the neighbors in Avoca and I had been worried that maybe she would have complications. There was nothing to worry about and for the next year Billy got her full attention as I navigated my business through exciting waters. The Irish economy was doing well, like the rest of Europe, as the economies of the world took off during the nineties. These were very different times to the strike-ridden seventies and the depressing eighties when I started my business. Unemployment was going down for the first time in living memory, and people were actually getting enthusiastic about Ireland and where we were heading as a country. Many American companies were setting up their overseas operations in Ireland due to the good work of the Irish government, the favorable tax rates if they used their Irish operations to create jobs, and this they did in their droves. For the first time in our history emigration was reversing into immigration as more jobs became available, and the economy benefited further with the construction industry taking off. All boats were rising.

Windows '95 had also arrived, and it changed everything for us. This was the latest and greatest operating system from Microsoft, which gave software houses far greater flexibility in the way they could do the things they couldn't do before, as they had been handicapped by the restrictions imposed by the old operating system. New, more feature-ridden software languages also came along that drastically reduced the time it took to produce better products. We also benefited hugely by the fact that our products had only been released a few years previously, whereas our competitors' products needed to be written from scratch. We were able to convert our products into windows much faster than our competition so that our products were in high demand as customers demanded the latest technology. At last things were turning our way.

For the next few years I started to make decent money on the strength of our Windows '95 products and the prospering Irish economy, and it made a huge difference. I no longer had sleepless nights worrying about personal guarantees on the business, and my staff numbers were becoming more manageable. I made the decision to buy my own property instead of wasting my money on exorbitant rents as the banks were now looking favorably on software companies now that they were gaining traction on world markets.

When I was a kid my parents would treat us to the occasional dinner in a place called Teddy's, an ice cream institution in our town that's still there and still selling the best ice cream around. I used to look forward to those occasions when my father could afford it, and I would always pick the same table by the window looking out over the Irish Sea, thinking nice thoughts. Now I had decided to buy that very same building for my business. I was going to convert the twin-level property into offices. When I got the keys, the first thing I did was sit at that same table I used sit at some twenty-five years previously with my parents, and boy did it feel good. The property allowed me to borrow using it as security instead of using my own personal house, allowing me to breathe more easily.

I knew every part of that town. I swam in the public baths, I was a member of the public library, played in the playgrounds, was an altar boy in the hospital, went to mass every Sunday in the old Catholic church, walked every side street and short cut that existed. I had worked for bars, hotels, and restaurants all over the town that was Dun-Laoghaire. Some people hated it, but I never had a problem with it. As I said, things were better than they had been in quite some time, and I was reasonably happy. My long-term plan was always to make my company salable, and the only way to do that I figured was to dominate my marketplace, to have so many customers that some big mega-type company would gobble me up and put me and those around me on easy street. I knew that it wouldn't happen overnight, but I also knew I had to come to their attention. To do that I had to attack them where they lived. I had to be a right royal pain in their arse.

As I reviewed my business I knew it was a totally different company to the one I had before I had torn it apart when I threw out the deadwood and had refocused. I had eliminated our hardware business, as we had never made any profit selling computers and printers. The only people making money from those efforts were the manufacturers, and we, like every other vendor, found it impossible to keep up with the ever-changing world of faster processors, forcing us to heavily discount our aging stock to buy the newer equipment. When we stopped selling the stuff, we found we never missed doing it, and again it released more personnel for other more important things. We had had the same result when we stopped overextending ourselves by supplying products to too many markets. We never missed those markets afterwards.

I was particularly delighted with our support services, both telephone support and training, ably run by my department manager Margie, a terrific girl who had been with me more or less from the start. She was someone you could totally depend upon. It's great when you have great people working for you, and I was very fortunate to have more than my fair share. Software support is practically nonexistent these days because it's impossible to get any human being on the other end of the line when you have a query or a problem, and it's more than infuriating sometimes. In our specialized business, dealing with professional accountants, you had better have a great service, or these guys will string you up without an anesthetic. We gave a great service due to Margie and her team who, despite a lot of abuse, remained very calm in the face of stupidity and adversity, took each call with the grace of an angel, explained everything with the patience of a kindergarten teacher, and moved on to the next call and the next call.

I would have bombed all of my customers with the subtlety of a B-52 and returned for reinforcements. I had no patience where that sort of thing was concerned, but at least I knew it. There were a number of careers for me that I knew were to be avoided at all costs, and I would never have involved myself with anything to do with bombastic, arrogant, or stupid people. They were a complete no-no where I was concerned, and my management knew this, so they kept me leashed to my desk, only to be released where a major charm offensive was needed or where some customers needed to be killed.

My sales team were good, two of them outstanding. As a sales person myself I knew the good ones and treasured the great ones. You only ever need two great ones to have a successful business as they'll keep the ship afloat and the monies rolling in. I counted myself among the great ones, and, with all humility, I was damned good at selling. The best people always know that they are the best, like great sports people who can be sent out on the field with only minutes to go and win the match for you. They know it, and you know it. So with the three of us there we never had any problems getting the numbers, and we carried the weaker guys. There was a natural aspect to being a great sales person. You either had it or you didn't. But like the best sports people, the more you practiced the better you became, and we never gave up learning, swapping ideas, examining our strengths and weaknesses constantly, checking each other's demonstrations and techniques, and I encouraged it. When we gave a large presentation, we would have the customers eating out of our hands. We were the top guns.

Of course we were only as good as our products, and by this time we had produced high-quality products better than our competition and the marketplace was hearing about us everywhere. When a product becomes a must-have, it makes selling it an awful lot easier. That's what we had managed to achieve. It had taken a lot of blood, sweat, and tears, but we had achieved that status. Accountancy practices from all over the UK and Ireland were hammering on our door, wanting to buy, and it doesn't take long before someone gets pissed, particularly the competition. That's what had brought us to the attention of the big fish, and they were knocking at our door.

I had always said that there were three types of opportunity: the one that people never see, the one that a person sees and is afraid of, and the one you see, grabs, run with like a prisoner on the lam. There's one other problem. You have to have your ears and your eyes open always in order to hear and see your opportunity knocking on your door. That's not always easy. Like the old man I told you about who attended my exhibition, whom I nearly ignored and turned out to be my most lucrative customer. I had done all the hard work of being the noisy neighbor and getting myself noticed, but I nearly blew it when they came knocking.

One day as I looked out my window I saw the mother of all downpours, so I decided to have an early night and head home. I was passing my secretary's desk when I happened to just ask her whether I had any messages, and she told me that there was nothing urgent other than some guy with a funny-sounding name had been ringing me a lot asking me to ring him back. She said it sounded like he wanted to become a dealer for our products, so I dismissed it and told her I was heading home. I had no coat, and I got soaked running across the road to my car. As I sat there about to turn the engine, I thought, *What the hell did that guy want?* It was going to be the most important question I ever asked myself.

I was always like that, a bit manic about being tidy. I hated loose ends. I could have done a number of things, such as forget about him and go to the pub or just go to the pub and forget about him, but as is my nature, curiosity always got the better of me. I got out of my car, and I ran across the road to my office. Remember, there were no cell phones in those days, so it was never as easy as it is nowadays when you can simply call somebody from your car. I grabbed the 3M sticker with the guy's name on it, and I rang him only to find that he wasn't looking to become a dealer. Instead he wanted to know if I wanted to sell my company. Now, I always wanted to sell my company, so my immediate answer was yes.

His name was Donnacha, the funny-sounding name that my secretary couldn't pronounce. He worked for Sage, a massive UK company that was listed on the London stock exchange, and he managed their Irish operation. Sage had been very active buying up companies in my marketplace. He told me that the British guys were fed up hearing our name everywhere and losing business to us, so they wanted to know if they could buy us. He was very straightforward about it. There was no pussyfooting about, which I liked. At that precise moment I had a vision of five hula girls dancing on a sunny Caribbean beach carrying trays of cocktails and ripe fruit to my sun bed.

"Are you there?"

Bang went the tray and the hula girls.

"Yes, of course. So what happens now?" I asked, looking around the office for my cocktail.

"Well, have you got a price in mind?"

"No, I haven't to be honest, but I'll have a think about it tonight, and I'll give you a call in the morning."

"Fair enough," he said, gave me his direct line number, told me that if he didn't hear from me that he would take it I wasn't interested, and hung up.

Now I'd been asked to sell my business a few times before this, most notably by people who wanted it for nothing or thought I was some gobshite who had just arrived from Outer Mongolia and who knew nothing about the value of my own company. I had gone down the road a bit with them, as you do, and told them to take a hike. But this sounded different. After all, this was a very reputable company that was starting a mating dance with me, and I didn't want to be the one that got thrown out because I didn't respect them. I wanted to be the one that got screwed like a very expensive whore who operated out of a five-star hotel. This was going to require some serious thinking.

So I stopped at my local on the way home, grabbed a quiet corner with a pen and paper, and tried to figure out how much I should sell it for. My accountancy background allowed me to work it out properly. I looked at earnings per share, balance sheets over the past three years, multiples of recurring income, revenue numbers, and combinations of all four, but when you boil it all down it's a guessing game between how much the buyer is willing to pay and how much you are willing to sell it for. That is always the bloody quandary because neither of you wants to look like a dickhead. Also, from my point of view, I was playing the biggest game of my life because if I cocked this one up I had no other games to attend. This was it. Whereas this deal to Sage was tiddlywinks as they were doing deals like this every week. *Oh bollocks*, I thought to myself, *come on, Bernie, don't fuck it up now, not now.*

I tormented myself with questions, so I had another pint. It's funny how the elixir of alcohol creates a warm glow of imperviousness within a man. When I had finished about three or four pints of lager I had taken over Sage!

I hardly slept that night, but by the time I had driven into work I had the number in my head.

You see, the multiples all told me that I was worth around six million, the recurring number told me seven million, while the turnover or generated revenues screamed about five million, so I rang Donnacha and told him I wanted twenty million. He never even coughed, and I'm sure he didn't blink either because he said okay, that he would relay my number and get back to me. I responded, as I usually do, in a high-pitched "Okay." That was the only visible or audible weakness I had all of my life. Whenever I got really excited I produced a high-pitched sound. It's why I never spoke when I played poker or when I was having sex. It was a sign of weakness. Anyway, it was out there now, the figure of twenty million together with my high-pitched sound, so there was nothing else for it.

It was time for a pint even if it was only ten o'clock in the morning. I was useless waiting around for their response. I kept telling myself that I'd blown it by asking for too much. They weren't stupid. They had teams of analysts employed that could give them an accurate valuation on my company in a hot snot. They were probably pouring over my accounts now, laughing themselves silly, saying what an idiot this Irish bloke was!

The next day went by, and not a word, then the next day the same.

"Bollocks, bollocks, bollocks!" I shouted at myself inside my soundproof office door. The glass wall allowed me to see my employees on the outside, who were now obviously looking at the wanted pages in the newspapers because their boss had obviously and finally flipped.

With that the phone rang. It was him, it was Donnacha.

Okay voice, I thought, *remain calm. No high-pitched stuff. Be good.*

"Donnacha, how are you?" I said, not giving a crap if he was dying from Ebola as long as he kept it to himself.

"They'd like you to come over and discuss it with you," he said.

"Okay," I said, and yes my voice was strong, it was holding up. Come on ye reds, come on ye reds! "When is it suitable to meet up?" I was playing a blinder—One nil, one nil, one nil, one nil—

"How about Monday next?"

So we coordinated ourselves and arranged where to meet, and he said that he would get back to me with the flight arrangements. I put down the phone, punched the air, and did a small victory walk around my office as the guys outside put away their newspapers and resumed working. I smiled at them to reassure them that their boss was more than okay. I couldn't wait for Monday, but when it did arrive I felt very much alone as I carried my half-empty but very impressive briefcase through the airport. I'd had this briefcase for what seemed like forever, and I never got to use it very much until now, so I threw a few papers into it to make it look good, and there was Donnacha waiting for me as arranged.

We had a coffee while we waited for our flight to Newcastle, the headquarters of Sage. I was dying to find out what the thinking was behind my suggested number. It was now a suggested number because the more I thought about it the more I realized I had spoken through my hole, so I wanted to dampen things down a little.

"What did they think of my suggested valuation?" I said, noting my beating around the bush tactics in full cry. God I was good—Nil all.

"Oh, they laughed a bit, a lot, actually, but don't let that bother you too much," he said. "Can I suggest something, Bernie?"

"Sure," I said, "please do."

He told me not to worry too much about the price, that Sage wanted to agree something with me and that I should be reasonable in my demands and not be too greedy. I was really warming to Donnacha, and then he told me that he had only recently started at Sage, that he liked the job but he didn't see it as a permanent position. We chatted away, and before we knew it we were at the headquarters of Sage, the UK's largest software company, and very impressive offices they were too.

I was nervous as we were sent up to meet the powers that be. I was confronted by about fourteen blokes of all ethnic persuasions, and out from their midst comes a little fella called Graham with his hand extended. He introduced himself as the chairman. The chairman no less! Well blow me down with a used condom!

So he started the introductions to his team, or teams, he had so many people. He then asked me where my team was. I turned around to see Donnacha had done a runner, although he wasn't on my team anyway.

"I'm it, I'm afraid," I said.

Graham looked behind me, sort of like the story I told you about the empty suitcase, so I turned around and came to the same conclusion. I was alone—definitely.

"That's not a problem," he said. "Now I'm going to leave you in the capable hands of some of my team, but before I go I just wanted to let you know that I want your company," he said as he smiled and made his exit. At that moment I turned to see his team wanting to throw up in the corner because their chairman had just scored an own goal by telling me that he wanted my company whether I liked it or not. At that moment I wanted to run after him, throw him onto his chairman's carpet, and have unprotected sex with him!

WeGraham introduced me to Jason, his chief negotiator, and we sat down at the boardroom table. These guys were good, they were very good, but I started to settle down after a nervy start, and I made a few decent passes myself.

"There's no way you're worth twenty million, Bernie," he opened.

Fifteen-Love.

"Your chairman seemed to think so," I responded.

Fifteen all.

"How did you calculate your valuation of twenty million?"

Thirty-Fifteen.

"Well, when you examine the figures for recurring income and combine it with future revenues, it comes out at around that number," I responded hopefully.

Second serve.

"I wouldn't agree with you at all. In fact, we would estimate that your company was barely worth half that number," he lashed.

Forty-Fifteen.

Welcome, ladies and gentlemen, to today's Wimbledon final, a match that sees the established frontrunner, Ms. Sage versus the newcomer from Ireland, an unknown novice playing in his first and probably last Wimbledon final. But the crowd love an underdog, and you don't come across a bloke like Bernie very often who should definitely be under some sort of dog, preferably somewhere else!

"I wouldn't agree with you," I said, wanting to take the little bollocks there and then for three rounds. *Relax, Bernie, think of those four or was it five hula girls!* "Because after all, you need to take into account that my company is beating the crap out of you everywhere you go in this country, and that is something that is not in any of the figures in front of you."

Ace! Forty-Thirty.

"And you should ask all of your sales teams if they would like to see me and my products as part of the Sage Group because I guarantee you that their answer will be a resounding yes."

Ace-Deuce.

"No, don't get me wrong. I understand about your position in the marketplace, which is the reason we wanted to talk to you. I'm just concerned about your valuation, as I have to reconcile it to my bosses, and I just don't see it, that's all." He was weakening.

Advantage Donnelly.

"Okay then, what valuation do you put on my company?" I asked.

Oh, bad play there from Donnelly. He played a weak ball. That was definitely out. Deuce.

"I'll be fair and give you our top-end figure, which would be thirteen million," he replied. That was twice the figure I had in mind.

Advantage Donnelly. This match is going the distance, ladies and gentlemen, and it looks like rain might stop play unless we get a winner very soon.

So we battled on for another four or five hours without a break. The hula girls were changing their dresses. I could feel closure, I could taste the cocktails.

"Make it fourteen million sterling, and you've got yourself a deal," I challenged.

The crowd is tense. They are on their feet. You could hear a pin drop, ladies and gentlemen.

"Done," he said and shook my hand.

I think I farted because there was an awful smell, and I think they noticed because we vacated the office pretty quickly.

Game, set, and match to Bernie, the underdog from Ireland leaving the courts with around thirty million dollars, give or take.

I met Graham on the way out, who told me he was delighted that we had struck a deal, and then he told me that my company had been a right royal pain in the arse. "Well done," he said. "You were the cause of your success, and you deserve the reward."

Then he handed me the Wimbledon trophy.

I sat in Newcastle Airport in a daze, exhausted but very happy. Then I snapped out of my daze, told the hula girls to wait for me, that I would be back eventually, because there were one or two things I needed to do.

First, I hadn't told anybody, particularly the other shareholders! "Minor problem, minor problem," I kept saying to myself in the hope that if I said it often enough it might actually be true.

CHAPTER 27

I KNEW IT WASN'T GOING to be easy. I knew that I tended to piss people off because I pushed things through, especially when I knew that what I was doing was correct, and I knew that the Sage deal was definitely the right thing to do. I arranged a meeting the following day with the two investors, one being a Canadian guy who had invested only the previous year and was due to see his investment double, the other being the investment bank, which would see its investment treble. I didn't foresee too many problems convincing them, but boy, how wrong can you be?

The banker guy with whom I had developed a friendly relationship was antagonistic from the start while the Canadian guy listened as I explained the deal. I told them that my company wasn't worth a quarter of what they were offering, but the banker said that I was talking through my anus and that we should hang out for a hundred million or more.

What is it with people when they start saying things that are totally ridiculous? I can only put it down to the craziness that existed in world markets then. Companies had been completely overvalued. Some had valuations of billions, and they had zero revenues. It was unrealistic, and that was why "real" companies, like mine, were put into the same category.

After listening to them for a while I turned to the Canadian and asked him if he had a lot of money. He said he had. Then I turned to the banker guy and asked him the same question. He said that he was very comfortable. Then I told them that I had no money whatsoever, and I asked them, if they were me, knowing that they were broke, would they take the money? I had learned over the years that people always wanted to tell you how well they were doing and how wonderful they were, so I knew they would give me the answer I wanted.

The Canadian was the first to admit to it when he told me to take the money. That forced the banker's hand. I had their agreement, but the banker guy was furious with me. I had barged the deal through so that by the time I got back to my offices to relay the good news to my other directors and investors the banker had already spoken to them and colored the waters. The four people who would stand to become millionaires and part millionaires were the people I had given the shares to some years previously for a very nominal sum as a reward for their loyalty and dedication, so I had assumed that as they were still only in their late twenties, that this was the opportunity of a lifetime for them. I was wrong, and they were sour from the moment I told them about the deal. I was nonplussed and quite shocked at their attitude, even when I brought them out for a celebratory dinner. I was even more dismayed when each of them stood up during the middle of the dinner and walked out, leaving me there on my own. I got a sheet of paper and I wrote down the following;

- That bloke you see up in the top office that looks like he hasn't slept in over a month, he's called the owner.
- The owner is the guy who gives all the personal guarantees to the banks to start the business and gives his blood to keep the business afloat.
- The owner is the guy who foregoes his wages every other month due to cash flow difficulties because his employees have not been selling enough.
- The owner is also the guy who has to defend his company against all lawsuits due to his employees screwing things up.
- The owner is also the guy who makes the most money should he be fortunate enough to sell his business. The other shareholders get paid their shares on the basis of their holdings in the company. That's why they are called shareholders. Simple, isn't it?

As an addendum to this, only six months after I closed the deal the stock market crashed, and I was reliably informed by my buyer that he wouldn't have given me a quarter of what he had given me if he had known what was going to happen. He told me this as we played golf at the European Golf Club, on the tenth hole, as I was about to drive off the tee. I missed the ball, by the way. Now, do you think that any of those wankers who made all that money from my deal ever contacted me at any time to apologize for being total wankers? I did hear that one them died recently. I hope that the rest of them will be okay!

Once I had all of their "agreements" to my deal, I informed the buyer, and they said they would start the due diligence right away. The next thing I needed to do was find myself a good lawyer, and I remembered this little Jewish fellow who had done some business for me. He had done a great job, so I told him about the deal, and he told me he'd be delighted to work for me.

Now I needed somebody good to handle my taxes. You'd think it would be easy to find an accountant who would guide you through the tax quagmire so that you ended up paying as little as possible of your hard-won jackpot. Not so, I'm afraid, as the first lot I talked to told me there was nothing I could do but pay all the taxes that were due. The second firm told me that life was too short to be wasting it on trying to reduce my tax bills, that I should pay up as well. *Bollocks,* I thought, *people are very bearish about my money.* We were talking about millions here. That buys an awful lot of happy meals, so I knew there had to be someone out there who knew what they were talking about. The problem was trying to find that someone.

Then I remembered this guy Alex who had done a lot of work for us on our taxation software. He had just opened his own practice, so I arranged to meet him in Jury's Hotel in Dublin one morning. After we chatted about football for a minute or so, I told Alex what was happening and asked if he had any suggestions how I might legitimately minimize my liability. He then went all serious on me, asked me a few questions, and took a piece of paper and seemed to write something on it. He pushed the paper over to me, and there was nothing written on it.

"Eh, Alex, it says nothing," I said.

"Is nothing not good enough?"

"If I booked a room upstairs, would you have time for sex?" I laughed.

We have been the best of friends ever since, and it will remain that way, otherwise I will tell people what happened afterwards in that hotel!

He explained to me the ins and outs of the tax plan, which was perfectly legal, using a system of loan notes whereby you actually lent your company to a potential buyer for a period of time. But there was a risk involved. If the buyer went bankrupt, so did you. It also meant that I would have to emigrate to either the Isle of Man or Portugal.

"So, Alex, where would you recommend?" I enquired.

"Well, my last client chose the Isle of Man, but he rang me after six months telling me to pay the bastards as it hadn't stopped raining since he had arrived there and he was drinking a bottle of whiskey a day."

"Portugal it is then." I said as I don't drink whiskey.

I had the deal going through, I had arranged the lawyers, and Alex was handling my tax affairs.

When I got home that day Angie wasn't in great form, and when I told her about the deal, that I was selling the business, she wasn't overly enthusiastic about any of it. I didn't understand her lack of logic. I also didn't think it was a great time to be telling her that she would be living in Portugal for a few years, so I chickened out. I had noticed that things had become strained with our relationship, but I put it down to having the baby, moving to a new house and the fact that I was immersed in my work. I promised her that we would take a long vacation just as soon as this business sale was over with.

The thing about going through a due diligence is you never know what they might uncover that would scupper the deal, but I was more than happy that everything was in ship shape as they sent their teams of accountants to both Manchester and Dublin. You can't believe the number of forms that you have to sign and the documents that you have to read. I was diligent with everything, asking questions and being methodical and professional about everything, but when the final day came to close the deal I was in a Manchester hotel, totally bollocksed, as I had been awake for many nights pouring through all sorts of legal documents. I would have signed an elephant's trunk in the middle of his sexual stampede if you could have managed to squeeze him into my hotel room. Professionalism went out of the window as the hula girls got closer and closer and I could taste the coconuts. I even gave the night porter five pounds every time he had to witness my signature. He was happy.

I must say that Graham and his guys were professional throughout, even as I pretended that all was well on my side while having apoplexy in the toilet as I tried to push the deal over the line. Graham pulled me aside and told me not to worry, that they did these deals every week and they always worked out.

Finally it did. It was all over, and we shook hands. Then he told me he wanted to go over to my Manchester office and speak with my management. It was then that I realized that they were no longer my offices or my management. They were his! After Manchester, we would then fly over to Dublin and do the same thing there. I said sure thing, and within two shakes of a lamb's tinker bell we were in his offices downtown.

I sat meekly in a corner, fading away fast as he addressed his new troops. After about twenty minutes I felt that my body was caving in, and Graham asked me to make him a coffee as he could see I was as much use to him as a tin of beans is to a mouse. After another hour I politely reminded him that we could miss our flight to Dublin if we didn't go now.

"Bernie, I own the plane!" he said, which put me back in my box. *Owned the airplane*, I thought. *Of course, Bernie, they owned the airplane, you dope!* So I sat very quietly in the corner, clutching my loan note.

The time came for us to fly over to Dublin. Now when I tell you it was my first time in a private plane, I wouldn't be lying. If Sage had added another hundred million to their buying price I would have bought one myself as it is the only way to travel. When your private pilot asks you if you are ready to leave and you scratch your arse one more time and only then do you give him the signal to push away, or when your own private stewardess asks you would you like some Columbian coffee or a foot massage while you sink into your deep armchair following your seamless check-in procedures, which don't exist because someone else has already done that silly stuff for you, then you know you've made it. It makes you appreciate this other side of living compared to the poor shmuck like me who has to contend with the airports that are rat mazes, designed to give you the maximum amount of torture in the maximum period of time. And then if you do manage to get to the mousetrap that doubles as your seat without having to swallow painkillers, you then have to contend with stewards barking orders at you as you sit there squashed and crying because a nasty four-hundred-pound gorilla is about to sit beside you for your ten-hour trip to Orlando.

Then Graham asked me if I'd like some champagne, and I said why not as we rose like a swan into the skies. In next to no time we were due to approach Dublin, and he asked me if I'd like to see anything special while we were up there. I looked at him, and I asked him if he wouldn't mind flying over my old school. I redirected the pilot, and it was at that time that I looked out of my window. I saw my old school, and I noticed this young fellow looking up at the school clock, praying for it to be time to go home because he hated school so much. The young fella looked up at this bloke in his private jet two thousand feet above him who had made himself a promise some twenty-eight years ago that he would one day be a multimillionaire.

"Are you happy, Bernie?" asked Graham.

"You bet your bollocks, Graham."

Epilogue

So there I was, a multimillionaire at last. I had a new son and was estranged from my four children. I had retired at forty-six years of age with no idea what to do with my life. My second marriage was shaky and I was still in remission from stage-four cancer. If you had told me that I was about to meet a person who would change my life completely, I would have scoffed at your suggestion. But then again, you never told me that you were talking about a person named Keiko.

Author Profile

BERNIE DONNELLY WAS BORN IN Dublin in 1953. He lived in Dun-Laoghaire (Pronounced Dun-Leary) a large town south of Dublin, all of his life. He formed his own software company at the age of twenty nine and became the largest provider of accounting solutions to the accountancy profession in Ireland, and one of the top three suppliers in the U.K. He had businesses in Ireland, England and India.

Following the sale of his business in 1999, he spent some years in Portugal, and in 2008 he emigrated to the U.S.A., arriving in Sarasota, Florida, where he remains to this day.

Bernie has five children and one step child. Dear Daughter is his first book, and plans are afoot to release a second volume.

He is a qualified C.P.A. and a venture capitalist. He is an avid reader of biographies and history and has travelled substantially.

www.berniedonnelly.com